ECOLOGICAL MODELS
OF ORGANIZATIONS

ECOLOGICAL MODELS OF ORGANIZATIONS

Edited by GLENN R. CARROLL

With a Foreword by AMOS H. HAWLEY

BALLINGER PUBLISHING COMPANY
Cambridge, Massachusetts
A Subsidiary of Harper & Row, Publishers, Inc.

International Standard Book Number: 0-88730-208-4

Library of Congress Catalog Card Number: 87-19618

Printed in the United States of America

Library of Congress Cataloging-in-Publication Data

Ecological models of organizations.

    Bibliography: p.
    Includes index.
    1. Organization. 2. Industrial organization. 3. Human ecology. I. Carroll, Glenn.
HM131.E24   1988   302.3'5   87-19618
ISBN 0-88730-208-4

CONTENTS

LIST OF FIGURES

LIST OF TABLES

FOREWORD

Amos H. Hawley

Ecology has become, if I may borrow a Biblical metaphor, "a house of many mansions." The most recent extension of the house had its inception in the seminal paper by Michael T. Hannan and John Freeman titled "The Population Ecology of Organizations," which appeared in 1977. These authors introduced a closely reasoned theoretical model that quickly attracted a growing number of vigorous researchers. The contributors to this volume are in the vanguard of the new application of ecological principles. But their many citations to the works of others engaged in the field points to the breadth of interest stimulated by the Hannan and Freeman formulation.

The terms population ecology and organizational ecology are closely akin. The former was introduced by bioecologists who turned their attention from a typological to a quantitative approach to their of field study. The questions raised concerned various aspects of the relations of populations to environmental carrying capacity. Population ecologists found the Lotka-Verhulst equations to be a useful way of modeling their problems.

Organization ecology is an adaptation of the population ecology model to populations of organizations. Environment in this case is the set of interrelated organizational populations, together with the conditions they engender, constituting an ecosystem. The relation of a population to its environment is expressed in terms of a small number of concepts, some carried forward from population ecology, some developed to fit the characteristics of organizational populations. Central to the theory is the niche concept, defined as resource space and regarded as a variable property of environment. Each population tends to become isomorphic to environment through the mechanism of competition among organizational foundings in excess of available resource space. Survivor selection differs with environmental change and type of organization, such as specialist versus generalist. Specialist organizations are more suited to rapid change, while generalist organizations accommodate more effectively to slow change. Or, in the Lotka-Verhulst model, specialist organizations prevail in the exponential phase of the curve, while generalist organizations have higher survival rates in the asymptotic or equilibrium phase. But that the Lotka-Verhulst model oversimplifies the process of number determination is demonstrated in the Hannan and Freeman chapter in this volume (Chapter 2). In a further development of their initial theory they show that founding rates of organizations are affected by niche density in a nonmonotonic fashion.

The versatility of the general model is manifested in its applicability to a variety of organization types. Exploitations of the theory in the following chapters display impressive ingenuity in research design and operationalization. The McPherson and Smith-Lovin chapter (Chapter 6) employs niche theory in an examination of the competition among voluntary groups of environments of potential members distributed in overlapping niches. Aldrich and Staber provide (in Chapter 7) additional support for the nonlinear pattern of founding and death rates in their study of trade association history. The multivariate analysis of community characteristics as affecting foundings of citizens' organizations opposing drunken driving, by McCarthy and colleagues, shows positive effects of demographic factors of environments (Chapter 5). Environmental niches in which political newspapers have been established and died in Finland are identified in the Amburgey-Lehtisalo-Kelly paper in terms of variations in political party membership and shifting government policy (Chapter 9). In their study of mortality rates of Knights of Labor assemblies, both specialist and generalist, Carroll and Huo observed a nonlinear life cycle effect, especially in specialist assemblies (Chapter 10). The niche for the wine producers analyzed by Delacroix and Solt (in Chapter 4) is conceived as the volume of wine consumption. Increases in the amount of imported wines contributed to new winery foundings through increasing the volume of wine consumption. A test of the competitive exclusion hypothesis with data on the semiconductor industry is presented by Brittain and Wholey (Chapter 11). Tucker and his associates examine (in Chapter 8) the effects of density variations on founding and death rates of voluntary social service organizations. And Boeker offers (in Chapter 3) an analysis of the relation of entrepreneurial characteristics to the founding of semiconductor firms in changing environmental circumstance.

One cannot read the papers in this volume without being impressed with several features of organization ecology. Foremost is the parsimony and the power of the theory to account for the numbers of organizations. That is due in no small part to a second characteristic: It brings into a single model both institutional and ecological variables. Environment, for example, is definable as a complement of institutions, a body of rules, an ideology, or as the attributes of client populations. The dependent variables, as already noted, are populations of institutions. Common to all institutional classes are environmental dependence and amenability to demographic measures, such as founding, death, and survival rates.

A third noteworthy property is the commitment to longitudinal analysis. That follows from the recognition of environmental variation and population dynamics. The shifting carrying capacities of environments, the foundings and deaths of organizations, the competitions among units, and the selections of organizational units that have achieved isomorphism with environments are events spread over a temporal continuum. Accordingly the research strategies in the following papers are designed to deal with those facts. All but one of the empirical papers employ either a time-series regression or an event-history model. The one exception, the McPherson and Smith-Lovin study of voluntary organizations in five countries, is based on cross-sectional data. It, however, develops propositions that lend themselves to historical analysis.

A fourth though less explicit feature of organizational ecology is its acknowledgment of the effects of microlevel factors. Although most of that lies in the assumptions made about the phenomena under study, it surfaces now and then as in Boeker's chapter on the role of entrepreneurs in organizational origins. But because individual attributes are treated in the aggregate, for the most part one might say that a theoretical reductionism is transposed in operationalization as methodological holism.

The net effect of the several features of organizational ecology is to move ecology from the periphery to the center of sociology. An important dimension is thereby added to the conventional approach to organizational study. The sociological import is further secured by the separation of ecological theory from economics. As pointed out in the Carroll and Huo and the Amburgey-Lehtisalo-Kelly chapters, organizational ecology makes no assumptions about efficiency or linearity of variation, and it employs variables that lie outside the purview of economics.

Fruitful as organizational ecology has proven to be, there are two questions unattended that, if answered, would allow an extension of the theory. One concerns a missing element in the model, the other an accounting for niche creation. Speaking to the first, in the conceptualization of change most of the elements of an evolution model are present, including niche crowding, competition, and selection. What is not there, however, is the element of variation as process. No analogue for genetic variation is offered. Clearly variation cannot be charged to competition, for that can account only for elimination from a niche. Nor does boundary permeability, as proposed by Hannan and Freeman in a recent paper published in *Sociological Forum,* do more than clarify some taxonomic problems. How new organizations are generated is still left unexplained. Part of the answer to that question, though only part, would seem to lie with niche emergence.

The theory as developed so far provides no clues as to how new niches come into being. Because the niche is viewed as a partition of environment, one might expect its appearance would find its explanation in environmental terms. But environmental variation is regarded in the main as merely nonlinear oscillation. A somewhat longer-run view would suggest the very plausible alternative of environmental accumulation, or rather ecosystem growth. Conceivably system growth is a process of new niche development. This seems to be recognized in the Delacroix and Solt chapter on wine industry foundings in California and again in Boeker's charting of environmental accretions as affecting births of semiconductor firms. But in neither paper is the theoretical significance of that observation developed. In short, it would seem that an answer to the question "Why are there so many kinds of organizations?," with which organizational ecology began, would have to include an explanation of how an organizational environment accumulates or, for that matter, how it varies from moment to moment. Such an explanation would call for an enlargement of the environment concept beyond a localized network of organizational populations with which a given population is interacting. If that were done, a new perspective on organization/environment interaction would be introduced.

Suggestions for theoretical extension are carried further in the final chapter of the volume by Fombrun. He takes issue with the neo-Darwinism of the organizational ecology approach, particularly with its assumption that organizations are passive actors in the selection process. It is his contention, supported by recent advances in cellular biology and genetics, that organizations enter into and reshape environments in what appears to constitute a projective adaptation. This calls for a rethinking of the strategy of organization ecology. The proposal is unquestionably constructive. Perhaps, however, it is looking further down the road than organizational ecology should travel at this time.

1 ORGANIZATIONAL ECOLOGY IN THEORETICAL PERSPECTIVE

Glenn R. Carroll

Although its adherents continue working at a feverish pace, the once hegemonic contingency theory of organization has been deposed by a paradigmatic revolution. The beginnings of the revolution can be dated sometime around 1975, a period marked by the appearance of four new seminal theoretical statements about organizations: (1) the book on transactions cost economics by Oliver Williamson (1975), *Markets and Hierarchies*; (2) the article on the population ecology of organizations by Michael T. Hannan and John Freeman (1977); (3) the article on institutionalized organizations by John Meyer and Brian Rowan (1977); and (4) the book on resource dependence theory by Jeffrey Pfeffer and Gerald Salancik (1978), *The External Control of Organizations*.

Each of these statements challenged the assumptions and tenets of contingency theory, each proposed a new and different set of assumptions and research problems, and each has in the decade since developed into a full-blown theoretical and empirical research program. The ultimate fate of each theoretical perspective remains to be revealed. Nonetheless, one thing is clear at this point: Intellectually speaking, contingency theory is dead. There is no longer any widespread interest in its progress or development, although it may take some time for this to be widely recognized.[1]

ADAPTATION AND SELECTION

Contingency theory assumed an adaptation model of organizational structure and performance, and three of the new theoretical perspectives do as well. According to this model, organizations are flexible social units. They are seen as changing regularly and adaptively in response to environmental, technological, and other types of exogenous change. The temporal horizon of this model is usually fairly short (that is to say, adaptations occur without great delay), and the types of adaptions emphasized usually represent some sort of organizational fine-tuning (such as the addition or deletion of a subunit). Surviving organizations are assumed to be well adapted, or at least not maladapted, an assumption revealing that the change process is implicitly thought to be in equilibrium.

Organizational ecology is the one new theoretical perspective that does not subscribe to the adaptation model of organizational change. Indeed, the ecological perspective challenges directly many of the fundamental features of the adaptation model and proposes instead a selection model of organizational change. By the view of the selection model, adaptive change is not impossible or even rare, but it is severely constrained (Hannan and Freeman 1984). By and large, organizations are seen as being characterized by strong inertial forces, and these are thought to limit the amount and degree of change. From a societal viewpoint, then, most organizational change occurring in any historical period is the result of processes of organizational selection and replacement rather than internal transformation and adaptation. Thus, organizational ecology calls for attention to patterns of organizational founding and mortality, the visible outcomes of selection processes.

POPULATION DEMOGRAPHY

At the time of Hannan and Freeman's (1977) revolutionary article on the population ecology of organizations, organizational theorists were ignorant about founding and mortality processes. In the intervening decade, knowledge of these topics has increased somewhat (see Carroll (1984) for a review). However, we are still a long way from any real understanding of either phenomenon. For instance, we do not yet even know fully the range and patterns of variation in observable organizational foundings and deaths.

The chapters in this book will move us along considerably in that quest. For the most part, they report empirical research on the topics of organizational founding and mortality. Most of them are drawn from larger research projects adopting an organizational ecology perspective and involving extensive data collection on particular "industries" as they evolved over long periods of time. The industries studied include semiconductor manufacturing, winemaking, newspaper publishing, labor organizing, social services, business interest organizing, voluntary formal associations, and social movement organizing.

The assortment of industries may seem odd, but it is the consequence of strong theoretical concerns. Founding and mortality processes are essentially population-level phenomena (an individual organization experiences only one of each type of event). The industries studied here were chosen because they each represent a demarcated population of organizations. This simply means that for one reason or another it makes sense to treat each of them as a single entity. Usually, the justification for so grouping a set of organizations is a similarity in function or purpose: Each organization does basically the same thing as the others, especially in comparison to other types of organizations.

The choice of exactly which population of organizations to study is a less rational matter. The reasons given by our chapter authors here reflect the variety of valid criteria a researcher might use. Most frequently, a strong substantive interest in a particular activity such as semiconductor manufacturing dictated the choice. In other instances, a theoretical goal, such as the wish to show the selection effects of political environments, guided the choice. And, finally, on many occasions the availability of data constrained the choice. Unfortunately, systematic data on failed organizations are extraordinarily difficult to find.

ENVIRONMENT

What can be learned from the analysis of organizational population data? The role of the organizational environment comprises the primary concern. As with most current organizational theory, organizational ecology posits that organizations and environments move toward isomorphism. Unlike other perspectives, however, the ecological view holds that the processes of organizational founding and mortality are the driving forces behind this matching of organizations and environments. This implies that there should be an empirical correspondence between environmental change and patterns of organizational founding and mortality. As environments shift, some organizational forms become obsolete and others become more viable. Thus, the founding and mortality rates of an organizational population depend on both its form of organization and the state of the environment.

A vulgar interpretation of the ecological selection model holds that efficiency and effectiveness are the only criteria that might account for why one population of organizations replaces another. Although efficiency and effectiveness may drive some organizational selection processes (such as profitmaking firms in competitive industries), they may be totally unrelated to others. Political, social, cultural, and institutional criteria can account for many selection processes among organizations. In what may be the most convincing demonstration of this point to date, the chapters that follow pursue these types of sociological arguments with great force and attention to detail. We can only hope that as one consequence the critics of organizational ecology will abandon their vulgar caricature.

ECONOMICS

Because the theory of the firm uses a selection model based on efficiency, organizational ecology has been likened to microeconomics (see Pfeffer 1982). The chapters below show that this comparison goes only so far and misses many of the most important features of organizational ecology. Besides the discovery of noneconomic selection criteria, the authors deftly illustrate the ability of ecological theory to explain the evolution of populations of nonprofit organizations, including some more often identified as social movements rather than formal organizations.

With one exception, the studies below also abandon the usual microeconomic assumption of temporal equilibrium. That is, they do not assume that the selection process immediately weeds out all organizations that do not match the environmental state. Rather, the process of elimination is seen as being imperfect and filled with delays. The system as a whole moves steadily in a particular direction toward a specific endpoint or equilibrium, but it takes so long to reach it that the environment is likely to change again in the interim. In technical terms, the selection process is said to be in temporal disequilibrium.

METHODS AND MODELS

Abandonment of the equilibrium assumption has major methodological implications (see Tuma and Hannan 1984). Specifically, cross-sectional data are no longer appropriate because they provide a misleading view of the process. Instead, longitudinal data and models for dynamic analysis are required. In the studies found here, two general types of dynamic models will be encountered. The first are time-series models. Based on the general linear model, these models are used in Chapters 4 and 8 to predict the number of organizatonal founding events occurring from one period to the next. Similar in interpretation to the conventional cross-sectional regression model, these models are dynamic because they include temporally lagged effects and they have explicit controls for the likely problem of autocorrelation.

The second type of model found throughout the book is the hazard function or rate model. These are used to model both founding and mortality processes from event-history data on the exact timing of the founding and death events. Technically, rate models use as the dependent variable an unobservable statistical construct known as the instantaneous rate of transition. It is defined as

$$r(t) = \lim_{\Delta t \to 0} \frac{\Pr[\text{event between } t, t + \Delta t \mid \text{at risk } a + t]}{\Delta t}$$

where the probability measures the propensity for an event in any arbitrary time interval and given that the unit is at risk to experience the event (organizations are founded and die only once). Intuitively, rate values of this kind have little appeal, but they can readily be transformed into constructs that do. The waiting time until an event, for instance, has an inverse relationship with the rate. So when an organization has a high instantaneous rate of death, the expected lifetime is short. For any given model specification, a more exact prediction could be derived.

Because negative rates are meaningless, the applications found below each use a nonlinear model to specify the effects of covariates on the rate. The simplest of these is the loglinear specification:

$$\log[r(t)] = b_0 + b_1 X_1(t) + \ldots + b_K X_K(t)$$

Because new organizations usually have higher death rates, models of mortality often include an age-dependent term that is expected to have a negative effect. In Chapter 8, this issue is addressed with the Gompertz model:

$$\log[r(t)] = b_0 + b_1 X_1(t) + \ldots + b_K X_K(t) + c_0 t$$

In Chapter 10, a constant-rate model with discrete "time-period" effects is used:

$$\log[r_p(t)] = b_{op} + b_{1p} X_1(t) + \ldots + b_{Kp} X_K(t)$$

where the p subscript denotes the separate time periods. Many of the other chapters use a more general, partially nonparametric specification known as the Cox (1975) proportional hazards model. It is

$$\log[r(t)] = h(t) + b_1 X_1(t) + \ldots + b_K X_K(t)$$

where $h(t)$ is an unspecified nuisance function that affects each unit in the same way. The Cox model is estimated with partial likelihood techniques; the other models are estimated with maximum likelihood procedures.

OVERVIEW

So far I have highlighted the common features of ecological analyses of organizations. Yet, as the following chapters also demonstrate, there are considerable differences of opinion and emphasis within the ecological perspective. To note an issue of debate pervading this book, some analysts see competition as the dominant force shaping organizational populations;

others place greater emphasis on institutional barriers and constraints. The difference is fundamental and affects the choice of variables as well as models.

Ecological study can also be conducted at different levels of analysis, and this too is sometimes a source of contention. The lowest level, the organizational, examines the organization in its environmental context and attempts to explain the development of the organization over time (for a recent example see Bidwell and Kasarda 1985). The next level, the population level, investigates how populations of organizations change in response to environmental changes. Research at this level typically uses a selection model and examines the relationship between the population's demographic events of founding and death on the one hand, and environmental characteristics on the other. Most of the chapters in this book use this approach. Finally, a third level of analysis, the community level, examines the interrelationships among populations and how they evolve over time. Less research of this kind has been conducted to date, but the last two chapters of the book suggest that this neglect may soon be remedied. Community ecology offers many new intriguing questions to organizations researchers.

Obviously, when compared to the other three theoretical perspectives on organizations—transaction cost economics, institutional environments, and resource dependence—organizational ecology shows the greatest generality. But that generality is of little use unless it can be drawn from to explain the specific patterns of organizational change found among particular types of organizations. In my opinion, the chapters that follow satisfy that requirement and thus demonstrate the power of organizational ecology. Advocates of the other theories would do well to take heed.

NOTES

1. "A new scientific truth does not triumph by convincing its opponents and making them see the light, but rather because its opponents eventually die, and a new generation grows up that is familiar with it." (Max Planck, quoted in Kline 1985: 160).

2 DENSITY DEPENDENCE IN THE GROWTH OF ORGANIZATIONAL POPULATIONS

Michael T. Hannan and John Freeman

Because organizations are the building blocks of modern societies, growth and decline in populations of organizations both signals and causes fundamental change in social structure. So theories about the causes of the expansion and contraction of populations of organizations are major ingredients in efforts to explain social change in the modern world. Population ecology theories of organization explore generic features of processes that control expansion and contraction in organizational populations. These theories focus on the interplay of the environmental constraint and competition within and between populations.

We focus here on ecological processes that constrain growth and decline in the *numbers of organizations* in a population. Consider what might have happened if the International Workers of the World succeeded in establishing the "one great industrial union" that was the object of their rallying cry. Without doubt, the articulation of worker interests would be much different if done entirely within the boundaries of a single union as compared with the more localized processes obtaining in a large number of diverse and more specialized unions. Moreover, unions are preeminently organizations devised to build the power of action through collective action. The power relationships between one giant union and other organizations

The research reported here was supported by National Science Foundation grant SES-8510277. Susan Olzak and Glenn Carroll made helpful comments on an earlier draft.

such as employers and government agencies are likely to be quite different from those obtaining with large numbers of organizations on each side. As this example suggests, changes in numbers of organizations imply changes in concentration of power and control.

The number of organizations in existence also has important implications for subsequent population dynamics. When organizations of a given type are rare, the factors Stinchcombe (1965) and others have analyzed as leading to a liability of newness are accentuated. On the other hand, when organizations with a particular form are very common, the competitive advantage on which a new entrant might trade is harder to identify. Claims on resources have been established by previous entrants whose organizations have been refined by practice. Further, existing organizations have survived previous selection processes, and new entrants do not face a random sample of historic entries but a sample biased in favor of functional competence.

In this chapter we explore the ways in which the size of populations (density) affects current dynamics. Our purpose is to show how the density of organizations can be built into models of population dynamics that will provide more specific content than the ordinary views of firm and industrial life cycles.

WHY ARE THERE SO MANY KINDS OF ORGANIZATIONS?

A typical organization's social environment includes many kinds of organizations. These include the states that claim jurisdiction in the realm of activity, schools that prepare cohorts of potential recruits, firms that supply technical, material, and symbolic inputs, organizations that produce similar products and services, and those that purchase or use the products and services. Change in the environment of one population of organizations usually means changes in the composition or activities of other organizational populations. If a particular social change alters the composition and activities of a focal population, these changes in turn reconstitute the larger social structure.

Modern population ecology concentrates on *numerical* aspects of population interactions. Analysis of the processes that constrain fluctuations in sizes of populations and in the number of populations illuminates fundamental ecological processes. Hutchinson's (1957) famous essay "Homage to Santa Rosalia" bears the subtitle "Why Are There So Many Kinds of Animals?" The essay makes clear that the subtitle poses a surprisingly deep question. Explaining the seemingly simple numerical features of ecology raises virtually all pressing theoretical issues in bioecology.

We use a similar strategy—we concentrate on *numerical* features of the world of organizations. In our earliest statements of the approach (Hannan and Freeman 1974, 1977), we paraphrased Hutchinson: *Why are there so many kinds of organizations?* This is a natural question for sociology because individual organizations can in principle grow without limit (Blau and Scott 1961). Under what conditions will one or a few organizations expand to take on many activities in society? When will the growth of organizations be constrained so that none grow really large and many kinds proliferate? We suggested that the social science literature did not have good answers to these questions and that trying to answer them would shed new light on the dynamics of the organizational world.

The actors in our scheme are *populations of organizations.* Our theoretical strategy depends on three assumptions about these actors. The *first assumption* is that populations can be defined so that they have what Hawley (1968) terms a *unitary character.* This means that the members of the populations must have a common standing with respect to the processes of interest. The most salient kind of unitary character for our concerns is *common dependence on the material and social environment.* A population of organizations has a unitary character in this sense if its members are affected similarly by changes in the environment (including other populations). So we must assume that populations of organizations can be identified in a way that the environmental dependence of the members are highly similar. This is equivalent to assuming that discontinuities in the world of organizations exist and can be identified.

Given the criterion of common environmental dependence, it might seem tempting to define populations *post hoc,* using information on the effects of observed environmental changes on the growth rate of members of many candidate definitions of populations. We do not do this because we want to make falsifiable predictions about the effects of interactions between populations on the growth rates of those populations. This requires that populations be identified *a priori,* using information on characteristics of the organizations or on the location of social boundaries to identify populations prior to collecting and evaluating evidence about outcomes. So the *second assumption* is that populations can be identified in a meaningful way on the basis of information about structures of organizations and social boundaries. We have discussed elsewhere how this might be done (Hannan and Freeman 1986).

Unlike the biotic case in which membership in a population is encoded in highly inert genetic material, individual organizations can and sometimes do make radical transformations in strategy and structure. In other words, they change form. If organizations can do so quickly and routinely, it is hard to claim that the populations have strong unitary character. Common environmental dependence of members is transitory in such a situation. No partition of organizations into populations provides stable dimensions for the space within which organizational evolution occurs. Unless the dimensions can be anchored, we cannot explain change over time.

The *third assumption* is that the characteristics that locate individual organizations in a population rarely change rapidly relative to the processes of interest. We assume that individual organizations are characterized by (relative) inertia in structure and the other characteristics that define membership in a population. In fact, we have derived this tendency as an implication of a social selection process (Hannan and Freeman 1984). But we do not assume that individual organizations never change form. Rather we assume that such changes are infrequent and cannot be timed precisely to coincide with shocks that favor a particular (destination) population.

THE PRINCIPLE OF ISOMORPHISM

Until fairly recently, the sociological literature lacked explicit treatments of the *causes* of organizational diversity. The absence of theory and research on this issue is doubtless due to the strong concentration of interest at the level of the *individual* organization. But recent theory on the organizational level does contain an implicit proposition about the causes of diversity. Most theory and research at the organizational level assumes that organizations adjust structure to ensure the continued flow of critical resources, as in the case of contingency theories. From an adaptationist perspective, organizations take on different structures only when crucial resources come in diverse streams. If key resources are few (or there are many but they can be exploited with a few strategies) and they are controlled by a few agents, there is no "need" for diversity. As the diversity of the resource base increases, the diversity in a set of adapting organizations increases.

An assumption of this kind lies at the core of sociological human ecology. Amos Hawley (1968: 334), the main architect of the neoclassical perspective in human ecology, proposed a "principle of isomorphism":

> Units subjected to the same environmental conditions or to environmental conditions as mediated through a given key unit, acquire a similar form of organization. They must submit to standard terms of communication and to standard procedures in consequence of which they develop similar internal arrangements within limits imposed by their respective sizes.

This principle implies that organizational diversity in any social system depends on the diversity of agents that control the flow of key resources into the system.

We noted earlier (Hannan and Freeman 1977) that Hawley's principle (like other adaptationist theories) does not apply when organizational resource environments are heterogeneous. But most organizations obtain resources from many other organizations. They may obtain trained personnel from educational organizations and apprenticeship programs of labor unions, financial capital from banks and venture capital firms, material inputs from firms in different industries (perhaps in different countries), and licenses from federal, state, and local agencies. Moreover, changes in the activities of agents who control key resources is often uncertain. For example, the policies of governmental agencies often change quickly when regimes change or when high courts issue rulings. In either case, the resource environment of each organization is heterogeneous, either at a point in time or over time (or both). Heterogeneous environments pose complicated problems of adaptation.

The recent literature suggests that organizations facing inconsistent demands from different portions of the environment try to create specialized structures to deal with the peculiarities of each dimension of the environment. This view reflects the long-standing tradition in organization theory emphasizing the tendency for organizations to develop differentiated substructures for performing specialized functions. The problem from our perspective is how to control and coordinate the actions of the various components.

Meyer and Scott (1983) suggest that organizations in the "institutional" sector deal with inconsistent demands from the environment by a strategy called *loose coupling*. According to Meyer and Scott, these organizations adapt to each environmental demand *symbolically* by creating a substructure that deals (or pretends to deal) with the problem. But the activities of these peripheral structures are kept "loosely coupled" with the activities of the core of the organization. In other words, the activities of the peripheral units are not allowed to interfere with the "real" work of the organization. Organizations that use the strategy of ritual conformity only *appear* to be isomorphic to several environments that pose inconsistent demands. They are symbolically or institutionally isomorphic to the environment.

The strategy of institutional isomorphism solves the problem of adapting to heterogeneous environments with the organizational equivalent of smoke and mirrors. Such solutions appear unlikely to work (that is satisfy the diverse actors in the environment) for long periods, especially when competition for resources intensifies. When resources shrink, as they have for public education in recent years, actors in control of key resources may investigate the tightness of coupling and may demand measures of the quality and quantity of outputs. In fact, the Meyer-Scott scenario reads like a description of one possible outcome of environmental heterogeneity for organizations like public schools. The larger environment fluctuates between two conditions. When resources are abundant, problems posed by inconsistencies among the various demands placed on these organizations are "solved" by creating special pools of resources for each problem and encouraging the target organizations to create specialized "programs" for each demand. When resources are scarce, public organizations are required to allocate limited budgets. The strategy of institutional isomorphism may be a good one when resources are rising; but it may not be such a good one when resources decline.

Perhaps some organizations can adapt to heterogeneous environments by multiplying peripheral structures and by weakening the link between public claims and actual practice. But this strategy handles only *cross-sectional* heterogeneity, variability among segments of the environment at a point in time. Once *temporal* heterogeneity is considered, the meaning of isomorphism to heterogeneous environments is once again unclear. When environments jump from one state to another over time, does isomorphism mean switching structures every time the environment changes or retaining a large number of peripheral structures at all times?

A general approach, one that deals symmetrically with cross-sectional and temporal heterogeneity in environments, seems needed. Below we show that a conceptualization based on niche theory provides one such approach.

Extending the principle of isomorphism to apply to heterogeneous environments requires specification of the underlying dynamic processes. The dynamic process of greatest interest to us is *competition*. We develop propositions about change in the structure of populations of organizations that (1) face cross-sectionally and temporally heterogeneous environments and (2) compete with other organizations (both within the population and with other populations) for limited resources.

THE NICHE

The concept of niche provides a useful way to express how environmental variations and competition affect the growth rates of populations. The imagery of the niche expresses the *role* of a population (or species) in a community, a population's way of earning a living. Elton (1927: 64), the pioneer in niche analysis in bioecology, put it this way:

> It is . . . convenient to have some term to describe the status of an animal in its community, to indicate what it is *doing* and not merely what it looks like, and the term is "niche." . . . when an ecologist says "there goes a badger" he should include in his thoughts some definite idea of the animal's place in the community to which it belongs, just as if he had said "there goes the vicar."

Although Elton's metaphor proved useful in naturalistic studies, it was not sufficiently precise for theoretical development. Modern niche theories began with Hutchinson's (1957) abstract geometric definition. He defined the niche as the set of environmental conditions within which a population can reproduce itself (in which its growth rate is nonnegative). Because growth rates usually respond to numerous environmental dimensions, the relevant environment consists of an N-dimensional space with each dimension telling the level of some relevant environmental condition (such as average rainfall, average diurnal temperature fluctuation). Each point in this space corresponds to a particular state of the N-dimensional environment. Hutchinson defined the *fundamental niche* of a population as the hypervolume formed by the set of points for which the population's growth rate (fitness) is nonnegative. In other words, the fundamental niche consists of the set of all environmental conditions in which the population can grow or at least sustain its numbers. It is called the fundamental niche because it refers to the physiological capacities of the members of the population.

The analogue for populations of organizations is straightforward. Classic theorists, notably Marx and Weber, paid much attention to the social, economic, and political conditions required to sustain particular organizational forms such as capitalist business enterprise or rational-legal bureaucracy. They suggested, for example, that the environmental dimensions that affect the growth of populations of rational-legal bureaucracies include the fraction of exchanges that are monetarized, availability of literate employees, and stability in flows of resources to the state. Taking the various dimensions together defines an N-dimensional social environment. The niche of rational-legal bureaucracy (or of any other organizational form) consists of the set of social arrangements in which this population can grow or at least not decline.

Specifying the niche of an organizational form requires intensive analysis of its "natural history," as we have discussed elsewhere (Hannan and Freeman 1986). Learning about the social, economic, and political conditions required to sustain a form of organization requires study of the details of the organizational form and the functioning of organizations that embody it. In fact, the concept of the fundamental niche of a form provides a felicitous device for incorporating institutional knowledge about kinds of organizations into systematic theory about population dynamics and evolution. It fits well with the actual practice of social scientists and others who provide detailed accounts of the functioning of various kinds of organizations.

A fundamental niche characterizes growth rates of *isolated* populations. The next step in the development of niche theory adds *interactions* among populations. From an ecological perspective, two (or more) populations interact if the presence of one affects the growth rate of the other(s). These effects may be either positive, negative, or absent. The term *competition* is often restricted to the case in which the negative effect is mutual—that is, to situations in which the presence of each population lowers the growth rate of the other. The predatory-prey (or host-parasite) case has one negative and one positive link. The case in which both links are positive is called *commensalism* or (sometimes *symbiosis*).

When populations interact, the presence of one population changes the niche of the others. If two populations compete, the presence of the competitor reduces the set of environments in which a population can sustain itself. Hutchinson called this restricted set of environments the *realized niche*. Two populations compete if and only if their fundamental niches intersect.

The development of competition theory in population bioecology was influenced strongly by Gause's (1934) experiments on coexistence of closely related species of beetles in controlled environments. He found that mixing two populations in the laboratory invariably caused one population to disappear. Gause summarized his findings by proposing a general ecological law. His *principle of competitive exclusion* holds that two species that occupy essentially the same (fundamental) niche cannot coexist in equilibrium.

Subsequent research has ruled out competitive exclusion as a general principle. For example, it turns out to be simple to produce coexistence of closely related species in the laboratory by making the environment more complex (essentially creating subenvironments in which the inferior competitor can find refuge or may possess an adaptive advantage). Nonetheless, this "principle" has proven useful in directing attention to the crucial role of *niche overlap* in competition processes. It has also stimulated the application of general models of population dynamics (discussed in the next section) to concrete ecological processes.

CLASSICAL COMPETITION THEORY

Lotka-Volterra Model

Alfred Lotka (1925) and Vito Volterra (1927) independently proposed models of population dynamics that incorporate effects of competition between populations. They began with models that imply that population growth of isolated populations has an S-shaped growth path. They assumed that the growth rate of an isolated population is given by the product of a growth rate, ρ, and the current size of the population, N:

$$\frac{dN}{dt} = \rho_N N \tag{2.1}$$

The growth rate ρ_N is defined as the difference between the birth rate, λ, and the death rate, μ, of the population:

$$\rho_N = \lambda_N - \mu_N \tag{2.2}$$

If the birth and death rates are constant (that is, if they do not vary with the size of the population), this model implies exponential growth. But such growth processes are not realistic in finite environments, as Malthus insisted. The growth model can be made more realistic by assuming that birth and death rates vary with density (the size of the population). Lotka and Volterra assumed that the birth rate falls (approximately) linearly with the size of the population:

$$\lambda_N = a_0 - a_1 N, \quad a_1 > 0 \tag{2.3}$$

and that the death rate increases (approximately) linearly with population size (assuming that the resources available are finite):

$$\mu_N = b_0 + b_1 N \tag{2.4}$$

Substituting (2.3) and (2.4) into the growth model (2.1) gives:

$$\frac{dN}{dt} = \pi_1 N - \pi_2 N^2 \tag{2.5}$$

with $\pi_1 = a_0 - b_0 > 0$ and $\pi_2 = a_1 + b_1 > 0$. This is the model of logistic population growth. It holds that the population grows essentially exponentially at low values of N, but that competition for fixed resources eventually drives the growth rate towards zero.

Note that (2.5) and the restrictions on the signs of coefficients implies a steady state for the population. Setting equation (2.5) equal to zero shows steady states at $N = 0$ and $N = \pi_1/\pi_2$. The non-zero steady state of the population is usually called the *carrying capacity of the environment for the population in question*. It has traditionally been denoted by K in population bioecology. The logistic model of population growth can be expressed in terms of the carrying capacity:

$$\frac{dN}{dt} = rN \left[\frac{K - N}{K} \right] \tag{2.6}$$

The coefficient $r = a_0 - b_0$ is called the *intrinsic growth rate*. It tells the speed with which the population grows in the absence of resource constraints. That is, when the population size is small compared to the carrying capacity, the growth rate essentially equals r. When the population size equals the carrying capacity, the growth rate is zero. If population size exceeds the carrying capacity (perhaps because some shock has reduced the carrying capacity), the growth rate is negative.

The parameterization in equation (2.6) provides a substantively appealing way to introduce competition. Two populations compete if the presence of either population lowers the carrying capacity for the other.

The Lotka-Volterra (LV) model of competitive interactions, which plays a prominent role in most contemporary population bioecology theory, assumes that the effect of the density of the competitor on the "realized" carrying capacity is *linear*. In the case of two competing populations, the model is

$$\frac{dN_1}{dt} = r_1 N_1 \; \frac{K_1 - \alpha_{12} N_2 - N_1}{K_1} \tag{2.7a}$$

$$\frac{dN_2}{dt} = r_2 N_2 \; \frac{K_2 - \alpha_{21} N_1 - N_2}{K_2} \tag{2.7b}$$

Comparing (2.7a) and (2.7b) with (2.6) shows that the presence of the competitor reduces the carrying capacity for the first population from K_1 to $K_1 - \alpha_{12} N_2$. The so-called competition coefficients, α_{12} and α_{21}, tell how the carrying capacity for each population declines with the density of the competitor. This model decomposes the growth rate for each population into effects of three components: (1) the intrinsic properties of the form that affect its speed of growth in the absence of resource limitations and competition, r_i, (2) limits on growth that reflect generalized conditions of resource availability, K_i, and (3) competition with specific populations, α_{ij}.

Even though the LV model builds on simple notions of density-dependence in birth and death rates and of the effects of competitive interactions, the system of equations in (2.6) does not have a known solution. Therefore, analysis of questions of coexistence of competing populations (the existence and stability of steady-states of models like (2.6) with nonzero sizes of both populations) relies on study of the qualitative behavior of the system of differential equations (see, for example, Wilson and Bossert 1971). The general result is that coexistence requires that the effects of density on mortality rates within populations must be stronger than the competitive effects between populations.

This is easy to see in the case of two competing populations. Setting equations (2.7) equal to zero and solving for the nonzero equilibrium values of N_1 and N_2 shows that stable coexistence requires that

$$\frac{1}{\alpha_{21}} < \frac{K_2}{K_1} < \alpha_{12}$$

Therefore, very similar populations (that is, populations whose competition coefficients are very near unity) can coexist only under a precise K_2/K_1 ratio. Any shock to the system that alters either carrying capacity is likely to drive the system away from the special conditions that support coexistence. Because this is an unstable equilibrium, the system will not tend to restore itself to the condition of coexistence.

Analysis of LV systems provides a way to assess Gause's principle. If two populations occupy essentially the same niche, both competition coefficients are close to unity (because addition of a member of the competing population has almost the same dampening effect on population growth as addition of a member of the population in question). Coexistence of competing species is extremely unstable when competition coefficients are close to unity. This does not mean that the principle of competitive exclusion follows logically from the LV model. But it suggests that the "principle" does describe accurately the instability of coexistence of populations that occupy the same niche.

The general (I-dimensional) LV system can be written as

$$\frac{dN_i}{dt} = r_i N_i \left[K_i - \sum_{i=1}^{I} \frac{\alpha_{ij} N_j}{K_i} \right] , \quad \alpha_{ii} = -1 \qquad (2.8)$$

The matrix of competition coefficients, sometimes called the *community matrix*, governs stability. Although this matrix is not generally symmetric, it does equal the product of a symmetric matrix of overlaps and a diagonal matrix whose entries indicate the total resource use of a population (Roughgarden 1979). The equilibrium point of this dynamic system satisfies the conditions:

$$\sum_{i=1}^{I} \alpha_{ij} N_j = K_j \qquad (2.9)$$

for all j. If one or more of N_j are zero or negative, it follows that not all I populations can coexist in a stable equilibrium (there is some competitive exclusion). If the vector n is strictly positive, the stability of the coexistence of all I populations depends on the properties of the community matrix.

Stable coexistence requires that the matrix of competition coefficients have a nonzero determinant. Levin (1970) proved that, in the context of populations whose growth depends on resources and constraints, this requirement means that at least I distinct resources (and constraints) are needed to support the stable coexistence of I populations. Thus the number of coexisting populations is constrained by the number of resources (and constraints). Earlier (Hannan and Freeman 1977) we suggested that this qualitative result be applied in organizational analysis. We proposed that the diversity of a community of organizations (the number of coexisting organizational populations) increases when new resources and constraints are added to social systems and declines when resources and constraints are eliminated.

Even though LV models do not have explicit solutions, they can still be estimated with data. Interestingly, the only attempts we have seen to do so with nonexperimental data are Carroll's (1981) analysis of growth and decline in populations of school organizations and Chapter 11 in this volume. (See also Tuma and Hannan 1984: chs. 11, 14.) By estimating an exact-discrete approximation to the LV model, Carroll was able to estimate competition coefficients directly from data.

Population biologists have typically not used the LV model or its relatives to estimate competition coefficients from nonexperimental data. Instead they rely on the close relationship between competition theory and niche theory to obtain indirect estimates of competition from overlap of observed niches (defined in terms of resource utilization). The profile of utilization of a population is a summary of its concentration on various levels of a continuous resource (or on categories of a discrete resource). We denote the utilization function of population i by $u_i(z)$. This indicates the intensity with which this population uses the resource at level z. In a typical biotic example, the resource is prey size. In a parallel organizational example, the resource might be size of a particular kind of transaction (contract for services, size of a loan, size of an order). Suppose that two populations, i and j, use the same resource base but with differing profiles of utilization. Macarthur (1968, 1970) defined the competition coefficient for this case as follows:

$$\alpha_{ij} = \frac{\int u_i(z)u_j(z)\ dz}{\int u_i^2(z)\ dz}.$$
(2.10)

This is the probability that a member of population i will encounter a member of population j at a particular resource position averaged over all resource positions divided by the probability that it will encounter a member of its own population at each position. The competition coefficient tells the probability of interpopulation interaction in resource acquisition relative to intrapopulation interaction.

When the resource has a discrete distribution, the corresponding measure of the competition coefficient is equivalent to an index well known to sociologists: Bell's (1954) p^* index of residential segregation. The p^* index was devised to measure the probability of contacts between racial or ethnic populations over neighborhoods or census districts. Olzak (1986) has generalized this index to measure occupational competition between ethnic groups, thereby highlighting the connections with general ecological theory. Her analysis treats occupations as resources and compares the utilization of these resources for different ethnic groups as the way to measure competition. A similar approach for measuring niche overlap of organizational populations appears to have considerable merit.

There are two approaches to analyzing LV-type systems empirically. One begins by estimating niches and niche overlap in order to estimate a set of competition coefficients. It then takes these estimates as parameters in evaluating the implications of the LV system in terms of growth rates and carrying capacities. The second approach estimates the effects of density of a population and of its competitors on the growth rates of a population, specifically on rates of founding, disbanding, and merger. In this sort of analysis, competition coefficients are estimated using models of growth rates and density rather than models of niche overlap.

DENSITY DEPENDENCE IN ORGANIZATIONAL POPULATIONS

We have found the general approach that underlies the LV model, though not always the models themselves, to be useful in framing questions about organizational ecology. We particularly value the three-way decomposition of population growth rates into components involving: (1) speed of expansion, (2) general environmental limits on growth, and (3) specific competition. The rest of this chapter discusses the analogues to these three components in the case of organizational populations. Does it make sense to assume that there are carrying capacity limits on the growth of populations of *organizations*? In motivating the LV model above, we noted that carrying capacities are simple functions of parameters expressing density dependence in founding rates and disbanding rates. The existence of a finite carrying capacity depends on the assumption that the founding rate falls with density and that the disbanding rate rises with density. Density serves as surrogate for the difficult-to-observe features of the material and social environment that affect the rates, particularly competition and legitimacy. Increasing density implies depletion of resources and increasing competition for the scarce remaining resources. Increasing density also strengthens the institutional standing of an organizational form. Below we develop particular models of these effects.

Why Study Population Size?

Population bioecology takes for granted that the relevant state space of the population growth process counts the *number* of members in the population. For example, the well-known studies of predator-prey interactions analyze counts of number of rabbits and number of foxes. In the biotic context, it is reasonable to assume that each rabbit exerts roughly the same demand on the resource environment. Likewise, one fox is pretty much like another. The density of populations of rabbits and foxes relative to some environmental condition is well expressed by the simple counts of numbers in each population (perhaps adjusting for age and sex distributions).

We follow a similar strategy of modeling the dynamics of counts of numbers of organizations in competing populations (such as the number of craft unions and the number of industrial unions). However, the sociological case is more complicated than the biotic one because populations of organizations sometimes exhibit considerable diversity in size among members. For example, some specialized (craft) labor unions that we studied had as few as 200 members; other broad generalist (industrial) unions have had close to two million members. The addition of a small union may have quite different consequences for existing unions than does the addition of a huge one. In this context, it may be useful to measure the size of an organizational population in terms of the aggregate size of all of its constituent organizations.

The case of labor unions, which we have studied extensively, illustrates the general issues well. Virtually all published research on growth and decline in the population of labor unions takes aggregate membership as the dimension of interest. Sociologists, economists, and labor historians have analyzed fluctuations in the total number of union members in the society or, more commonly, fluctuations in the fraction of the labor force that union members comprise. From this perspective, issues concerning carrying capacities focus on the availability of members and on legal and social constraints on the process of enlisting members. Such research, even when it does not employ the notion of a carrying capacity, recognizes that changes in the social composition of the labor force, in the industrial composition of the economy, and in laws regulating conditions of collective bargaining affect the number of members that could be mobilized by the population of unions at a particular environment. (It may well be that under certain conditions, this carrying capacity is the size of the labor force.)

We agree that the dynamics of aggregate membership involves interesting social processes. However, we do not think that understanding such dynamics is the only way—or even the best way—to analyze change in the world of labor unions. We think that the *number* of unions in a society is an interesting sociological variable in its own right. A society in which, say, all union members belong to a single union has a quite different structure from one in which the same number of members are organized into a thousand unions. For one thing, the average (and maximum) size of unions differs greatly in the two cases; and size is associated with a great many dimensions of internal structure. For another, the totality of collective actions by unions will obviously be more diverse in the second case than in the first.

In our empirical research on the ecology of labor unions, we based our research designs on a strategic bet that there are regularities in the processes that constrain growth and decline in numbers of unions (Hannan and Freeman 1987, in press). More generally, we assume that such regularities apply to all kinds of organizations and that analysis of such regularities can illuminate basic processes of organizational ecology.

Founding Rates

We assume that density affects founding rates of organizational populations by several processes. Knowledge about organizational strategies and structures is often available only to "insiders" (those already participating in such organizations). This is commonly the case when organizational functioning is shielded from public observation and when essential features of the organizational form have not been codified. In such situations, existing organizations are the only training grounds for knowledgeable organization-builders. The number of foundings in such populations depends on the number of jobs in existing organizations that give the requisite training (Brittain and Freeman 1980). Marrett (1980) argues that high density increases the founding rate by widening and strengthening the networks that connect persons with the inclination and skills to succeed in creating a certain kind of organization.

Institutional processes also link density and founding rates. If institutionalization means that certain forms attain a taken-for-granted character, then simple prevalence of a form gives it legitimacy. When numbers are small, those who attempt to create a form must fight for legitimacy. They must argue both for the special purposes of a proposed organization and for the design of the form. Once a sufficient number of instances of the form exist, the need for justifications (and thus the costs of organizing) declines. Other things being equal, legitimation of a form increases the founding rate of populations using the form. If, as we argue here, legitimacy increases with prevalence of the form in society, then legitimation processes produce positive density dependence in founding rates.

The main source of *negative* density dependence is competition within and between populations. The more abundant the competitors, the smaller the potential gains from founding an organization (and the bigger the cost to potential competitors) at a given level of demand for products and services. Fewer resources are available and markets are packed tightly in densely populated environments. For these reasons, collectives with the knowledge and skills to build organizations are less likely to make attempts in densely populated environments. Capital markets and other macro structures often reinforce this effect. For example, investors may be reluctant to participate in new ventures in dense markets. Likewise, professional associations often try to restrict entry when density is high.

In general terms, high density implies strong competitive interactions within populations dependent on limited resources for organizing (when levels of such resources have been controlled). As density grows, supplies of potential organizers, members, patrons, and resources become exhausted. Moreover, existing organizations respond to increasing competitive pressures by opposing attempts at creating still more organizations. For both of these reasons, the founding rate declines as the number of organizations in the population decreases.

Use of a simple model of the process helps convey the main point of our argument (see Hannan in press). To keep the exposition simple, assume that legitimacy (L) and competition (C) are the only relevant factors. We propose that the founding rate ($\lambda(t)$) is proportional to the legitimacy of the population and inversely proportional to the level of competition within the population:

$$\lambda(t) = a(t) \cdot \frac{L_t}{C_t} \tag{2.11}$$

and that L_t and C_t are functions of density (N_t):

$$L_t = f(N_t) \text{ and } C_t = g(N_t)$$

The crucial modeling questions concern the forms of these relationships. Unfortunately institutional and ecological theories have not addressed these issues. Our reading of the two bodies of theory suggests that both of the relationships are nonlinear. Consider the dependence of legitimacy of an organizational form on the number of copies of the form in existence. From the perspective of legitimacy as taken-for-grantedness, it seems clear that extreme rarity of a form poses serious problems of legitimacy. If almost no instances of a form exist, how can it be taken as the natural way to achieve some collective end? On the other hand, once a form becomes common, it seems unlikely that increases in numbers will have a great effect on its taken-for-grantedness. Therefore, we assume that density increases legitimacy at a decreasing rate, that legitimacy is sensitive to variations in density in the lower range but that there is something like a ceiling effect on the relationship—that is,

$$\frac{dL_t}{dN_t} > 0 \text{ and } \frac{dL_t^2}{d^2N_t} < 0$$

In the case of competition, variations in the upper range have more impact on founding rates than variations in the lower range. When numbers are few, addition of an organization to the population increases the frequency and strength of competitive interactions slightly at most. But when density is high, addition of an organization strongly increases competition. So we assume that increases in density increase competition at an increasing rate:

$$\frac{dC_t}{dN_t} > 0 \text{ and } \frac{dC_t^2}{d^2N_t} > 0$$

Moreover, we propose that the legitimacy process dominates when N_t is small but that the competition process dominates when N_t is large. That is, the effect of density on the founding rate is nonmonotonic. This is the core idea of the modeling effort.

The next step is to build a model based on particular functional forms of these relationships that agree with these qualitative restrictions. We use a simple model that is consistent with these assumptions and with the restriction that the rate be nonnegative:

$$L_t = f(N_t) = \alpha N_t^\beta, \quad \alpha > 0, \quad 0 < \beta < 1 \tag{2.12}$$

and

$$C_t = \gamma e^{\delta N_t^2}, \quad \gamma > 0, \quad \delta > 0 \tag{2.13}$$

Inserting these equations into equation (2.11), the simplified model of the founding rate, yields the basic parametric model:

$$\lambda(t) = \phi(t) N_t^\beta e^{-\delta N_t^2} \tag{2.14}$$

where $\phi(t) = a(t)\alpha/\gamma$.

This model was chosen because its qualitative behavior agrees with the theory. In particular, it implies that there is a *nonmonotonic* relationship between density and the rate. To see this, note that

$$\frac{d\lambda(t)}{dN_t} = \phi(t) N_t^{\beta-1} e^{-\delta N_t^2} \left[\beta - 2\delta N_t^2 \right] \tag{2.15}$$

There is a point of inflection (a minimum) at

$$N_t^* = \sqrt{\frac{\beta}{2\delta}} \tag{2.16}$$

The rate declines with density until N_t reaches this level and then rises with increasing density.

In empirical testing the key issue is whether this nonmonotonic model improves over a simpler model with only monotone dependence of the rate on density. A secondary but still interesting issue is whether the point of inflection falls within the observed range of density. So in estimating models with this form, we check first to see that the estimated parameters have the predicted signs and second whether the implied behavior of the process over the range of density is nonmonotonic. If the founding rate rises initially and then falls with increasing density, the process implies the existence of a carrying capacity for the population. So it is important for evaluating this theoretical approach to learn whether founding rates vary with density and, if they do, whether the dependence is nonmonotonic.

This model of density dependence in founding rates is more complicated than the corresponding assumption in the LV model. Whereas the LV model is built on the assumption of linear density dependence in this rate, the model presented here implies nonmonotonic dependence. This added complexity in the model reflects the greater complexity of organizational ecology.

We have estimated this model with partial likelihood using data on the times of foundings of national labor unions in the United States over the period from 1836 to 1985—there were 479 foundings (see Hannan and

Freeman 1987 for details). Here we report estimates of the model in (2.14) using data on the yearly counts of foundings of national labor unions over the 150 years from 1836 to 1985 and the entries of firms into the U.S. semiconductor manufacturing industry using thirty-one years from 1951 through 1981. In each case we estimate model (2.14) using maximum likelihood and the method of Poisson regression. The models analyzed included the effects of prior foundings (see below) and period effects in addition to the measures of density in the prior year. For labor unions our maximum likelihood estimates (and asymptotic standard errors) of the effects of density on the founding rate are

$$\hat{\beta} = .386 \qquad \text{s.e.}(\hat{\beta}) = .086$$
$$\hat{\delta} = .0000379 \qquad \text{s.e.}(\hat{\delta}) = .000007$$

These estimates agree with our findings using partial likelihood (Hannan and Freeman 1987); they also agree with our qualitative predictions in (2.12) and (2.13). They imply that the founding rates rise sharply with increasing density until the number of unions reached approximately eighty-eight (the range of density is from 0 to 211). At this point the founding rate was about five times larger than the rate at zero density. From that point on, the founding rate fell with increasing density. By the time density had reached its observed maximum, the founding rate was at about the same level as when $N = 10$. These findings, which are robust with respect to the inclusion of environmental covariates in the model, agree with the view that a combination of competitive and institutional processes shape founding rates in populations of organizations.

In the case of semiconductor manufacturing firms, the event is entry into the industry (as indicated by a listing in the appropriate sections of the *Electronics Buyers Guide*). So far we have analyzed the data for the period from 1950 through 1981 and find 783 entries into the industry. In preliminary analyses of yearly counts of entries over this period we find a pattern that agrees with the findings for labor unions. The maximum likelihood estimates of a simple version of (2.14) with just the density terms are

$$\hat{\beta} = .609 \qquad \text{s.e.}(\hat{\beta}) = .072$$
$$\hat{\delta} = .0000035 \qquad \text{s.e.}(\hat{\delta}) = .0000016$$

However, these findings do not appear to be robust. That is, adding measures of the demand for semiconductor products and for the cost of capital tends to eliminate the effect of N^2 (without diminishing the effect of N). So we do not yet have convincing evidence that competitive processes have shaped the flow of entries into this industry. Still, in all the specifications we have tried, density does affect the entry rate. Additional analysis is required to discern whether the effect of density on this rate is monotonic or nonmonotonic.

The populations of national labor unions and semiconductor manufacturers differ in several important ways. Although labor unions fought to establish their legitimacy over a very long period of time, and their density reflects success in winning that battle, semiconductor electronics firms were always legitimate. Their leaders did not have to contend with marauding bands of company detectives or state legislatures inclined to declare their illegality. Challenges to their existence came from two sources: the market for their products and the technology. Both developed rapidly over the thirty years under study, and both were characterized by extreme turbulence (Braun and MacDonald 1978; Brittain and Freeman 1980).

The semiconductor industry is a relatively young industry. Small, entrepreneurial firms are being started yearly, and only after our data stop, in the mid-1980s, does it appear that oligopoly is a real possibility. Consequently, an expanding market for the devices produced by the organizations under study means a growing upper limit on the number of such organizations that can exist. That is, the carrying capacity is expanding throughout the time period under study.

We assume that the processes by which density affects founding rates also apply to disbanding rates with some modifications. The modifications follow from the observation that founding rates pertain to attempts (and the absence of attempts) to create organizations, while failure rates pertain to existing organizations. Disbanding rates presumably depend on properties of individual organization such as age and size as well as on population characteristics such as density. But founding rates depend only on population characteristics (because a founding that does not occur cannot be associated with an organization's characteristics).

Some of the processes by which density affects disbanding rates operate mainly at low densities and others at higher densities. At low densities, the growth of populations of organizations is constrained by the novelty and rarity of the form. The fact that there are few organizations in the population presumably makes it difficult to convince key actors (such as banks and government agencies) to transfer material and symbolic resources to organizations in the population. It may likewise be difficult to convince talented people to join such organizations and to remain in them.

Above we suggested that rarity of an organizational form cast doubts on its legitimacy. Most organizations theorists assume that legitimacy decreases disbanding rates (Meyer and Rowan 1977). Thus, increasing density will lower disbanding rates by increasing the legitimacy of the form (and of populations using the form). Low density also hampers attempts at coordinated political action to protect and defend claims of the population or of some of its members.

Increases in numbers alleviate these problems. Growth in numbers of organizations gives force to claims of institutional standing and also provides economies of scale in political and legal action. That is, increases in numbers lower the disbanding rate.

At high density, competitive interactions intensify. Growth in numbers increases the likelihood and intensity of both *direct competition* between pairs of organizations and *diffuse competition* among all (or many) of them. Individual organizations can easily avoid direct competition with others for members and other scarce resources when there are few organizations in the system. As the number of potential competitors grows, avoidance becomes more difficult.

For example, labor unions competed for the services of skilled organizers and dedicated staff, political support and influence, attention from the news media, and so forth. Sometimes such competition involved direct rivalry, as when two or more unions seeking to organize the same workers competed for support of and membership in a national federation such as the AFL and CIO. More often the competition was diffuse—it had more the character of congestion than rivalry. As the number of unions grew large, more of the resources used to build and sustain unions were claimed by unions that could defend themselves against raids. Such diffuse competition lowers the life chances of new unions and also affects the life chance of existing unions. In other words, when density is already high, further growth increases disbanding rates.

We assume that the disbanding rate at age u, $\mu(u)$, is proportional to the level of competition and inversely proportional to the legitimacy of the population:

$$\mu(u) = b(u) \cdot \frac{C_u}{L_u} \tag{2.16}$$

As in the case of the founding rate, we assume that density increases competition at an increasing rate but increases legitimacy at a decreasing rate.

There is no obvious reason not to use the same parametric assumptions regarding the dependence of legitimacy and competition on density as made above for the founding process. However, there is no reason to assume that the parameters of each part of the process are identical for the two rates. So we assume that

$$L_u = \nu N_u^{\varkappa} \quad \nu > 0 \quad \varkappa > 0 \tag{2.17}$$

and

$$C_u = \varsigma e^{\lambda N_u^2} \quad \varsigma > 0 \quad \lambda > 0 \tag{2.18}$$

With these assumptions the model for the disbanding rate is

$$\mu(u) = \psi(u) N_u^{-\varkappa} e^{\lambda N_u^2} \tag{2.19}$$

where $\psi(u) = \zeta/b(u)v$. What matters are the functional form and signs of parameters. Again the crucial qualitative feature of the model is that the effect of density on disbanding rates is *nonmonotonic*. The model implies that *the disbanding rate falls with increasing density up to a point (the neighborhood of the carrying capacity) and then rises with increasing density*. (Note again the departure from the LV assumption of linear density dependence.)

In our empirical research with this model (Hannan and Freeman, in press), it turned out to be difficult to obtain convergent estimates of the model in (2.19). Therefore we used an alternative specification whose parameters have essentially the same qualitative interpretation:

$$\mu(u) = \psi(u)e^{(-\theta_1 N_u + \theta_2 N_u^2)} \qquad (2.20)$$

Differentiating the rate with respect to density, we have

$$\frac{d\mu(u)}{dN_u} = \mu(u) \cdot [-\theta_1 + 2\theta_2 N_u], \quad \theta_1 > 0 \quad \theta_2 > 0$$

Again the model implies a point of inflection (a minimum), this time the minimum is given by

$$N^* = \frac{\theta_1}{2\theta_2} \qquad (2.21)$$

Below this level of density the rate declines with increasing density; above this level the rate increases with increasing density.

We used the same two data sets (national labor unions and semiconductor companies) to estimate the model in (2.20). Of the 621 unions observed between 1836 and 1985, 191 disbanded; the rest ended in merger or were still functioning in 1985 (that is, they are right-censored). We estimated models with the functional form of (2.20) and added the effects of aging, the type of starting event, and effects of historic periods. Our partial likelihood estimates of the theoretically relevant parameters are

$$\hat{\theta}_1 = -.020 \qquad \text{s.e.}(\hat{\theta}_1) = .007$$
$$\hat{\theta}_2 = .000090 \qquad \text{s.e.}(\hat{\theta}_2) = .000035$$

Again these estimates agree with our qualitative predictions in (2.20). These estimates imply that the disbanding rate falls with increasing density until density reaches about 100. At this point the disbanding rate is only about 40 percent as high as at zero density. From this point on the disbanding rate rises with increasing density. So as was the case with the founding rate, the disbanding rate of national labor unions has a nonmonotonic relation to density within the observed range of density.

We have estimated comparable models for exits from the semiconductor industry using data for the 1950–81 period. These models include the firm's age (measured as the number of years since it appeared in the semiconductor industry) and period effects as well as the effects of density. Partial likelihood estimates of the effects of density on the exit rate (using the model in (2.20) are

$$\hat{\theta}_1 = -.014 \qquad s.e.(\hat{\theta}_1) = .000049$$
$$\hat{\theta}_2 = .003 \qquad s.e.(\hat{\theta}_2) = .000008$$

These estimates are strikingly similar to those yielded by the union data.

Using the relationship in (2.21), these estimates imply that the exit rate reaches a minimum when the number of firms in the industry reaches 250 and rises with further increases in numbers. The point of inflection again falls within the observed range (the maximum level of density observed is 335). So the predicted nonmonotonic pattern does seem to have characterized the early history of the semiconductor industry. Despite the many obvious differences in the ecologies of unions and semiconductor manufacturing firms, our analysis suggests that the exit rates, defined broadly, of both kinds of populations were affected similarly by density, in a manner that agrees with our hypothesized model of legitimation and competition. These results strengthen our hope that density dependence will prove useful as an ingredient in general models of organizational population dynamics.

Merger Rates

Fluctuations of numbers in organizational populations are also affected by merger rates. Merger is a more complicated kind of event than disbanding or exit from an industry. For one thing, merger requires the coordination of two or more organizations. For another, organizations merge both because they are failing and because they are succeeding. That is, some mergers reflect attempts to incorporate successful technologies and organizational forms, as when established giant firms acquire newer, innovative firms. Other mergers reflect the low valuation of merger targets— firms that are faring poorly can often be acquired cheaply. So the merger rate depends on organizational outcomes in a very complicated way. We suspect that it also depends on density in a complicated way as well. We have not yet succeeded in modeling this process.

Competition among Populations

The various processes responsible for density-dependence within populations have strong parallels in processes occurring between populations.

Just as the addition of an organization to a population affects the founding and disbanding rates in that population, the addition of an organization to a competing population may also affect these rates. These are two kinds of density dependence. The only distinction is whether the effect occurs within a population or across the boundary between populations.

In conceptualizing interactions among organizational populations, we retain the classic sociological distinction between competition and conflict. As Durkheim and Simmel insisted, conflict is a social relation that requires interaction between the parties. Parties to a conflict take each other into account. Competition by contrast is often indirect. The growth of one population of organizations may depress the growth of another even though the members of the two populations never interact directly. In fact, the members of the populations may not even be aware that they stand in a competitive relation if they compete indirectly for resources. In one classic form of competitive situation, the undominated market of many buyers and sellers, no actor needs to know the identity of its competitors.

Our analyses rely on competition between populations for limited material and social resources for building and sustaining organizations. We do not assume anything like a fully competitive "market." Our theories hold even when the number of competitors is sufficiently small that the actions of one competitor can change the terms of trade significantly. In these circumstances, competition often causes conflict. There is no reason for us to assume the absence of conflict. In fact, we think that the usual state of affairs is for intense, localized competition to turn into conflict. However, we do not assume the existence of conflict as a precondition for our arguments.

We investigate whether the density of other populations affects the founding and disbanding rates of a target population. If such a link exists and the density of population B decreases the founding rate and/or increases the disbanding rate of population A, we infer that population A competes with B. If, in turn, the density of A depresses the founding rate and/or raises the disbanding rate of B, we have an example of classic reciprocal competition. But if the density of A raises the founding rate or depresses the disbanding rate of B, the interaction has the predator-prey form. Several other cases are possible, including symbiosis in which the density of each population increases the founding rates and/or decreases the disbanding rates of the other.

Although there may be particular cases in which the legitimation of one population depends on the *size* of some other population, it seems unlikely that this is the case generally. However, whenever two populations seek to exploit the same limited resources, the density of each affects the strength of competitive interactions, as we noted above in discussing the LV model. Therefore, in developing a multipopulation model, we specify only competitive effects between populations. It seems likely (as Lotka and Volterra assumed for the biotic case) that the strength of competitive interactions increases monotonically with density. So assume that the strength of competitive pressures on the first population has the form:

$$C_{12t} = g(N_{1t}, N_{2t}) \tag{2.22}$$

with

$$\frac{dg}{dN_{1t}} < 0, \frac{d^2g}{dN_{1t}^2} > 0$$

and

$$\frac{dg}{dN_{2t}} > 0, \frac{d^2g}{dN_{2t}^2} > 0, \frac{d^2g}{dN_{1t}N_{2t}} > 0$$

In other words, we assume that the effect of density of the competing population is monotonic.

A simple parametric model consistent with these assumptions (and with the constraint that rates be nonnegative) is

$$C_{12} = \exp(\beta_1 N_{1t}^2 + \beta_2 N_{2t}) \tag{2.23}$$

This assumption when combined with the assumption made above about legitimacy implies the following form of density dependence:

$$\lambda(t) = \phi(t)N_{1t}^{\alpha}\exp(-\beta_1 N_{1t}^2 + \beta_2 N_{2t}) \tag{2.24}$$

The cross-effect of density (β_2) captures the effect of *interpopulation competition*. Whenever the two populations use the same resources, the cross-effect is negative for both populations.

Elsewhere (Hannan and Freeman 1987) we estimated the model in (2.24) using data on the times of foundings of the two main forms of labor unions: craft and industrial unions. We found evidence of asymmetric competition. The effect of the density of industrial unions on the founding rate of craft unions was negative and significantly different from zero. However, the density of craft unions had no systematic effect on the founding rate of industrial unions.

CONCLUSIONS

We have suggested that population of organizations facing finite environments display density-dependence in rates of birth and death. Although we loosely follow the lead of population biologists in formulating models of density dependence in such rates, we think that organizational ecology is more complicated than biotic ecology. In particular, we think that density dependence in the growth rates of organizational populations reflects opposing forces of legitimation and competition. Our model of these processes suggests that the joint effect of density-dependent legitimation processes and density-dependent competition processes produces non-monotonic density dependence in birth and death rates.

We have explored the implications of this model with data on the histories of two populations of organizations: national labor unions and manufacturers of semiconductor electronics devices. Overall we find a robust pattern of effects that agrees with the model, with the exception of the somewhat fragile findings regarding entry rates for the semiconductor population. The predicted nonmonotonic pattern of density dependence holds for many different specifications using many different covariates describing the environmental conditions facing the population. The fact that the pattern occurs in two such different populations at different times in U.S. history gives us some confidence that we have identified a generic organizational process. We look forward to exploring this process with data on other kinds of organizational populations.

3 ORGANIZATIONAL ORIGINS
Entrepreneurial and Environmental Imprinting at the Time of Founding

Warren P. Boeker

Organizations, like other social systems, have histories. The process through which organizations come to develop the characteristics they currently exhibit is strongly delimited by this earlier history. The founding of the organization has an especially influential effect on the structure, processes, and strategy the organization develops and continues to exhibit over time.

Stinchcombe (1965) was one of the first organizational theorists to emphasize the importance of the founding period. He argued that events surrounding the creation of a new organization have a long-lasting effect on its subsequent development. Others have since echoed his thesis. Kimberly (1979: 438), for instance, observes that

> There is the possibility, at least, that, just as for a child, the conditions under which an organization is born and the course of its development in infancy have important consequences for its later life. Just as one might be interested in similarities and differences in the backgrounds of executives as one important element in an explanation of their personal success, so might one be interested in the backgrounds of organizations.

Pennings (1980: 254, emphasis added) argues similarly:

> The creation of a new organization is one of the most salient moments of its life cycle. Organizational birth is salient not only because it is the starting point of that life cycle but also because it is an overriding factor in molding and constraining the organization's behavior during the subsequent stages of its life cycle. Foundation

involves a decision as to location that constrains the organization geographically. The entrepreneur acquires equipment and other assets and selects markets that put further limits on adaptation. The initial stage entails a learning process that results in decision-making patterns, an authority structure, and rules and procedures that are relatively permanent and evoke pressures toward organizational inertia. While organizations undergo modifications and display varying degrees of flexibility, *they are cast at birth into a mold that is discernible in all subsequent stages of their life cycle.*

Particularly interesting from a theoretical viewpoint is Stinchcombe's notion of "imprinting." Stinchcombe argues that organizations, at the time they are established, have incorporated elements of the larger societal social structure of the period into their basic structures. That is, the social conditions prevalent at the time of founding become imprinted into newly founded organizations. Because these traits are viewed as being highly inertial, the imprinting hypothesis implies that an organization reflects the historical circumstances of its founding period throughout its existence.

Stinchcombe's imprinting hypothesis has been utilized widely by organizational theorists but its empirical status remains ambiguous. We have yet to see any rigorous empirical examination of the argument. Such evidence is especially important to the perspective of organizational ecology because it implies an imprinting assumption (Hannan and Freeman 1977, 1984; Aldrich 1979).

More specifically, ecological theorists have argued vociferously that organizations exhibit strong inertial properties that limit change (Hannan and Freeman 1984). Choices made early in the development of organizations are seen as serving both to shape their subsequent characteristics and to constrain the range of future options available to them (Miles and Randolph 1980). If inertia exists and change in the core properties of organizations is limited, then the founding of the organization provides the initial template from which subsequent organizational actions are derived.

Newly formed organizations are characterized by high levels of uncertainty in decisionmaking (Greiner 1972). Work routines must be identified and assigned, and new roles and relationships must be negotiated and developed. Enactment of the new setting provides information that the organization uses to convert heretofore nonroutine portions of the setting into routine activities (Nelson and Winter 1982). The organization's strategy, its structure, and patterns of influence that develop among organizational subunits and participants gradually become established to govern decisionmaking and behaviors.

Consider the conditions at the very outset of an organization's founding. It presumably has some consensus on its mission and some resources to draw upon, but likely has very little else—no existing structure, standards, internal ideology, or facilities. It is incumbent on the entrepreneur or founding leader to establish the initial structure, acquire the facilities, hire the initial employees, and create the conditions that are subsequently imprinted. Thus, the organization's founding entrepreneur is particularly important to the imprinting hypothesis of Stinchcombe. He or she serves as a primary conduit by which larger social conditions become incorporated into organizational strategy and structure. However, the entrepreneur is only one possible conduit. It is therefore useful to consider separately the roles of entrepreneurs and the environment.

THE ROLE OF ENTREPRENEURS

Entrepreneurs often have strong ideas about how to organize their firms for maximum effectiveness. Decisions about how to divide up product lines, market areas, and functional responsibilities become intermingled with assumptions about internal relationships and with theories of how to get things done. These assumptions and theories derive from the social background of the entrepreneur starting the organization.

Histories and cast studies of organizations reveal how the personal beliefs and preferences of entrepreneurs on a matter can mold an organization at its founding and for some time afterwards (Chandler 1962). Freeman (1984: 8) notes that

> No one who starts a new organization is fully free to structure it as he or she might wish. Few would quarrel with the existence of such constraints as legal regulations, or the limitations of technology. Entrepreneurs are also limited by their own experience. People starting new organizations have limited experience to use for guidance and limited time to be used in organizational tinkering.

Strategy formulation is seldom such an analytically objective process that we may exclude from consideration the values and assumptions of those who form the firm's dominant coalition (Cyert and March 1963). Past studies of the role of top management indicate that personal values are important determinants of strategy (Guth and Tagiuri 1965; Andrews 1971). Most entrepreneurs possess personal conceptions of what their organization's strategy either is or ought to be. These conceptions, however idiosyncratic, are likely to reflect the entrepreneur's own background and prior experience. Most entrepreneurs starting new firms tend to behave in ways that reflect their own cognitive biases and their own preferences when choosing among alternative strategies.

Decisions articulating the firm's strategic direction are hardly separable from the personal assumptions of executives who make the choice. Those who direct company mission or strategy do not look exclusively at what the company might do and can do. They are often more heavily influenced by personal preferences. This view is captured by Sarason's (1972: 24) discussion of the importance of founder's values in the development of the organization:

> if you wish to understand the creation and development of the Ford Motor Company, you have to understand the kind of person Henry Ford was: his habits, ways of thinking, goals, values and so on. Or if you want to understand how the Menninger and Mayo Clinics were created and developed, you have to know what the brothers Menninger and Mayo were like—their personal, intellectual, and professional histories. Or if one wants to understand "The Harmony Society," one of many religious-communist societies of the nineteenth century described by Nordhoff (1966), one has to understand its founder, George Rapp.

The personal assumptions, perceptions and biases of entrepreneurs starting a new company play a central role in both the formulation of strategy and the manner in which influence will be distributed within the firm. Entrepreneurs create organizations that are in many ways a reflection of their own past backgrounds and experiences.

Entrepreneurs are likely to seek models to imitate in order to avoid the task of reinventing each organizational role (Brittain and Freeman 1980). The entrepreneur's own past experience forms the basis for the models used; new organizations do not spring from the minds of entrepreneurs as totally original creations. The nascent firm's memory lies within organizational actors (Nelson and Winter 1982) rather than in existing structure and processes. The newly founded organization's structure arises out of the previous experiences of the entrepreneur and is much more dependent on their input than is the structure of an established firm.

PAST RESEARCH ON THE INFLUENCE OF ENTREPRENEURS

Kimberly's (1979) study of events surrounding the creation of a new medical school provides support for the view that individuals and their own value systems are more critical in newly formed organizations. Kimberly argues that although aspects of the founding process can be interpreted in terms of the organization's technology and environment, such interpretations ignore many of the prerequisites necessary for the founding to occur. When describing the role of the medical school's founder and first dean, he says (1979: 454): "call him an entrepreneur, a leader, or a guru, the fact is that his personality, his dreams, his flaws, and his talents were largely responsible for the school's early structure and results."

More recently, Schein (1983) investigated the role played by three entrepreneurs in the organizations they founded. In all three cases the founders' personal assumptions of the organization's future direction and mission became institutionalized and remained so, even though the firms grew much larger, modified aspects of their businesses, and changed leaders. Pettigrew (1979) analyzed the origins and subsequent development of a school's culture through retrospective interviews and archival data. His study identified key events in the school's history and demonstrated the central roles played by the school's founder as well as subsequent headmasters. Clark (1972) used retrospective approaches to reconstruct the histories of several colleges. In these "sagas" the values and visions of the early founders were shown to have inspired the school's early employees and definitively shaped the future course of the institution.

Past research on the role of entrepreneurial influence in the creation of new organizations seems to support the view that the characteristics of the organization's founders are reflected in the design of the new organization and its method of operating. Because organizations are primarily begun by individuals, these individuals (the founders) play a central role in guiding the organization's creation process. As Weber (1947) observed with respect to the charismatic leader, it is the founder who is the earliest and most important progenitor of the organization's priorities, shared assumptions, and strategy.

THE ROLE OF THE ENVIRONMENT

Entrepreneurs are unlikely to exhibit unilateral influence on the strategy and social structure of newly created organizations. If, as Stinchcombe (1965) argued, organizational structures and processes are natural products of earlier environmental conditions and cultural norms, then initial choices of strategy, technology, and structure also arise from environmental conditions at the time of founding. As Freeman (1984: 11) observed: "In the extreme, when inertia is very high, current technological and environmental conditions have nothing to do with explaining the current structure. Rather, one must look to those characteristics at the time of founding, when the organization was smaller than it is today."

Examining the relationship between the date of organizational founding and the orientation and structure of a group of rehabilitation organizations, Kimberly (1975: 1) states that

> As open systems, organizations engage in various transactions with their environments. These transactions are complex, variable across organizations and environments, and reciprocal. At a given time, however, there are various environmental constraints which limit the structural form that organizations can adopt. Thus, the etiology of organizational configurations is, at least in part, a function of environmental influences, and variability in these configurations should be predictably related to variability in environmental influences.

Earlier works by Stinchcombe (1965) and by Chandler (1962, 1977) both point to the influence of specific historic and cultural factors on subsequent organizational development. Environmental conditions determine not only the needs for particular goods and services but also many of the characteristics of the organizations created to provide them.

Stinchcombe argued that organizational structures, processes, and norms of behavior imprinted at a point in time tend to persist, even though environmental conditions may have changed dramatically. He further asserted that imprinting tends to restrict the adoption of new structures and processes unless changes in environmental conditions are especially stark and dramatic. For example, even in the twentieth century most railroad companies had structures, staffing patterns, and managerial views of the market that in many ways were a manifestation of the environmental conditions in the period of their founding during the nineteenth century.

RESEARCH ON ENVIRONMENTAL EFFECTS

Research on the effects of early environment on organizational characteristics is not as extensive as that of the influence of the entrepreneur on the organization. The small amount of work that has been done seems to support the idea that events surrouding the founding and early history of the organization have important influences on subsequent organizational activity. Stinchcombe (1965) has demonstrated how the character and structure of an organization formed during its creation persist even when the context within which the organization was created has changed. Kimberly (1975) further demonstrated Stinchcombe's notion of organizational imprinting in a longitudinal study of sheltered workshops, in which characteristics prevalent during the period of the organization's founding persisted for several decades. Differences in environmental constraints at founding were closely related to the organization's rehabilitation orientation as well as other organizational characteristics. Empirical work by Carroll and Delacroix (1982) and Carroll and Huo (1986) demonstrates how characteristics of the environment at the time the organization begins affect subsequent death rates in a sample of newspapers. In addition, the case studies of organizational creation and early development by Sarason (1972) and Kimberly (1979) have provided evidence of the constraints that the early environment imposes on subsequent organizational behaviors and outcomes.

To summarize, differences in both the past experience of entrepreneurs starting new organizations and environmental conditions at founding can, at least in part, explain why organizations begun at different times have different forms and might pursue different strategies when they start. To study this issue empirically, I examine the influence of *entrepreneur characteristics* and *environmental conditions* at the time of founding on the strategy *initially* adopted by organizations in the semiconductor industry.

The semiconductor industry is a particularly attractive venue for this study because of its relatively brief history. The industry itself dates from the late 1950s, and information on firm founders and events surrounding the founding of the firm are generally available.

DESCRIPTION OF VARIABLES

Organizational Strategy

Research on business-level strategy has evolved considerably in recent years, moving from earlier case studies of the detailed histories of single firms to comparative studies across several firms (Hambrick 1980). A recent approach to operationalizing business-level strategy is through strategic typologies (Porter 1980) or strategic groups (Oster 1982). Strategic typologies are especially useful for parsimoniously conveying fundamental differences in strategic approach. Each strategic type is viewed as having its own distinct pattern of characteristics. Typologies are developed to capture both the comprehensiveness and the integrative nature of strategy.

The usefulness of any strategic typology depends on the dimensions that the typology attempts to explicate. A strategic typology that seems particularly well suited for technology-based industries was first introduced by Ansoff and Stewart (1967) and more recently has been extended by Maidique and Patch (1982). They define four broad strategies commonly found in high-technology industries in terms that are relevant to a technology-intensive environment. These strategic types, which can usefully capture differences in the strategies used by semiconductor manufacturers, are defined below (adapted from Maidique and Patch, 1982: 276):

1. The *first-mover* or first to market strategy aims to get the product to the market before the competition. It provides the advantages of a temporary monopoly in exploiting a new technology during the period preceding the adoption of the new technology by competitors. The benefits of this strategy can be exploited by either of two principal approaches: (a) skimming by pricing high to achieve an immediate profit or (b) through an experience curve approach, achieving learning economies through earlier production of the device, which can maintain technological leadership as well as building customer loyalty.
2. The *second-mover* or "fast follower" strategy involves quick imitation of innovations pioneered by a competitor. Emphasis generally focuses on attracting customers away from the technological innovator. Second-movers attempt to learn from the innovator's mistakes, so as to develop an improved, more reliable product that may include

features desired by customers while avoiding those products that prove to be market failures.

3 . The *low cost producer* or cost minimization strategy achieves a relative cost advantage over competitors through economies of scale in manufacturing and distribution, through process and product design modifications to reduce costs and through overhead minimization and operating cost control.

4 . The *niche* strategy focuses on serving small pockets of demand with special applications of the basic technology. Large size or mass production competence is not required for this strategy and may even be a handicap because scheduling and control requirements for a large number of special applications can be exceedingly complex.

Characteristics of the Entrepreneur

Characteristics of entrepreneurs thought to affect the strategy the organization adopts and the way it is structured include (1) the entrepreneur's previous functional experience, (2) the company the entrepreneur had worked for previously, (3) the entrepreneur's educational experience, and (4) the entrepreneur's age.

Functional Background. Founders of semiconductor firms appear to come from roughly three types of functional backgrounds or experiences: (1) research, design, and development, (2) manufacturing and production, or (3) marketing, sales, and customer service. Although entrepreneurs may have held several jobs over their careers, in the vast majority of cases their primary work experience comes from within one of these three areas. Entrepreneurs are likely to have spent their earlier career specializing and gaining experience in a particular functional area. Founders are expected to make strategic choices that reflect these previous functional experiences.

Hypothesis 1: The previous functional experience of the entrepreneur will influence the strategy initially adopted by the newly created firm.

H1a: Firms employing a first-mover initial strategy will be disproportionately founded by entrepreneurs with previous functional experience in research, design, or development.

H1b: Firms employing a second-mover initial strategy will be disproportionately founded by entrepreneurs with previous functional experience in marketing or sales.

H1c: Firms employing a low-cost initial strategy will be disproportionately founded by entrepreneurs with previous functional experience in manufacturing or production.

H1d: Firms employing a niche producer strategy will be disporportionately founded by entrepreneurs with previous functional experience in marketing or sales.

The reasoning for hypotheses 1a and 1c follows directly from arguments advanced earlier. Founders with experience in research or development are expected to rely more heavily on innovativeness and being first to the market with a new product. Founders with experience in manufacturing or production are likely to place more emphasis on efficiency and being a low-cost producer.

Hypotheses 1b and 1d reflect the emphasis that founders with experience in marketing or sales are expected to have on serving customer needs. Both the niche strategy and the second-mover strategy are attempts to satisfy specific customer needs or requirements that are not served by existing organizations. In the case of the niche strategy, the firm actually focuses on a small subset of the market. Managers of firms pursuing a second-mover strategy attempt to create imitations (often improved imitations) of products that have already been introduced by other organizations. Management of the second-mover is aware of customer needs and demands and, by creating slightly modified copies of existing products, can serve customer needs that are not currently being met.

Company Previously Worked For (the Incubator Firm). Characteristics of the firm an entrepreneur previously worked for are likely to affect the way in which the entrepreneur organizes his own firm, as well as limiting the range of strategic options considered by the founder. The organization an entrepreneur comes from, which Cooper (1971) terms an *incubator,* provides the entrepreneur with experience that leads to particular managerial skills and industry knowledge. Cooper noted that the founding of new firms, "seems to be closely related to the characteristics of established incubator organizations." Because the new business draws primarily on the knowledge and skills of the entrepreneur, one might expect that the choice of strategy would be closely tied to the experience gained in the incubator organization.

Hypothesis 2: The strategy employed by the firm the entrepreneur previously worked for will influence the strategy initially adopted by the newly created firm.

H2a: Entrepreneurs who previously worked for a firm with a first-mover strategy will disproportionately adopt a first-mover strategy in their own organization.

H2b: Entrepreneurs who previously worked for a firm with a second-mover strategy will disproportionately adopt a second-mover strategy in their own organization.

H2c: Entrepreneurs who previously worked for a firm with a low-cost strategy will disproportionately adopt a low-cost strategy in their own organization.

H2d: Entrepreneurs who previously worked for a firm with a niche strategy will disproportionately adopt a niche strategy in their own organization.

Formal Education.   A founder's formal educational background may be viewed as an indication of his or her knowledge and skill base. Although most entrepreneurs in the semiconductor industry have at least some technical training, they differ in the extent of their training (such as B.S., M.S., Ph.D.). Entrepreneurs who are more highly educated are more likely to stress the importance of technical innovation and sophistication in their own competitive approach. It is expected that entrepreneurs with more extensive technical training are likely to be more familiar with recent innovations, will compete in leading-edge products and processes, and will pursue strategies stressing innovation.

Hypothesis 3:   Entrepreneurs who are more highly educated in a technical field (engineering or science-based) will be more likely to pursue a first-mover strategy.

Age.   Several studies of entrepreneurship (such as Collins and Moore 1970; Boswell 1973) have found an inverse relationship between youth and risk, with younger managers pursuing more risky strategies. The age distribution of semiconductor firm founders is probably narrower than that of entrepreneurs in other industries—most entrepreneurs in our sample are ages 35 to 50 when they begin their firms. This lower degree of variability might limit the effects of founder age. But it is likely that the age construct is actually a measure of two separate factors which may influence risk or innovativeness: (1) Following traditional arguments from the entrepreneurship literature, younger entrepreneurs are more risk seeking than older entrepreneurs; and (2) given the rapid changes in technology that have occurred in the industry, obsolescence of past technical training can occur relatively quickly. Because of technological obsolescene, the effects of founders' age are expected to be strengthened.

Hypothesis 4:   Younger founders will be more likely to pursue a first-mover strategy.

Environmental Characteristics: The Development of the Semiconductor Industry

Hypothesis 5:   Environmental conditions at the time of founding will influence the strategy initially adopted by the newly created firm.

The environment of the industry is viewed by many (cf. U.S. Department of Commerce 1979; Hanson 1982; Dataquest 1984) as consisting of roughly four separate periods of development:

1958–66: the Military Market.   The earliest period of the industry was characterized by the domination of government and military purchases, offering producers an assured demand for integrated circuits at premium prices. Semiconductor producers were free to experiment with new products and original designs, encouraging firms to pursue strategies stressing innovation.

H5a: Semiconductor firms started between 1958 and 1966 will disproportionately pursue a first-mover strategy.

1967–73: Symbiotic Competition.   The development of the computer and industrial electronics market in the United States during this period increased the demand for semiconductors dramatically. Existing firms could not meet this emerging demand and opportunity developed for new firms to enter the semiconductor market by offering imitations of products that were pioneered by earlier producers.

H5b: Semiconductor firms started between 1967 and 1973 will disproportionately pursue a second-mover strategy.

1974–79: Expansion of the Consumer Market, Entry of the Japanese.   The development of large-scale integrated circuits in the early 1970s lowered the cost and broadened the appeal of semiconductor technologies. As technical advances permitted competition on cost and drove the price of an electronic function progressively downward, the circuits themselves became commodity items. Further influencing the emphasis on competition and competitive pricing during this period was the entry of the Japanese.

H5c: Semiconductor firms started between 1974 and 1979 will disproportionately pursue a low-cost strategy.

1980–84: Advent of the Custom Market.   The most recent stage of the semiconductor industry's evolution has witnessed a shift toward customization, driven by the strong demand for unique, cost-effective products and the lack of large-scale integrated circuits that are feasible for many unique applications.

H5d: Semiconductor firms started between 1980 and 1984 will disproportionately pursue a niche strategy.

Methodology and Measurement

The hypotheses are tested using information gathered through structured interviews as well as archival data. Initially the participation of sixty-two semiconductor firms was solicited, representing a comprehensive estimate of the entire population of merchant semiconductor firms in the Santa Clara–San Jose Area (which is headquarters for the majority of semiconductor firms in the United States). Six organizations were removed from the sample after being contacted because they no longer produced semiconductor devices or because at the time of the interview they produced devices for only internal consumption. Five other firms refused to participate. The semiconductor firms that were selected for the study but did not participate do not differ significantly from the final sample in terms of size, complexity, or any other apparent characteristics.

Interviews were conducted with presidents and top-level managers of fifty-one merchant semiconductor firms, comprising over one-half of the semiconductor producers in the United States. The interview focused on the president or chief executive officer of the firm. In the few cases where the president or chief executive was not available, they were asked to recommend another individual familiar with the firm's strategy and policies. In several cases, especially with larger semiconductor manufacturers, numerous people were interviewed in addition to the president. Questionnaire and interview data was augmented with information collected by and made available through semiconductor market research firms such as Dataquest, Data Resources Inc., and Gnostic Concepts. Firm-level information was also obtained through articles in the business and electronics press.

MEASUREMENT OF VARIABLES

Organizational Strategy

The determination of business-level strategy is somewhat subjective because it requires inputing a motive to the business. The appraisals of top managers within the firm (gathered through the structured interviews) were used to provide assessments of how firms differ in their competitive emphasis within the industry. The measurement of initial strategy is taken from the self-reports of the company because the top management of the firm is more likely to be aware of the initial strategy taken by the organization than are those working outside the organization. The strategic typology previously described consists of four relatively distinct patterns of organizational response in the semiconductor industry. Scaled responses were utilized to create a more "fine-grained" measure of strategic tendency than many past strategy studies, which have measured only modal strategic approach. Strategy is measured proportionally on a 100 point (total) scale by permitting the respondents to allocate points representing the extent to which the organization pursues each of the four strategies (first-mover, second-mover, low-cost producer, niche producer) at the time of its founding.

Each organization was characterized by the extent to which its initial strategy was that of a first-mover, second-mover, low-cost producer, or niche producer. The firms had a value of zero in one or more of the four strategy types in over 70 percent of the cases (that is, a particular strategy was in no way descriptive of the firm).

Entrepreneur Characteristics

Functional Background. Functional background consists of the primary functional experience of the entrepreneur prior to starting the new firm. The functional background of the entrepreneur is measured categorically as falling within one of three areas: (1) research and development, (2) manufacturing and production, or (3) marketing, sales, and customer service. Whenever possible this is determined through interviews. In cases where respondents indicated a lack of knowledge regarding the entrepreneur's functional background, archival data from the business and electronics press is utilized.

In all of the firms in this sample this categorization was comprehensive and mutually exclusive. In all but one of the cases the founder's primary work experience could be categorized as coming from within one of these three broad functional areas.

Company Previously Worked For (Incubator). The founder's previous organizational experience is measured in terms of the strategy pursued by the firm the founder previously worked for. In the vast majority of cases (forty-five of fifty-one) founders of semiconductor firms had previously worked for other semiconductor firms. Therefore, the measurement methodology is similar to that outlined above for organizational strategy. Incubator strategy is measured proportionally as falling within the four strategic groups (first-mover, second-mover, low-cost producer or niche producer). Although the measure is not a precise evaluation of incubator strategy, it does provide a good indication of the strategy favored by the organization the founder emerged from.

Age of Entrepreneur.   Age of the entrepreneurs in the sample is measured as age at the time of new firm founding. It was gathered through interview responses or the electronics and business press.

Entrepreneur Education.   Entrepreneur education is measured by the highest degree obtained, categorized as: (1) obtained a bachelor's degree, (2) obtained a master's degree, or (3) obtained a Ph.D.

Industry Environment

Industry environment is measured categorically as the period during which the firm was first started. Four distinct periods of development were identified in the semiconductor industry:

1. 1958–66: the military market,
2. 1967–73: symbiotic competition,
3. 1974–79: expansion of the consumer market. Entry of the Japanese,
4. 1980–84: the advent of the custom market.

RESULTS AND DISCUSSION

Effects of Entrepreneur Functional Background on Initial Organizational Strategy

Hypotheses 1a, 1b, 1c, and 1d are tested by regressing the scores for each firm's initial strategy (first-mover, second-mover, low-cost producer, or niche) against the independent variable of entrepreneur functional background.

Tests of Hypothesis 1 demonstrate strong support for the predicted relationship between initial strategy and functional background as indicated at the top of Table 1 (Hypothesis 1). The prediction of hypothesis 1a— that founders with backgrounds in research, design, or development will be more likely to pursue a first-mover initial strategy—was strongly supported. Similarly, a strong effect was found for hypothesis 1c. Entrepreneurs with previous functional experience in the areas of manufacturing and production were most likely to begin firms with a low-cost strategy. Hypothesis 1b—predicting that entrepreneurs beginning organizations with second-mover strategies would have prior functional experience in marketing or sales—was unsupported, although the relationship was in the predicted direction. Finally, hypothesis 1d did receive significant support. Entrepreneurs forming organizations with a niche strategy were more likely to have prior functional experience in marketing or sales.

Table 3–1. Models of Founding Strategy of Semiconductor Manufacturing Firms.

Independent Variables	Dependent Variable			
		Initial Strategy		
	First Mover	Second Mover	Low-Cost Producer	Niche Producer
Entrepreneur functional background				
R&D	26.5[a]	1.6	− 4.3	1.4
Manufacturing	—	—	27.5[a]	—
Marketing/sales	− 1.8	12.1	—	21.6[a]
Constant	21.3	17.6	16.3	14.3
R^2	.12	.04	.14	.11
Incubator strategy				
First-mover	.63[a]	.47	− .17	− .09
Second-mover	− .17	.30	—	.48
Low-cost	− .36	—	.83[a]	—
Niche	—	.27	.00	.46
Constant	31.9	− 11.9	5.9	1.9
R^2	.06	.05	.08	.03
Education	12.2[a]	2.2	− 4.2	1.4
Constant	3.1	23.1	26.1	24.2
R^2	.06	.01	.00	.02
Age	− 2.1[a]	− .33	1.2	− .56
Constant	116.3	45.0	− 18.6	62.3
R^2	.09	.01	.03	.00
Environment				
1958–66	32.7[a]	− 5.0	− 5.7	3.2
1967–73	4.4	8.9	10.3	5.1
1974–79	5.1	3.2	17.4[a]	—
1980–84	—	—	—	31.4[a]
Constant	18.8	28.0	31.8	15.0
R^2	.14	.08	.10	.20

[a] $p < .05$.

The overall patterning of the findings from three of the four subhypotheses (1a, 1c, and 1d) provides strong support for the causal relationship suggested by hypothesis 1. The functional experience of an individual appears to delimit substantially the range of strategic options they consider when beginning a new organization of their own. Earlier experience in a particular organizational function apparently provides an important basis for an entrepreneur's perceived set of distinctive competencies as well as their view of the basis on which their own firm can successfully compete.

Effects of Incubator Strategy on Initial Strategy

The prediction of hypothesis 2a, that founders emerging from firms with a first-mover strategy will be more likely to pursue a first-mover strategy in their own firm, was moderately supported in the model. Additionally, founders previously working for a firm with a low-cost strategy were significantly more likely to adopt a low-cost strategy in their own organization, supporting hypothesis 2c. In contrast, no apparent support was demonstrated for either hypothesis 2b or hypothesis 2d. Entrepreneurs from incubator firms with second-mover or niche strategies demonstrated no proclivity to mimic these strategies in their own firms.

Hypothesis 2, therefore, receives varying amounts of support depending on the type of incubator firm the entrepreneur emerged from. In all cases, the amount of variance explained was small. First-mover and low-cost producer firms appear somewhat more likely to be founded by individuals with earlier experience in firms using a similar strategy. Firms that are first movers in the industry and leaders in innovation apparently serve as the breeding ground for founders of new first-mover firms. Similarly, semiconductor producers emphasizing cost efficiency apparently spawn new firms pursuing similar low-cost strategies. Neither second-mover nor niche strategies appear to produce any particular type of entrepreneur.

Effect of Education on Initial Strategy

Hypothesis 3 was tested by regressing each firm's score for first-mover strategy on the founder's highest level of education (B.S., M.S., Ph.D.). By assigning a B.S. degree a score of 1, M.S. a score of 2, and Ph.D. a score of 3, education was measured with a quasi-interval scale. Whether three-point ordinal scales can be considered to have interval properties is debatable. The statistical analyses shown in Table 3–1 (Hypothesis 3) follow the statistical assumptions of Labovitz (1970) and Kim (1978), who state that multivariate parametric statistical techniques can be used with ordinal-level measures. Results indicate a strong and significant relationship between the level of formal education of the entrepreneur and the degree to which the firms initially followed a first-mover strategy. There was no significant effect of education on the likelihood of pursuing other strategies.

Effects of Age of Entrepreneur on Initial Strategy

Hypothesis 4 is tested by regressing initial strategy on the age of the founder. As indicated in Table 3–1, a significant negative relationship exists between the extent to which the firm pursues a first-mover initial strategy and the age of the founder. No significant effects occur with the other strategies.

These findings may be interpreted in terms of the constraints that entrepreneurs face. Although not formally precluded from pursuing any strategy, entrepreneurs may in practice be limited by the relative obsolescence of their technical training and the consequential extent of their understanding of recent innovations. A wider variety of opportunities may be available to younger founders of organizations, whose more recent technical training provides them with a better understanding of recent technological issues.

Effects of Environment

Tests of hypotheses 5a through 5d indicate support for the relationship between period of founding and initial strategy, although the results are mixed. As predicted, firms founded in the earliest era (1958–66) were significantly more likely to pursue first-mover strategies. However, firms started in the period from 1967 to 1973 did not demonstrate the hypothesized propensity to pursue second-mover strategies. Firms started between 1974 and 1979 were more likely to adopt low-cost initial strategies as predicted, and low-cost strategies were also popular for firms begun between 1967 and 1973 (although not significantly so). Finally, the niche strategy has been pursued most frequently as an initial strategy by firms founded most recently, in the period from 1980 to 1984.

The effects of the environmental period demonstrate, to a limited extent, the importance of industry evolution in favoring the formation of firms with strategies that meet the dominant environmental requirement. As Stinchcombe (1965) noted, different sets of environmental conditions favor the formation of different types of organizations. An entrepreneur's choice of strategy, although guided strongly by his or her own social background, is also significantly linked to the period of founding.

Combined Effects of the Independent Variables on Interdepartmental Influence

To determine the *relative* contribution of each independent variable to the organization's initial strategy, a multivariate model combining all the independent variables was tested. Only variables that were specified explicitly in the hypotheses were included in this full model. In order to retain maximum degrees of freedom, independent variables were excluded from the model if they did not have direct theoretical relevance (for example, the effect of education on propensity to pursue a second-mover initial strategy). The results of the overall model are shown in Table 3–2.

Incubator strategy no longer shows a significant effect on the adoption of any of the four strategic types in the full model. The entrepreneur's

Table 3–2. Combined Model of Semiconductor Manufacturing Firms Founding Strategy.

Independent Variables	Dependent Variable			
	Initial Strategy			
	First Mover	Second Mover	Low-Cost Producer	Niche Producer
Entrepreneur functional background				
R&D	25.2[a]	—	—	—
Manufacturing	—	—	25.78[a]	—
Marketing/sales	—	11.52	—	18.57[a]
Incubator strategy				
First-mover	.50	—	—	—
Second-mover	—	.33	—	—
Low-cost	—	—	.71	—
Niche	—	—	—	.19
Education	12.8[a]			
Age	– 1.30[a]			
Environment				
1958–66	31.5[a]	—	—	—
1967–73	—	11.01	—	—
1974–79	—	—	18.5[a]	—
1980–84	—	—	—	34.4[a]
Constant	17.82	19.87	27.74	21.09
R^2	.46	.19	.30	.32

[a] $p < .05$.

functional background, age, and education and the period during which the firm is founded continue to be significant determinants of which firms will pursue a first-mover strategy. The functional background of the entrepreneur and the period of founding also have a significant effect on the adoption of either low-cost or niche strategies. Finally, as in the earlier model, none of the hypothesized effects were significant for the second-mover strategy. The most important findings from this analysis appear to be the strong and consistent effects of entrepreneur functional background and environmental period on the organization's initial strategy for three of the four strategic types.

DISCUSSION

Early strategic decisions and patterns of organizing are bounded by both entrepreneur and environment. By focusing on an organization's creation and the development of its initial strategy, we can come to understand both the entrepreneur's leadership role and the existing environmental context that inevitably limits that role. The demonstrated link between entrepreneurial, environmental, and strategic characteristics suggests that historical factors need to be examined more closely for their contribution to our understanding of the organization's creation as well as its subsequent evolution.

To understand more fully the process of imprinting in organizations, we need to know how the intentions of individual entrepreneurs come to be shared by other members of the newly formed organization. These intentions and personal conceptions can be differentiated into an external and an internal set of issues. The external issues have to do with the entrepreneur's perception of the organization's environment and how to compete successfully in it; the internal issues have to do with the entrepreneur's definition of how to organize relationships among members of the organization that permit effective performance and the creation of consensus within the organization.

One of this study's most significant implications is that organizations are set on a course at founding from which change may be costly or difficult. Most organizations prefer to apply familiar solutions to new problems, and it is the general tendency of managers to preserve, rather than radically change, their organization's strategy. Early patterns of organizing also set boundaries on the range of strategic actions that are likely to be successful for the organization. When an organization adopts a particular strategy, a great number of interests simultaneously become vested in this way of doing things, and the organization's strategy can take on the character of an independent, autonomous goal. Factors such as capital investments, specialized skills and knowledge, and internal political processes all act to support a particular strategic approach. Only very strong external or internal events are likely to motivate change from earlier established patterns.

The founding of the organization provides the initial patterning of influences: These in turn are central to the early strategic decisions that are made. The founding of the organization provides an opportunity for entrepreneurs to embed their own assumptions about the task and the means to accomplish it in the newly created organization. Strategy represents the outcome of a selectively interpreted organizational environment that reflects, in many respects, the past experience and personal predispositions of the founding entrepreneur as well as the environmental context at the time of founding.

4 NICHE FORMATION AND FOUNDINGS IN THE CALIFORNIA WINE INDUSTRY, 1941–84

Jacques Delacroix and Michael E. Solt

In this chapter, we link the foundings of new wineries in California between 1941 and 1984 to a qualitative change in the increasing demand for wines taking place during this period. We interpret this qualitative change as defining a new niche for wineries.

A long-term rise in the demand for a product may be met through increased production by existing firms or through an increase in the number of firms in production. From an organizational standpoint, it is important to know which solution will prevail. In the first case, competition tends to be between more or less like firms. These may be few in number and they often engage in a degree of mutual accommodation. This is roughly the situation prevailing in the U.S. automobile industry between the end of World War II and the early 1960s. If, on the other hand, growing demand is met by the recurring entry of new firms, competition will tend to approximate more closely the ideal conditions posited by classical economic theory. Furthermore, new entries into an industry provide the raw materials for the competitive processes that are the heart of the logic of organizational ecology described in Hannan and Freeman (1977). Finally, the environmental circumstances favoring the second solution constitute a crucial ingredient of *entrepreneurship*, narrowly defined as the founding of new business organizations or "organization creation" (Gartner 1985).

We thank our colleague Ed Omberg for helpful suggestions in the early stages of this chapter.

We are interested in this environmental ingredient of entrepreneurship thus defined because this topic seems to fall between several disciplines. The management sciences have, in the tradition of Schumpeter (1958), concentrated on commercial innovation in general, without paying special attention to the multiplication of firms. Correspondingly, they have included under the topic entrepreneurship a variety of intraorganizational processes encouraging or discouraging innovative action. (See, for example, Chandler 1977.) Yet they have shown limited interest in the external conditions that might be propitious to the founding of new business entities. Traditionally, microeconomics also has little to say about the antecedents of startups. Thus, even Samuelson (1980), who tries for the broadest coverage, makes only two fleeting references to entrepreneurship. Likewise, the field of managerial finance, in spite of its pronounced interest in investors' intertemporal decisionmaking, rarely goes into details about the antecedent conditions of foundings (see, for example, Weston and Copeland 1986).

We link the propensity to found wineries to satisfy growing demand to a set of environmental variables inspired by organizational ecology. This chapter therefore comes in the wake of Nielsen and Hannan (1977) and of Delacroix and Carroll (1983). It explores the possibility of tying organizational ecology with entrepreneurship research by casting an ecological light on the decisions and actions that lead to the launching of reasonably autonomous business organizations.

NEW NICHES AND FOUNDINGS

We define *niche* informally, but without contradicting more rigorous usage, as organizations' resources space—that is, as any fairly systematic way in which a population of organizations draws sustenance from its environment. A new niche may become available for a given type of organizations with the advent of new technologies to perform old tasks, with the opening of new environmental resources hitherto not accessible for tapping, or with the emergence of new ways to obtain resources from the environment on the basis of unchanged technology. We focus on this latter process of niche formation.

The genesis of this third process of niche formation often lies in changes in consumer taste. Changes in consumer taste, in turn, may result from little-understood processes in the evolution of collective preferences, from industries' deliberate strategic collective actions, or from the unintended consequences of competition between firms within an industry. However, it seems that more and more frequently the origin of change in consumer preferences is found outside conventionally defined markets. Thus, U.S. buyers' turn to small cars (which notably, predate the gas crisis of the mid-1970s) may have been largely triggered by the availability of imported compacts.

We think that wine imports during the period of observation similarly contributed to the definition of a new niche where domestic wineries were soon able to earn a living. We argue further that the formation of this new niche favored the foundings of new firms within the wine industry, rather than merely providing expanded opportunities for existing firms.

New niches should be perceived as comparably favorable occasions for entrepreneurs to launch new organizations and for established firms to spin off autonomous units. Newly defined niches should be perceived as favorable to new ventures for two reasons. First, and by definition, new organizations are free of structural inertia. They may design structures and adopt procedures specifically tailored to exploit the new niche. By contrast, old organizations must expand efforts of adaptation to cope with the new niche. Second, new organizations are also usually small organizations. In a new and therefore relatively unstabilized niche, the economies of scale accruing to older and larger organizations will be viewed as less instrumental to success than they would be in a clearly defined older niche.

We are discussing here a matter of perception only. We do not argue that new organizations will *perform* well in new niches because this is a largely unexamined question. Rather, we propose that private and corporate entrepreneurs should be encouraged to found new organizations disproportionately when a new niche is appearing. Thus, we do not concern ourselves with the fate of these start-ups (most of which can probably expect a quick demise, as shown by many organizational ecology studies). Instead, we examine below the possibility that changes in the nature and volumes of wine imports account for the pattern and frequency of foundings of California wineries during the period 1941 to 1984.

CALIFORNIA WINERIES AS A DYNAMIC ORGANIZATIONAL POPULATION

The organizational population of interest in this chapter is the complete set of California establishments producing wine for commercial purposes between 1941 and 1984. We choose this particular population in this particular period because it constitutes a privileged arena wherein to study entrepreneurship in a fairly pure form.

Wineries (unlike restaurants, for example) have the potential to become genuine, sizable industrial concerns. Yet barriers to entry into the wine industry are not formidable (unlike the barriers to entry into the automotive industry, for example). Thus, in 1985 Gallo, a vertically integrated concern that manufactures its own bottles and caps, generated approximately $1 billion in revenue by shipping 150 million gallons, largely in its own fleet of trucks (Fierman 1986). In spite of the domination of the industry by such giants as Gallo, wineries are comparatively easy to start. The mammoth Gallo company itself, was launched in the late 1930s with capital of $6,000 (Fierman 1986). A recent study (Castaldi and Folwell 1986) puts the contemporary investment outlay for a small winery at about $270,000. (The study does not entertain equipment leasing solutions, which would lower this figure.) One should note, in particular, that access to land is not an absolute necessity because winegrape is readily available on the open market and through contractual agreements. (Gallo is said to purchase 95 percent of its crush.) Distribution may also appear comparatively unproblematic for two reasons: (1) As a member of the general category "alcoholic beverages," wine can be piggy-backed into well-established retail networks; and (2) in California, where wineries are tourist attractions, direct sales to consumers are common.

In sum, the founding of a commercial winery from scratch seems to require mostly skills and will, in addition to modest amounts of capital. Hence, Ernest Gallo, interviewed in 1958, described the rebirth of the industry immediately following the repeal of Prohibition "the people who rushed into the wine business at repeal were people who were attracted because they saw a new industry coming into being. They jumped in with no experience, training or capital, hoping to find a quick way to make money" (cited by Teiser and Harrown 1981: 190).

We restrict our attention to California wineries specifically, although in 1983, admittedly a peak year, there were wine-producing establishments in thirty-nine states, including Minnesota (*Wines and Vines* 1983). California, historically, is home to about 90 percent of all U.S. wineries that account for approximately 90 percent of U.S. production. Nevertheless, we refrain from generalizing the propositions of this study to the whole of the domestic industry because some of our inferences require the existence of a mature wine-consuming milieu that may not be present in other regions.

Our period of observation extends from 1941 to 1984. Foundings data are available from the year 1940, but we begin our period of observation one year later, to sidestep left censoring problems.

For practical purposes, 1940 or 1941 can be considered the beginning of the U.S. wine industry as we know it. The twenty-first amendment to the U.S. Constitution repealed the Prohibition Act and was ratified in December 1933. A number of wineries managed to survive Prohibition by dedicating themselves to the production of sacramental and "medicinal" wines and through other subterfuges. Their narrow product lines and their narrowly specialized distribution channels (overt and covert) and the absence of competition from new entries ensured that the pre-1934 wine industry was very different in character from what followed (see Potorski 1985). Nevertheless, the survival of some wineries during this period contributed to the preservation of oenological skills that might otherwise have been lost in this country.

It must have taken five to seven years after Prohibition ended for entrepreneurs to convert land to winegrape use, to plant and allow vineyards to come into production, and to organize distribution. Production jumped 40 percent between 1939 and 1940 (Department of Commerce 1939). This rise may have been a fortuitous event owing more to natural circumstances than to intent. However, the onset of World War II in Western Europe helped consolidate this auspicious start by limiting imports from Italy and France, the two largest suppliers and both chronic overproducers. Hence, we think of the year 1941, our first year of observation, as coinciding with the rebirth of the industry. This fact adds to the desirability of the population of California wineries as a locale for the study of foundings. We are, in effect, observing the foundings of new firms in a new industry.

OVERVIEW OF THE CALIFORNIA WINERY POPULATION, 1941–84

Figure 4–1 shows the pattern of new wineries foundings between 1941 and 1984 and the progressive growth of this population during the period. All

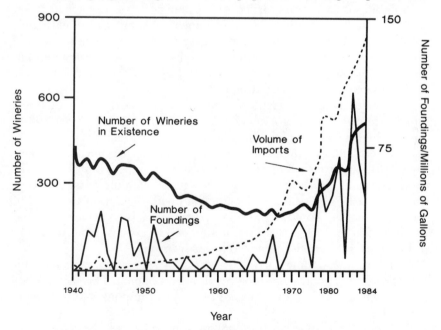

Sources: *Wines and Vines;* National Association of Beverage Importers.

Figure 4–1. Yearly Number of Foundings, Number of Wineries in Existence, and Volume of Imports, (millions of gallons) 1940–84.

data on wineries are from the annual directory of the industry publication *Wines and Vines*. We define a founding as the first appearance of a winery name in this publication, corresponding well with the commercialization of its products. This periodical is a family enterprise linked to the early rebirth of the industry and generally considered trustworthy. *Wines and Vines* obtains its data from the Federal Bureau of Alcohol, Tobacco, and Firearms (BATF) and does some cross-checking of its own. All establishments engaged in the commercial production of wine must be registered with BATF. Hence, we are confident that our data comprises the near totality of the California wineries population. This is a population study, not a convenience sample study.

The most likely underinclusion bias would concern very small establishments and establishments founded during the yearly period immediately preceding the publication of the directory. This yearly period shifted from September to December during the period of observation. We believe that this inclusion defect and this calendar change are of little consequence.

Figure 4–1 shows that in 1941, the first year for which we have uncensored data, there were already 381 commercial wineries in existence, an expression of the enthusiasm with which entrepreneurs had greeted the end of Prohibition, seven years earlier. An all-time peak was reached in 1984, when our study ends, with 534 establishments in simultaneous existence.

The upward "wineries in existence" growth curve in Figure 4–1 simply results from the excess of foundings over disappearances in the relevant period. Between 1941 and 1984, there were about 850 foundings, while approximately 700 wineries disappeared.

The foundings curve in Figure 4–1 exhibits patterns of troughs and peaks familiar from other studies of foundings over long periods (see Carroll 1984). Spells of high numbers of foundings are followed by troughs where few new firms are created, as if the environment were perceived momentarily as incapable of supporting a larger population after each spell. Few of the peaks are interpretable on the basis of common sense, with the possible exception of the 1947–48 peak, which coincides with the optimistic mood of the end of the war. Possibly, one might argue that it is no coincidence that the high 1977 and 1983 peaks occur after two recessions. However, other recessionary subperiods are not followed by peaks.

Notably, the foundings curve does not track wine production and consumption curves, which are smoothly upward slopping. This fact inhibits simple explanations of foundings as mechanical responses to increasing demand.

The foundings curve has some rough isomorphy with the curve representing total imports volumes, also shown in Figure 4–1. These grew from 3.5 million gallons in 1940 to 141.7 million in 1984.

All wine import data are from the *Quarterly Bulletin of the National Association of Beverage Importers*. Wine imports volumes are expressed in millions of wine gallons per year. Total imports are obtained by aggregating quantities of sparkline wine, table wine, vermouth, fortified wine, and a small residual category labeled "Other."

ACCOUNTING FOR FOUNDINGS: GENERAL DESIGN

We attempt to account for the pattern of foundings shown in Figure 4–1 by constructing a time series model where number of foundings in a given year is the dependent variable and several temporally lagged variables are the righthand side covariates.

Harvey (1981: 38) notes that when some of the covariates are lagged values of either the independent or the dependent variables, a dynamic element is injected into the equation. This model serves our purpose because we are interested both in understanding the general form of the relationships that we hypothesize and in the intertemporal dimensions of these forms.

Following Stinchcombe (1965), who defines opportunity as the intersection of resources and information, we construct this model in two stages. In the first stage, we construct a version of a primitive macroeconomic model of foundings. The independent variables incorporated in this first submodel constitute a crude but credible expression of resources available to launch enterprises: product demand and capital availability. In a second state, we add to this macroeconomic submodel independent variables designed to capture relevant information available to entrepreneurs and deemed to guide their decisionmaking processes. The variables included in this second stage are "entrepreneurship" variables in the sense that they are unlikely to exercise a direct, structural influence on foundings and that they must act as signals to a wider process.

Then, we reestimate the complete model with a dummy variable to evaluate its overall appropriateness to the period covered by our observation. In a later analysis, we estimate yet another time series model to establish more firmly our interpretation of the first model.

The purpose of the analysis is to devise a plausible scenario of winery founding and not to demonstrate or to adjudicate between rival hypotheses. We expect our findings to be suggestive and tentatively applicable, in their general form, to all classes of organizations that share the high entrepreneurial quality of the California wine industry from 1941 to 1984.

A SIMPLE MACROECONOMIC MODEL OF FOUNDINGS

In the macroeconomic submodel, yearly number of foundings is viewed as a joint function of apparent *consumption* and of *capital availability*.

Consumption is represented by the quantities of wines of all kinds withdrawn from bonded warehouses and for which the excise tax was paid, in a given year. The assumption here is that the payment of taxes is a good sign of intent to sell shortly. Consumption (withdrawals) figures are obtained from several issues of the *Survey of Current Business*.

Capital availability is expressed by nonresidential fixed investment in producers' durable equipment, compiled by the Bureau of Economic Analysis of the Department of Commerce. A nationwide formulation is used because capital markets for the period considered are of national rather than of regional scope. We believe that this quantity is an adequate proxy both because of its face-value validity and because it is highly correlated with numerous other indicators of economic activity. (It has a high negative correlation with prime rates, in particular.) We choose this variable rather than alternative indicators because it provides the best regression fit. We are thus giving the macroeconomic submodel maximal opportunity to account for the variance in the dependent variable.

Both of these macroeconomic independent variables are used in their *change* form because we are interested in building a substantively credible model. This, in turn, requires that independent variables measures precede, with a believable interval, the phenomenon that they are purported to account for. Hence, we use as independent variables the lagged values of these macroeconomic measures. The lags are determined by each relevant substantive process hypothesized. This substantive interest imposes change measures of the macroeconomic variables because the raw measures are so highly intercorrelated across time as to be virtually useless for the purpose of identifying believable time lags. Second, the raw measures' high intercorrelations would lead to artificially inflated R-squares. We must avoid such inflated R-squares because our assessment of the credibility of the entrepreneurship submodel rests on its contribution to R-square. Finally, reliance on change values is also theoretically justified: Entrepreneurial activity is more likely to be stimulated by changes, which are highly perceptible, on a human life scale than by current levels, which are historical abstractions.

The capital availability measure is lagged four years. The consumption measure is lagged two years. In each case, we selected from among substantively credible lags those lags contributing most to the explanation of the variance in the dependent variable.

AN ENTREPRENEURIAL MODEL OF FOUNDINGS

To the macroeconomic submodel we add three measures designed to mimic a plausible entrepreneurial process of foundings. Specifically, we wish to infer from observable events entrepreneurial decisionary processes that can be tied logically to number of foundings.

The first entrepreneurship variable is simply the number of foundings in a judiciously selected previous year. Delacroix and Carroll (1983) have shown that prior numbers of foundings may positively affect latter foundings within the same industry. Similarly, we hypothesize that entrepreneurs watch closely the industry where they contemplate launching a new venture. We speculate further that they take the present as a guide to the future. Hence, decisions to act and the first concrete steps toward a future founding may well be determined by the observation of a spell of foundings. The time elapsed between (1) the observation of a spell and initial steps and (2) the moment when the new business enters the record by engaging in sales is largely determined by the material instrumentalities of the creation of the new enterprise. In the wine industry, assuming that capital is available, these are planting of the desired grape variety, maturation of the vineyard to harvest, fermentation, aging (if any), and sale. (Distribution lead times are not considered because our data mark a winery as being in operation as soon as it sells wine to anyone.) Most sources in the wine industry consider that the above steps take four to six years (Adams 1978: 542–43). We hypothesize below that many of the winery foundings during the period considered are oriented to a strategy requiring some control over the grape varieties utilized but not aging because white table wines and sparkling wines do not require it. We include the fairly lengthy planting phase in our lag, excluding the sourcing strategy used by many bulk producers who purchase rather than grow grape. All these reasons make us choose a lag of five years for the measurement of the *previous foundings* variable.

The second entrepreneurship variable comprises two differentially lagged versions of *change in total volume of imports*. The selection of these two measures of the same variable requires separate consideration. Accordingly, the two next sections are devoted to a substantive discussion of the putative links between change in imports and the process that we hypothesize to underlie the pattern of foundings exhibited in Figure 4–1.

IMPORTS AS NICHE DEFINERS

Conventionally, economics will consider imports primarily as substitutes for domestic products in a market tending toward equilibrium. Thus, a recent set of exhaustive studies of the impact of imports on fourteen different U.S. industries arrives at uniformly negative conclusions (Sonfield 1985). Closer to home, Wohlgenant and Knutson's (1985: 24; see also Wohlgenant 1985) massive econometric study of the impact of wine imports, prepared in support of a 1985 complaint to the U.S. International

Trade Commission, concludes that, "In 1984 alone, the loss in total revenue due solely to increased table wine imports was more than 20 percent of total actual revenue."

It is easy to jump from such findings—which we do not dispute—to the diffuse popular impression that "imports hurt the industry." By implication, it might seem superficially reasonable to assume that imports discourage entrepreneurs from entering the field with new establishments. We explore, instead, the idea that imports induce the creation of new wineries by contributing to the definition and to the creation of a new niche within the wine industry. This formulation contains an indeterminacy not resolved in this study. The findings below are compatible with the idea that imports merely signal the emergence of a new niche. The same findings could be used to argue that imports create as well as signal a new niche. In either case the relation between wine imports and the new niche depends on the meaning of the word *wine*.

The term *wine* designates a motley category of products whose sole commonality is their origin in fermented grape juice and in the techniques used to produce them. Among other dimensions, wines differ in both their alcohol content and in their sweetness. Some wines are naturally sweet; some have a naturally high alcohol content. The two traits can be combined artificially by interrupting the fermentation of grape sugar through the admixture of distilled alcohol. The resulting products are called *fortified wines*. They include such names as port, sherry and Madeira. Vermouths are derived from a similar process. In addition, the symbolic meaning attached to sparkling wines differentiates them from still wines. This heterogeneity allows for varying consumption motives and for diverse consumption patterns within the bounds of seemingly unchanging quantities. Different consumption patterns may also, of course, combine with changing quantities over time.

Impressionistic, anecdotic evidence strongly suggests that U.S. wine consumption since World War II has been radically altered from one characterized by the dominance of sweet, still wines high in alcohol and of vermouth, to one where relatively light, tart table wines and sparkling wines gain steady ground. Domestic figures for the period considered are not explicit enough to allow for a thorough verification of this widespread impression. Nevertheless, it is noteworthy that the ratio of sparkling to still wines in the domestic production grew from 2 per thousand in 1940 to 8 percent in 1984, a fortyfold increase that occurred more or less continuously during this period (Department of Commerce 1961, 1984).

More detailed import figures, which represent well what U.S. consumers are willing to purchase, tell a fuller story. As shown in Figure 4–2, in 1940, vermouth and fortified wines of the port and sherry kinds made up fully 77 percent of the total volume of wine imports into the United States. By 1984 this percentage had declined to less than 4 percent. This decline

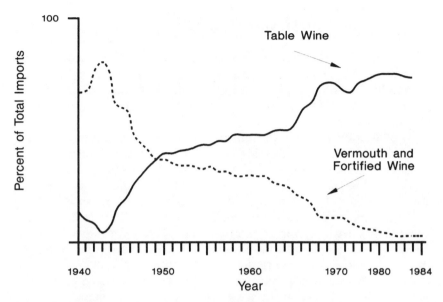

Source: National Association of Beverage Importers.

Figure 4–2. Percentages of Vermouth and Fortified Wine and of Table Wine in Total Volume of Wine Imported, 1940–84.

in the relative import of sweet and fortified wines and of vermouth between the two dates describes a smooth, steadily descending curve with hardly a return to earlier levels. This, in spite of the fact that these imports increased by 360 percent, in absolute terms, during the 1940 to 1984 period. Hence, this decline in the *relative* share of imports of sweet and fortified wine does not signify a return to low-alcohol virtuousness (a phenomenon that may be occurring as we write). Plenty of Americans were still drinking fortified wines and vermouth at the end of the period.

Nevertheless, the share of (unfortified) table wines in imports rose even faster during the same period. Hence, in 1940 table wines (including, undoubtedly, some dessert wines but not fortified and not vermouth) accounted for 16 percent of the volume of imports. By 1984, this share had grown to nearly 85 percent. This increase is described in Figure 4–2 by a smooth, monotonically ascending curve.

The curves pertaining to the respective percentages of vermouth and of fortified wines on the one hand, and of table wines, on the other, are strikingly symmetrical. But one must remember that imports of the first category also grew, in absolute levels.

This fairly simple picture can, perhaps, be fleshed out. We undertake this task below, without benefit of additional data.

A NICHE-OPENING SCENARIO

After World War II Americans were, to a great extent and, outside ethnic enclaves, drinking wine after the British fashion. British-style wine drinking involves libation of sweet, alcohol-fortified variety before and after dinner (port and sherry) and reliance on vermouth as a comforting wrapping for gin.

By 1984 a distinctively Continental mode of wine consumption was clearly in evidence, with red table wines taken during meals, after the Italian and French fashion. Even the divergent and apparently indigenous innovation of drinking slightly sweet white Chardonnays before dinner can probably be traced to Germany. By that time, also, the European custom of celebrating the slightest occasion with libations of sparkling wine, although by no means new, had spread through wide swatches of the population.

From the standpoint of wine producers, one would say that a new niche had opened. It was a niche in the rigorous sense (Freeman and Hannan 1983) that the new wine consumption patterns represented a different way to make a living based on the same raw materials, the same equipment, and about the same technologies relied on by producers of fortified wines. (Indeed, perusal of the detailed data available for a subset of wineries shows that it is not uncommon for the same establishments to supply at once fortified wines and table wines—although sparkling wine producers only rarely produce still wine.)

This niche opening scenario raises further questions: How did large numbers of U.S. consumers acquire a taste for the rather alien, watery, and sour beverages hitherto favored mostly by the Italians, the French, the Spaniards, and sundry effete cosmopolitan elites? How did sparkling wines—which, after all, had been around since before the American Revolution—become such common objects of consumption in the relatively short span of forty-four years?

A likely answer is that these developments constitute yet another instance of the worldwide convergence of lifestyles in process since World War II. This convergence, facilitated by the tremendous growth of international travel, by the amplification of global trade, and by the routine exchange of movies and television serials (Delacroix 1984) may have been triggered, in the case concerning us, by returning GIs of the generation of Henry Miller. The diffusion of the Continental wine drinking model was helped by general U.S. prosperity. Most important, a steady and considerable reduction in trade barriers and generally favorable exchange rates (Hervouet and Blandford 1986) brought to the U.S. market European wines untailored for that market.

In short, we speculate that European influences opened a new niche in the California wine industry by making novel products acceptable to the U.S. consumer. Imports—especially imports of table wines, which grew 150-fold during the period—were the most tangible expression of this radical change in the environment of wineries.

In principle, it should not have been impossible for well-established large wineries to preempt this new niche. However, well-established organizations enjoy little competitive advantage in availing themselves of new opportunities. It is also often the case that their vested interest in ways of doing things that have proved successful makes them slow to react to new opportunities. If they do react, they may do so by spawning separate, new organizational entities in order to protect their core technologies from the hazards inherent in new ventures and to maintain their familiar image to the consumer. The opening of a new niche is the time most propitious for would-be entrepreneurs. (This is a relative concept; it implies that this is the best time to try. Most entrants can expect a quick demise.) The opening of a new niche is also the time when established organizations are most likely to launch autonomous spin-offs. Hence, foundings are expected to increase while a new niche emerges both because of new entries by outside entrepreneurs and because of the entrepreneurial activities of established firms.

In summary, we suspect that as more wine is imported into the United States, the new niche appears clearer and the propensity to found wineries becomes greater.

This expectation of a positive link between imports and foundings may be in contradiction with a negative relationship that is often implicit in macroeconomic models. We allow this contradiction to play itself out by incorporating twice into the whole model the variable *change in import volume*. This variable is placed in the model once with two-year lag and again with a three-year lag. The correlation between these two measures is positive but moderate (Pearson $r = .28$). The two lags are *ad hoc* and not justified *a priori*. This combination of lags is used in lieu of the more conventional insertion of a squared form of this variable. The squared formulation was tried and identified no significant effect, indicating the absence of a curvilinear relationship between change in import volume and number of subsequent foundings. We think that our two-differentially lagged measures formulation gives the hypothesis of a negative effect of imports on foundings a fair chance of being verified.

FINDINGS

The macroeconomic submodel in equation 1 of Table 4–1 gives a mediocre accounting of foundings. The R-square associated with this equation is only .47. This explained variance is provided entirely by the

Table 4–1. Effects of Changes in Capital Availability, Consumption and Imports, Past Foundings, Population Size, and Time Period on California Winery Foundings; Effects of Changes in Capital Availability, Change in Imports, and Past Foundings on Changes in Imports (standard errors shown in parentheses).

Equation	Dependent Variable	Constant	ΔCapital Availability (4-year lag)	ΔConsumption (2-year lag)	ΔImports (2-year lag)	ΔImports (3-year lag)	Number of Foundings (5-year lag)	Population Size	Dummy Variable for Time Period	Adjusted R^2	Durbin-Watson Statistic
1	Winery foundings	7.86[a] (3.57)	2.15[a] (.39)	.17 (.22)						.47	2.02
2	Winery foundings	−2.41 (2.24)	1.18[a] (.25)	.34[a] (.12)	1.26[a] (.31)	−.64[a] (.30)	.80[a] (.11)			.86	2.09
3	Winery foundings	5.18 (12.60)	1.27[a] (.29)	.34[a] (.12)	1.36[a] (.36)	−.57 (.33)	.78[a] (.12)	−.05 (.07)		.86	2.09
4	Winery foundings	11.33[a] (1.76)	5.76 (5.28)	1.25[a] (.59)	1.50[a] (.52)	−1.23[a] (.44)	.70[a] (.20)		−4.00 (11.49)	.81	1.64
5	ΔImports (2-year lag)	1.86 (1.07)	.11 (.13)			.25 (.17)	.001 (.013)			.04	2.09

[a]$p \leq .05.$

capital investment variable. The coefficient associated with the consumption variable is not statistically significant.

Equation 2 of Table 4–1 shows the complete model with all the variables discussed above entered at the same time. This model is designed to assess the contribution of the variables expressing entrepreneurship processes in addition to the macroeconomic processes.

The R-square associated with this equation is .86, a significant advance over the previous submodel. All variables in the equation have effects significant well above the .05 level. This includes the consumption variable whose effect was suppressed in the macroeconomic submodel. All signs are in the expected direction.

Capital availability does have an influence on the propensity to found wineries in equation 2, although this effect is much reduced once entrepreneurship variables come into play.

The strongest effect is positive and associated with number of foundings lagged five years. As hypothesized, spells of foundings invite further foundings within a lapse of time that is in keeping with that required by entrepreneurs to create grape variety-specific wineries.

The effect of change in wine imports lagged two years is positive. This supports the niche-creation argument. It appears that growth in the volume of wine imported—increasingly composed of still, tart table wines and of sparkling wines—encourages entrepreneurs to persevere in their founding projects. However, change in import volume lagged three years has a negative effect on number of foundings. This is what we would expect if imports had a dampening influence on foundings because they displace domestic production. Yet this effect is weak, although its coefficient is significant in this equation and above the .05 level. However, numerous other exploratory runs (not shown in this paper) indicate that this association is tenuous and elusive (as shown in equation 3 of Table 4–1). It does not take much by way of added controls to eliminate its significance. This last finding, unlike the others, is not robust. Hence, we are left with the distinct impression that the positive influence on foundings of change in import volume much overshadows any negative influence the same variable may have. The thesis that imports encouraged population growth by defining a new niche receives better support than the traditional view that imports dissuade domestic producers.

Equation 2 is reasonably trustworthy. The highest initial Pearson coefficient between the independent variables—that between change in capital investment lagged four years and number of foundings lagged five years—is only .43. Because it is not likely that the number of foundings of wineries affects capital availability at the national level or that the change in capital availability doubles back on itself to influence the number of foundings in a previous year, we are confident the two effects are separate and complementary. This second equation looks fairly good in every way. It has smaller residuals than equation 1, and its residuals approximate more closely a normal distribution. The Durbin-Watson coefficient associated with this equation is a near perfect 2.09, indicating an absence of autocorrelated error terms.

In equation 3 we introduce a measure of (human) population size into the model to show its imperviousness to secular trends. This equation also serves to illustrate the relative fragility of the coefficient associated with change in import volume lagged three years. Equation 3 does not differ from equation 2, except that in the former, the significance of the coefficient pertaining to change of import volume lagged three years disappears altogether.

One more concern relative to the appropriateness of equation 2 to the whole period of observation must be addressed. The foundings curve in Figure 4–1 suggests that patterns of foundings may differ drastically between a long, early period extending to 1976 and a short, latter period from 1977 to 1984. During this last period, yearly number of foundings increases rapidly in a manner that is out of proportion to what is seen in the first period. Hence, the concern arises that equation 2 may provide a close approximation of the processes at work until 1976 and yet be inappropriate for the latter 1977 to 1984 subperiod.

We assess this eventuality in equation 4 by reestimating equation 2 with a dummy variable denoting the latter period, as recommended by Hanushek and Jackson (1977: 101–08). In this period-controlled model, a dummy variable is created that takes value of 1 for the years 1977 to 1984 and of zero for previous years. All independent variables are multiplied by this dummy variable, and the dummy itself is entered into the equation. This procedure is designed to pick up any interaction that might obtain between the suspicious time period and the independent variables, thereby pointing to an eventual inadequate fit for the subperiod under suspicion.

The reestimation confirms that the model in equation 2 is largely valid for the latter subperiod. The coefficient associated with the primitive value of the dummy variable is not significant. All coefficients retain their sign and their significance with one exception. The coefficient associated with change in capital availability is not significant in this last estimation. We must proceed cautiously in interpreting this difference with equation 2. First, the addition of another variable makes it marginally more difficult for any coefficient to appear statistically significant. Second, the Pearson r between this *interactive* variable and its dummy component is a high .75. This degree of collinearity makes it difficult to interpret with certainty the loss of significance of change in capital availability. Nevertheless, we note with interest that the apparent lack of effect of capital availability is quite compatible with a situation where a new niche has been established and where late in the period, entrepreneurs feel unconstrained by narrow economic calculations and launch new wineries with abandon.

Such an absence of effect would also be compatible with a situation where investment capital is sectorially available in the wine industry, independently of its availability in the wider national economy. Both hypothetical situations would support the niche argument.

THE AUTONOMY OF CHANGE
IN IMPORT VOLUME

We argue that increases in import volume that took place between 1940 and 1984 prompted the founding of new wineries because much of this increase contributed to the definition of a new niche. The empirical support we bring to bear relies heavily on the assignment to imports of the role of niche definer.

For this use of the evidence to be wholly convincing, ideally, several other conditions regarding the autonomy of import changes would have to be demonstrated. We do not have the space here to examine the independence of imports from the many other general macroeconomic processes, not represented in our equation, taking place during the period. However, we will at least show that change in imports is not temporally dependent on other variables in the model.

The different lags in equation 2 leave open the possibility that changes in imports are only a consequence rather than a primitive cause of other variables in the equation. Thus, capital availability lagged four years may influence import change lagged two years inasmuch as capital availability reflects a general prosperity conducive to heightened consumption of everything, including of imported wine. Thus, if change in capital availability positively affects subsequent change in imports, the relationship between the latter and subsequent foundings may be spurious.

We explore the likelihood of this and of other spurious relationships permitted by different time lags by estimating how change of imports lagged two years is affected by the three independent variables that are measured before it in equation 2. We construct a model that respects the substantive lags between these variables in equation 2. These variables are change in capital availability (lagged four years), number of foundings (lagged five years), and change in imports (lagged three years). The estimation of the exogenousness of import volume change is shown in equation 5.

None of the coefficients in this new equation is significant, and the R-square associated with this equation approximates zero. This last test confirms that the strong positive effect of imports on subsequent foundings is independent of other effects in the model, in conformity with our argument that imports autonomously contributed to the definition of a new niche for wineries.

CONCLUSIONS

The analysis above illustrates the plausibility of a process where the observation of new entries into the wine industry and of changes in volume of imports of a qualitatively different nature prompt and encourage entrepreneurs to found new wineries. This example demonstrates how the ecological concept of niche can be used to cast a distinctive light on a phenomenon of great economic interest: The multiplication of firms in the same industry. This exercise also led us to a plausible but quite counterintuitive explanation of the impact of imports on domestic industries.

Pareto (Powers 1987) turned to sociology because of questions he was unable to answer as an economist. In similar vein, we think that the role of organizational ecology is less to contradict conventional economics than to extend their reach. A recent econometric study of the factors affecting U.S. imports of wine from France can help illustrate this claim.

Hervouet and Blandford (1986: 4) report that "(ordinary) Table wine imports are more sensitive to variations of price and income than still quality wines" and also that "As imports have increased, consumer response to changes in price of imported French wines becomes inelastic."

Those are credible conclusions. Unfortunately, their discussion stops there, without drawing out the implications for the wine industry as a whole. We think that if the authors of this study had employed the concept of niche, they would have been tempted by inferences similar to ours: The relative indifference of U.S. consumers to cost considerations as perceived quality (defined by French producers, according to their own alien value system) goes up, and the progressive character of this indifference, both suggest that imports create new opportunities for the domestic industry even while inflicting damage upon it.

We have also attempted to sketch how ecological conceptualizations might be useful where they are least expected to be. We showed how the application of the ecological concept of niche to readily available archival data could help bridge the gap between macroeconomic research, on the one hand, and mainstream studies of entrepreneurship, on the other. The latter (see Kent, Sexton, and Vesper 1982, for a bird's-eye view) abound in descriptions of the psychological traits of entrepreneurs and of the structural features of the microenvironments believed to nurture entrepreneurship. Rarely do they attempt to link this management orientation with objects of interest to the discipline of economics. Even more rarely does one encounter efforts systematically to exploit quantitative data to bridge these two shores of economic reality. Hence, we are left with an intellectual chasm that may only be overcome through leaps of faith.

The developing field of organizational ecology has the potential to build refutable models across this chasm. Refutable models, however rickety, are to be much preferred to faith.

5 THE FOUNDING OF SOCIAL MOVEMENT ORGANIZATIONS
Local Citizens' Groups Opposing Drunken Driving

John D. McCarthy, Mark Wolfson, David P. Baker,
and Elaine Mosakowski

During 1978, 1979, and 1980 a few local citizens' action groups formed
to reduce the extent of drinking and driving in the hope of reducing the
resulting automobile fatalities. One of the first groups formed during this
period, Remove Intoxicated Drivers (RID), began in Schenectady, New
York, in 1978. In 1980 the first chapter of Mothers Against Drunk Driving (MADD) was formed in Sacramento, California, by Candy Lightner
after the death of her daughter after being struck by a car driven by a
chronic drunk driver. Since then more than 400 local groups have started
nationwide and have directed the efforts of thousands of volunteers toward
reducing the amount of drinking and driving in their communities. During the few short years since the founding of RID and MADD, a widespread
and vigorous citizens' movement has emerged.

Despite the breadth of the movement and the publicity surrounding
it, however, these local citizens' organizations are quite modest in size and
in their control over resources. In 1985 the typical group had a membership of thirty-six people, a mailing list of 120 people, and an annual budget

An earlier version of this paper was delivered at the 1986 annual meeting of the American
Sociological Association in New York, N.Y. The research is supported by a grant from the National Science Foundation (#SES-8419767) as well as by continuing support from the Center
for the Study of Youth Development at Catholic University of America. We thank David Britt,
Glenn R. Carroll, Doug McAdam, and Susan Olzak for comments on an earlier draft of this
paper, Teresa Ankney for research assistance, and Nancy J. Walczak for computer assistance.

of $1,500.[1] Most groups depended exclusively on volunteer labor and operated from the group president's home. Founders of anti–drunk driving organizations are typically people with little or no previous experience in mounting citizens' action campaigns, and the majority (75 percent) of local leaders are women.

Yet the recent development and modest power base of these groups does not mean that their impact has been slight. In alliance with others, including state agencies, law enforcement officials, and insurance companies, they have worked to bring about changes in citizen attitudes toward drinking and driving, shifts in law enforcement patterns directed toward drunk drivers, legislative and administrative changes focused on the control and punishment of drunk drivers, and attention to their own leaders and activities. Many of these efforts have been successful.

But the pattern of emergence of these local groups has been uneven. Many communities still lack an organization working exclusively on the issue of drinking and driving, and other communities have only recently seen one formed. Why do some communities develop these local citizens' groups early on, others not until years later, and still others not at all? In this chapter we describe an analysis that begins to assess how various environmental factors influence the spread of a local citizens' movement.

THEORETICAL ISSUES

This chapter investigates the temporal and geographic patterns of founding of local social movement organizations across communities. Although some researchers have encouraged the systematic analysis of social movement organizations as a way of understanding broader social movement phenomena (McCarthy and Zald 1977; Zald and McCarthy 1980), the systematic application of quantitative evidence to the founding patterns of social movement organizations has been quite rare. Several studies, however, have examined the founding and prevalence of voluntary associations of many types across communities (Lincoln 1977; Marrett 1980). And Gamson (1975) investigated the founding of social movement organizations nationally in the United States, linking time with founding incidence rates.

By using the local community as the unit of analysis and the founding of a local anti–drunk driving group as the outcome, we investigate which community characteristics influence the cross-community variation in the timing of founding. Our expectations of which characteristics are worthy of investigation are drawn from previous thinking about both the emergence of social movements and the emergence of other complex organizational forms.

Founding Motivations

It is often assumed that individuals who are aggrieved by some state of affairs are most likely to organize to attempt to ameliorate the problem. The assumption of the importance of grievances has occupied a prominent, if controversial, place in debates about the founding motivations of social movements. Most analysts believe that common grievances are a necessary ingredient for the subsequent development of organized social action, although there has been disagreement over their relative importance.

The most aggrieved citizens of the drinking and driving problem are those who have lost a loved one in an alcohol-related crash. Between 1980 and 1983 the number of Americans who lost their lives in such crashes ranged between 22,500 and 28,000, annually (Fell 1983). Each of these deaths leaves behind friends, relatives, and co-workers all of whom may be potentially mobilized into collective action. Activists in the movement typically refer to the surviving relatives of persons killed in alcohol related crashes as *victims*. The movement is predominantly led by such victims and consists primarily of a victim membership. Our study, as well as several others (Weed 1985; Ungerleider, Bloch, and Connor 1986), shows that about one-half of the local organizations' presidents are victims and about 35 percent of their members are victims.

All citizens in a local community might support efforts to reduce drinking and driving, but it seems reasonable to believe that victims would be most concerned with these efforts. At the same time, local communities differ greatly in the number of alcohol-related fatalities that they experience. As a consequence, we are led to expect that the greater the volume of victims of alcohol-related crashes in a community, the greater the likelihood that an organization will form to address the issue locally.

Collective Action Repertoires

The prevalence of victims alone must not be enough to account for the timing and location of the emergence of these local organizations; otherwise we should have seen such groups arise decades ago. Indeed, the sheer annual number of fatalities in alcohol-related crashes has declined substantially over the last decade. In addition to the presence of victim pools, we argue that the founding of local groups is based on the presence of shared understandings of the problem and possible solutions. The idea that drinking drivers are responsible for an important share of automobile fatalities and the idea that aggrieved citizens can mitigate the extent of drinking and driving were not commonly shared social constructions until quite recently. Because a more unified definition of the problem has emerged, citizens have become more likely to come together to act to combat drinking and driving as a perceived social evil.

This common social construction of the problem has emerged over several decades. Joseph Gusfield (1975, 1981) has carefully chronicled the active development of the idea of the "killer drunk" through the efforts of the National Safety Council and others. As the idea became widespread that drunk drivers were responsible for many automobile fatalities, the concept of taking countermeasures against the threat emerged in the newly created National Highway Transportation Safety Administration (NHTSA). Through the 1970s this federal agency supported a variety of such countermeasures in many local communities around the United States.

The NHTSA also publicized the idea that local citizens' groups could affect the problem. In 1979 the agency published and widely distributed a guide describing in great detail how to start a citizens' group opposing drinking and driving. The effectiveness of this guide as an organizational template for local groups is evidenced by the correspondence between its suggestions and the basic structure of the local citizens' groups we have studied. Mothers Against Drunk Driving (MADD) and Remove Intoxicated Drivers (RID), the two national umbrella organizations, also made similar organizational templates available to any individual who contacted their central office expressing a desire to begin a local group. The availability of this organizational technology no doubt facilitated the growth of local groups around the country in much the same way that franchise models facilitate the development of local firms (Reinarmann 1985).

By the late 1970s, then, a repertoire of citizen actions for organizing to combat drinking and driving was available. The massive wave of publicity that attended the early efforts of local groups no doubt made this repertoire even more widely available.

Environmental Conduciveness

Most analysts of organizations do not believe that strong motivations to found purposeful organizations and uniform common conceptions of their form and substance are sufficient to account for founding patterns (Stinchcombe 1965). The environment within which such organizations might form and develop also are thought to be of major importance.

First, the size of a community should have consequences for the founding and development of most organizational forms. The larger the population of a community, the more likely that any kind of organization will form, other things being equal. Also, recent population increases may increase founding rates through what Pennings (1982) calls the "unpredictable change" produced by rapid growth. Lincoln (1977), in his study of voluntary associations in ninety-three large urban areas in the United States, found that population size and change in population size were the best predictors of the prevalence of most types of voluntary associations.

Both organizational ecologists (Carroll 1985; Carroll and Huo 1986; Hannan and Freeman 1977, 1984) and resource mobilization theorists (Oberschall 1973; Tilly 1978; McCarthy and Zald 1977) have suggested a link between community resources and the birth and growth of organizations. The more plentiful both material and human resources are in a community, the more likely is the development of most organizational forms. One way in which resources may affect the likelihood of founding and growth of local citizens' groups is through potential support constituencies. The more resources available to potential activists, the more likely such groups are to form and grow. More affluent and better-educated individuals are, in general, more likely to form groups; so communities in which these types of people live should be expected to more quickly spawn a local citizens' group opposing drunk driving.

Another way in which community resources may affect the potential of organizational founding and growth is through the resources of governmental authorities, because these authorities can and do provide many resources to groups of this kind (McCarthy and Zald 1977). Many of the local anti–drunk driving groups that we have studied have close ties with local and state governmental agencies and receive considerable support from them. For instance, local police agencies are often quite supportive of these groups, and state highway safety offices, encouraged by mandates and funds from NHTSA, also encourage local citizen efforts. These are exactly the types of institutional resources that Wholey and Brittain (1986) see as most important in understanding the founding of organizations like those opposing drunken driving.

In the remainder of this chapter we attempt to evaluate the relative importance of the several theoretical factors that we have discussed. How important are grievances in accounting for the founding rate of anti–drunk driving groups? If grievances are relatively unimportant, what other county-level factors can account for group formation rates? We begin by describing the data that we have assembled in order to address these questions.

DATA

We assembled two data sets to describe each of the 3,137 counties or county equivalents in the United States. We chose the county as the boundary for the local community for several reasons. First, the county is the common geopolitical unit in which the emergent organizations exist. Second, MADD, the largest of the coalitions of organizations with about 75 percent of the local groups affiliated with it, uses county boundaries to organize its chapters. Third, counties have the basic local responsibilities for criminal justice, and therefore they should be important in focusing the activities of these groups. Last, the county is the most disaggregated geographic unit common to each of our data sets.[2]

Census of Local Citizens' Groups

To the data on county characteristics we added information about local citizens' organizations opposing drunken driving, which were founded in approximately 14 percent of all counties. We developed this data with a census of all such organizations in existence in the United States in 1985. Chapter rosters of the two umbrella coalitions, RID and MADD, and various newspaper and periodical indices, organizational newsletters, and personal communications with local activists were used to build a list of all such local groups. This census includes 369 local MADD groups and fifty-three local RID groups.[3]

Our interest lies in the timing of the founding of the first local citizens' organization opposing drunken driving in a county. We have allocated organizations to the county in which they reside. The founding dates of the organizations were generated either from the reports of the local groups or from other sources of information, such as the umbrella group rosters.

It should be noted that many of these organizations can be ephemeral. Some leave almost no trace after very short corporate lives. Information gathered from the umbrella coalitions suggests that the mortality rate of organizations is somewhere between 5 percent and 25 percent of all groups formed between 1978 and 1985. This means that between twenty-five and 125 local groups may have failed prior to our census and have not been included in our analysis.

Alcohol-Related Motor Vehicle Fatalities

To estimate the size and nature of the pool of potential activists created by drinking and driving fatalities, we drew on the Fatal Accident Reporting System (FARS) data compiled by NHTSA (U.S. Department of Transportation 1980). This data set was designed to include information about the circumstances, including time and place, and individuals involved in all fatal automobile crashes. With it we were able to construct a set of county-level variables to reflect the annual incidence of alcohol- and nonalcohol-related crashes. The FARS data set has been collected annually since 1975, but this analysis uses only the 1980 data.

We use in this analysis the following four measures of grievances: The number of fatal *crashes;* the number of fatal accidents in which one or more of the drivers registered a .05 or greater blood alcohol concentration (BAC), which we call *alcohol crashes;* and the number of fatalities resulting from a crash in which one or more of the drivers had at least a .05 BAC, which we call *alcohol fatalities.* Finally, we use the number of fatalities in all crashes that were under age 21 and were killed on late nights or early mornings on weekends. Such a measure is commonly used as a surrogate for alcohol involvement in automobile crashes because crashes during these hours typically are the most likely to involve alcohol. We call this measure *youth fatalities*. Each of these variables was normalized by county population for the purposes of this analysis. We expect that each of these measures of automobile fatalities will be positively related to the rate of founding of local organizations.

Community Characteristics

Other characteristics of local communities were measured with information drawn from the U.S. Census Bureau's County Statistics File 1 (Bureau of the Census 1984a, 1984b) for 1980.[4] This data source includes information gathered from many sources for (in most cases) each of the 3,137 counties or county equivalents in the United States. It includes 827 variables generated by the Census Bureau, other federal agencies, and several private organizations on a wide variety of topics, including demographics, commerce, income, labor, and crime (Bureau of the Census 1984a, 1984b).

We drew a number of indices from this source to tap what we viewed as the important dimensions of community conduciveness. Unless otherwise specified the variables represent 1980. First, we used five variables to index community size: The logarithm of 1980 population *size,* the logarithm of population per square mile in 1980 (*density*), percentage population *change* between 1970 and 1980, *land area* in square miles, and *rural* population, which is the proportion of the county population classified as rural. Second, we used five variables to index the human and material resources of each community: *College,* which is the proportion of the adult population with some college education; *median income,* which is 1979 median household income (in hundreds of dollars); *middle class,* which is the percentage of households earning between $15,000 and $24,999 in 1979; *white population,* or the proportion of the population that is white; and *outcommuters,* or the percentage of the population that works outside of the residence county. Finally, we used three variables to index local government activity: The logarithm of government *revenue,* which is the local government general revenue in 1977; *revenue change,* which reflects the percentage change in general revenues between 1972 and 1977; and the logarithm of *police expenditures,* which includes local expenditures on police activities.

FINDINGS

First we map the pattern of foundings of local groups and then present the results of our analysis of the rate of founding.

History of Local Citizens' Group Formation

Figure 5–1 depicts the pattern of formation of local organizations across time. Only a few groups formed each year between 1978 and 1980, and a burst of foundings occurred in 1981. The peak year of new foundings was 1983, with the number of new groups founded dropping off through 1984 and 1985. Although this analysis ends with 1985, it is our impression that the decline in the rate of founding of new groups continued through 1986.

Influences on Founding Rates

We are interested in explaining the connection between the founding of groups opposing drinking and driving and characteristics of their local communities. To examine this connection, we model the rate of founding of local organizations (Tuma and Hannan 1984). The dependent variable is the instantaneous rate of founding of the first organization in each county based on historical time. We estimate this rate model using a partial likelihood technique (Cox 1975; Efron 1977) to control for the time dependence of organizational founding.

Number of Groups

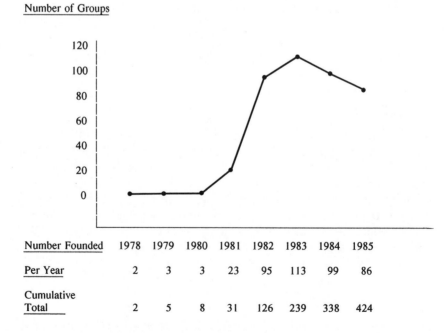

Number Founded	1978	1979	1980	1981	1982	1983	1984	1985
Per Year	2	3	3	23	95	113	99	86
Cumulative Total	2	5	8	31	126	239	338	424

Figure 5–1. Pattern of Founding of New Anti–Drunk Driving Local Organizations, by Year of Founding.

The findings of our analysis are shown in Table 5–1.[5] Coefficients were estimated for four hierarchically related models. Model 1 includes five variables representing the population and physical size of counties. As we predicted, the coefficients for population size and population change between 1970 and 1980 are positive and significant. The proportion of the county population classified as rural is negatively related to the founding rate, as anticipated. Population density, measured as population per square mile, and land area are seen to be negatively related to the organizational founding rate.

Model 2 consists of five variables measuring several aspects of the potential human resource base for organizations in each county added to the cluster of variables assessed in Model 1. A likelihood-ratio chi-square difference of 67.68 (d.f., 5) indicates that the addition of the human resource base variables results in a significant improvement in the explanatory power of the model. Specifically, the relative size of the middle-class population and household income are found to be positively related to the founding rate and are significant at the .05 level. A relatively large number of individuals working outside of the county of residence is found to retard the founding rate. The coefficients for the proportion of the population that is white and the proportion that has some college education are positive but not significant. With the exception of population density, which drops toward zero, each of the coefficients from Model 1 retains its original sign and statistical significance.

Model 3 adds three variables measuring potentially facilitating resource levels of local governments to the variables contained in Model 2. None of these coefficients was found to be significant. Moveover, the coefficient for land area, which was significant in Models 1 and 2, is no longer significant. The likelihood-ratio chi-square test indicates that Model 3 significantly improves on Model 2.

Model 4 adds four grievance variables to the clusters of variables tested by the earlier models. Although none of the coefficients of these new variables was found to be significant, the likelihood-ratio chi-square test suggests that the inclusion of grievance variables enhances the model's explanatory power. We also find in the final model that the coefficient for rural population becomes nonsignificant and the coefficient for college educated population remains significant, as it is in Model 3.

DISCUSSION

We will begin by briefly summarizing our findings. Then we will address the relative importance of the various community factors that we investigated to organizational foundings. We then discuss the importance of theoretically separating organizational founding from organizational growth and development. Finally, we speculate on the temporal pattern of founding that we have observed for these organizations.

Table 5–1. Partial Likelihood Estimates of the Effects of
Environmental Factors on the Rate of Founding of Local
Anti–Drunk Driving Organizations in U.S. Counties,
1978–85 (standard errors in parentheses).

| | Models | | | |
Independent Variables	(1)	(2)	(3)	(4)
Population				
Size	2.879[a]	2.165[a]	2.762[a]	2.365[a]
	(.2339)	(.2412)	(.4667)	(.4853)
Change	.0075[a]	.0111[a]	.0096[a]	.0111[a]
	(.0018)	(.0020)	(.0027)	(.0028)
Density	− 1.150[a]	− .2824	− .2068	− .3020
	(.2039)	(.2222)	(.2351)	(.2431)
Land area	− .0002[a]	− .0001[a]	− .0001	− .0001
	(.0000)	(.0000)	(.0000)	(.0000)
Rural	− 1.334[a]	− .7774[a]	− .7324[a]	− .5548
	(.2891)	(.3275)	(.3399)	(.3477)
Human resources				
College		1.109	1.236[a]	1.288[a]
		(.6760)	(.6937)	(.7068)
White population		.8258	.8367	.6976
		(.5147)	(.5221)	(.5251)
Middle class		3.839[a]	3.600[a]	3.622[a]
		(1.741)	(1.746)	(1.766)
Median income		.0036[a]	.0043[a]	.0046[a]
		(.0021)	(.0022)	(.0022)
Outcommuters		− .0689[a]	− .0702[a]	− .0709[a]
		(.0107)	(.0112)	(.0112)
Government resources				
Revenue			− .7653	− .5707
			(.5054)	(.5069)
Revenue change			.0425	.0446
			(.1742)	(.1777)
Police expenditure			.1191	.2653
			(.3878)	(.3935)
Grievances				
Crashes				− .8995
				(.5925)
Alcohol crashes				− 1.132
				(3.153)
Alcohol fatalities				− .0035
				(2.549)

Table 5–1. *Continued*

Independent Variables	Models			
	(1)	*(2)*	*(3)*	*(4)*
Grievances continued				
Youth fatalities				– 2.744
				(2.831)
N	3,132	3,132	3,109	2,966
Chi squared	976.58[a]	1,112.12[a]	1,126.36[a]	1,112.49[a]
Likelihood ratio *Chi*-square test		67.68[a]	19.64[a]	13.88[a]
		(5 df)	(3 df)	(4 df)

[a]$p < .05$ one-tailed test.

Our final model (4) illuminates the connection between various ecological factors and a community's propensity to have a local citizens' group form within its boundaries. Along with several other researchers, we found that the sheer number of people and rapid population growth are positively related to the rate of founding. On the other hand, the physical environment in which the population lives has little independent impact on the founding rate. Resources, in the form of aggregate qualities of the community's population, are also important determinants of the founding rate. Four out of five indicators of personnel resources are significant in the final model. As we hypothesized, counties with larger pools of educated or middle-class persons are more likely to form citizens' organizations. Also, the data suggest that as the percentage of adults working and living in the same county increases, the rate of founding also increases. We find, also, that the level of local governmental resources is not a very important independent influence on the founding rate. In an analysis not reported here, we found that when each grievance measure was used as the sole explanatory variable in the rate model, it positively contributed to the rate. When other community characteristics are added to the model—especially population size—the significance of the grievance measures is substantially reduced.

Our theoretical expectations have been influenced by current thinking about the growth of existing organizations as well as thinking about the founding of new organizations. In an earlier analysis (Baker et al. 1986) we found that the relationship between the organizational age of these groups and their state of development is subject to substantial variation. Many older groups flounder, and many newer groups grow quickly. It may be the case that environmental factors we initially thought important in understanding founding rates, such as grievances and government resource levels, are in fact more important in explaining the growth patterns of these groups across communities.

Because we used a partial likelihood analysis to estimate the rate equation, we cannot directly address the form that time dependence took in our data. We can, however, speculate on the independent influence of time on the rate of foundings and what might be the underlying causes of this time dependence. One account of the temporal pattern of foundings may lie in the diffusion of ideas. Founding patterns may be similar to the diffusion of collective behavior patterns such as innovations, collective violence, or fads (Hamblin, Jacobsen, and Miller 1973; Olzak 1986). The availability of a social construction of the problem and possible solutions to victims in local communities—which will increase over time—should be important in explaining the founding of local organizations. Communities with large enough pools of victims must have some threshold of awareness of appropriate social constructions. Once such a level is reached, the likelihood of a founding increases (Granovetter 1978). We have not yet been able to measure the importance of social construction factors; however, they may explain the rising incidence of foundings from 1978 to 1983 shown in Figure 5–1 above. But how can we explain the declining incidence of foundings after 1983?

One account depends on a possible decline in the public availability of common constructions of problem and solution. In Figure 5–2 we show the national attention given to the issue of drunken driving in the print media. This curve mirrors very closely the organizational founding curve. It is plausible that as the issue of drinking and driving received less attention, victims and other potential founders were decreasingly likely to be aware of available commonly understood modes of citizen action. As a consequence, new victims during the decline in attention would be less likely to act on their grievances, and the rate of founding would decline.

Another account of the temporal pattern would consider the idea of natural limits to numbers of groups founded. Although we have linked each group to a single county in our analysis, many groups serve more than one county. The consequence of this fact is that the number of "counties at risk" for a new founding actually declines over time, even though we observe many counties without an organizational founding. As this limit is approached, the rate of founding must also decline. The fact that the counties within which an organization had been founded by 1985 contained approximately 50 percent of the total U.S. population is consistent with this account.

The data set that we have employed here is most useful in raising and addressing questions of organizational founding and growth. Its major strengths, however, will become increasingly clear as we continue to explore

Number of Stories

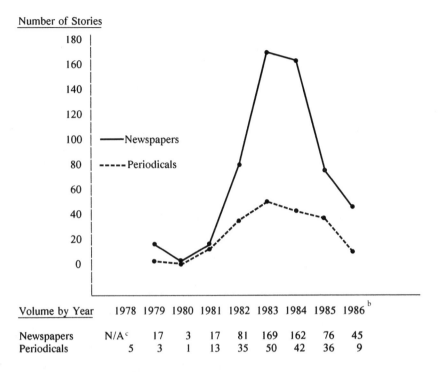

Volume by Year	1978	1979	1980	1981	1982	1983	1984	1985	1986 [b]
Newspapers	N/A [c]	17	3	17	81	169	162	76	45
Periodicals	5	3	1	13	35	50	42	36	9

[a]Newspaper volume is based on count of stories in the National Newspaper Index, 1979–86 (Information Access Corporation, Menlo Park, Calif.). This database indexes stories in *The Christian Science Monitor, The Los Angeles Times, The New York Times, The Wall Street Journal,* and the *Washington Post.* Periodical volume is based on counts of stories in the *Magazine Index,* 1978–86 (Information Access Corporation, Menlo Park, Calif.). The database indexes stories in 370 popular periodicals.

[b]The 1986 extrapolations are derived by doubling the volume reports of the January to June reports for both sources. If the 1984 to 1985 trend continues, these estimates should be inflated ones.

[c]The *National Newspaper Index* begins in 1979.

Figure 5–2. Volume of National Newspaper and Periodical Coverage of Drunk Driving, by Year.[a]

both the consequences of using other definitions of community boundaries and also our future success in measuring community variation in additional factors that we believe to be theoretically important to our understanding of organizational founding and growth.

NOTES

1. These figures are preliminary median estimates based on completed protocols for the first 300 responding local anti–drunk driving organizations. The Project on

the Citizens' Movement Against Drunk Driving has gathered systematic information about organizational structure, organizational activities, and community relations from approximately 400 of the local organizations.

2. Other approaches to operationalizing the boundaries of the local community, or "catchment area," of each organization are possible, including multicounty boundaries, SMSA boundaries, media markets, and congressional districts, among others. In the future we will explore a number of these other approaches to conceptualizing the community context of each organization.

3. We have identified approximately forty local groups working exclusively on drinking and driving issues that are not affiliated with either RID or MADD. We call these groups *outliers.* They include, for instance, Concerned Citizens and Victims of Drunk Drivers, begun in Northern Nevada in 1979, and the Alliance Against Intoxicated Drivers (AAIM), a coalition of local groups in the state of Illinois. We do not include these groups in the present analysis because we have not yet completed gathering information from them all. Neither do we include the few cases (twelve) of second organizational foundings in a county.

4. We chose 1980 as the most appropriate year for indexing local community characteristics because the local census data is available for that year but also because 1980 immediately precedes the major period of organizational founding that we are exploring here. We chose 1980 as the year for indexing automobile fatalities for similar reasons.

5. The results reported here represent the outcome of extensive preliminary analyses with many different indicators of the community-level factors that our theoretical expectations suggested should be important in understanding the founding rate. The variables included in these final models are chosen as the most robust and plausible of the many variables that we explored.

6 A COMPARATIVE ECOLOGY OF FIVE NATIONS
Testing a Model of Competition among Voluntary Organizations

J. Miller McPherson and Lynn Smith-Lovin

In research on voluntary organizations, attempts at making structural comparisons have been attempted in two limited ways. First, researchers have compared individual measures of organizational affiliation such as the mean affiliation rate across aggregates, communities, or nations. The strength of these studies is that they can be based on high-quality, system-wide probability samples and therefore have a known relationship to the system population. The weakness of such comparisons is that they cannot ordinarily tap structural features of great theoretical interest such as the relations among organizations. The second type of study, which uses case study or ethnographic techniques, admirably represents these structural elements; but here, comparisons are difficult because the representations for different systems are not standardized.

Recent advances in organizational ecology have suggested a different approach. McPherson (1982) showed how association membership data from a probability sample of individuals could be used to study some characteristics of the population of organizations. A later paper (McPherson

Work on this paper was supported by National Science Foundation Grants SES-812066 and SES-8319899 (to McPherson) and National Science Foundation Grant SES-8122089 (to Smith-Lovin). The data are from the Interuniversity Consortium for Political Research. We would like to thank the Structuralist Seminar at the University of South Carolina—Bruce Mayhew, Euihang Shin, John Skvoretz, David Smith, Jimy Sanders, and Don Tomascavich-Devy—for their useful comments. All interpretations and conclusions are solely the responsibility of the authors.

1983) develops an ecological model of the competition of social organizations for members. Here, the concept of an ecological niche is quantified explicitly in a way that allows us to use data from individuals to study how populations of organizations fit together into communities. The representations of the competitive structure are easily understood and may be compared across systems. Thus, the model allows us to compare communities of organizations in a systematic and quantitative way. This new capability should enhance the development of comparative theory in the organizational literature.

In this chapter, we apply this ecological model to data from the Five Nation Study by Almond and Verba (1963, 1968). We have two goals. First, we test the new ecological model in five different national settings. Second, we use the model's representation of the competitive structure of organizations in the five nations to compare the structure of their organizational communities, and to test several macrolevel hypotheses.

THE ECOLOGICAL MODEL OF ORGANIZATIONAL COMPETITION

The Niche

The most important idea in the ecological model is the organizational niche. In general, the niche is a location in multidimensional space defined by the resources in the environment. The concept has been used extensively in organizational ecology (Hannan and Freeman 1977; Aldrich 1979) but has only recently been quantified (Freeman and Hannan 1983; McPherson 1983). McPherson's (1983) definition of niche is simple: Because organizations consume the time, energy, and resources of humans, the characteristics of people affiliated with an organization define that organization's niche. These characteristics may include the sociodemographic characteristics of the people, their physical location, and their availability in time (although data on geography and time are seldom available in standard surveys). An organization almost always recruits from a limited segment of the community—this restricted part of the population of individuals is its social niche.

An example of niche differentiation in one dimension would be the extreme differentiation of business/professional organizations and unions on education. In 1960 the typical member of a business or professional organization in the United States had at least a high school diploma; most had some college or an advanced degree. These organizations only rarely recruited members from the high school dropout population. On the other hand, high school graduates were at the top of the educational range for unions. The average union member had eight years of education. Obviously, this differentiation on education meant that unions and business/professional groups rarely competed for the same members.

Figure 6–1 shows the power of the niche differentiation idea when it is extended to multiple dimensions. Each type of organization is represented as a rectangle in two-dimensional space, describing the social space that the organizations occupy. Operationally, the rectangles are formed by taking a two-standard deviation range about the mean, for each dimension. We call this window around the mean the *niche breadth*. For instance, the mean education for the members of civic organizations in Germany in 1960 (Figure 6–1) was approximately 5.4 years, with a standard deviation of about 1.2. The two standard deviation niche breadth on education captures the majority of members of the organization and allows a concise description of the location of these members on the education dimension. In Germany, civic organizations recruit from an older, less-educated population than business/professional groups. The extension of this basic imagery to more dimensions is straightforward mathematically, although difficult to visualize.

The difference in niche volume between the two organizational types in Figure 6–1 is apparent. The niche volumes are simply the area of the

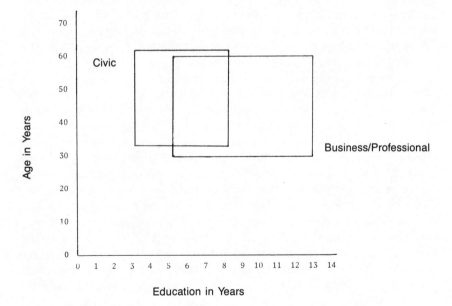

Source: Data from Almond and Verba (1963, 1968: Germany).

Figure 6–1. An Illustration of Niche Overlap in Two-Dimensional Space for Two Organizational Types.

boxes in two-dimensional space. The civic groups have a niche width of about 4.8 years of education and a width of about age 30. The business/professional organizations recruited from a less restricted age range (age 33) and have wider range of education (8.1 years). The civic organizations therefore have an area of 4.8 × 30 = 144 units, while the business/professional organizations have an area of 8.1 × 33 = 267 units. Clearly, the civic groups occupy a narrower niche than the business/professional organizations; they are more specialized, while business/professional organizations are more generalized. Specialists focus on a narrow range of possible resources, while generalists cast their nets more widely.

Competition in Social Space

In the McPherson model, the location of organizations in the niche space is the most important feature of the system. If the boxes in the niche space overlap, the organizations are recruiting from the same aggregate of individuals; they are competing. The extent of their competition can be quantified in the same way as the niche volume, by calculating the volume of their overlap. The rectangular representation of organizational niches forces the overlaps to be rectangular also. These overlaps can be calculated just as easily as the niche volumes because the volume of any box is simply the product of its dimensions, no matter how many dimensions there are. For example, in Figure 6–1 (considering just the two dimensions and the two organizations represented there) the area of overlap between the two types of organizations is three years of education (8.1 − 5.1) multiplied by twenty-eight years of age (65 − 37). Because rectangular shapes will have rectangular overlaps no matter how many dimensions are involved, the model can be extended to any number of dimensions.

The key idea is simply that because individuals have finite time, each organization limits the ability of the others to grow. Thus, when two organizations rub shoulders in niche space, they are competing ecologically with one another because they are recruiting the same kind of people. The available people in the niche space define the carrying capacity of the community for that type of organization. These people are the potential members of the organization. For the civic groups in Figure 6–1, the carrying capacity of the system for these groups would be the number of people who had between 3.1 and 8.1 years of education and between 37 and 67 years of age. In the absence of competition, the model suggests that an organization would grow until it contained all of the potential members in its niche space. However, there is competition for members; other organizations overlap in the niche space.

Because the basic imagery of the model is geometric, the system can easily be mathematized. As McPherson (1983) shows in detail, the system for two types of organizations can be represented by

$$M_i^* = K_i - a_{ij}(M_j^*)$$

and $\qquad\qquad\qquad\qquad\qquad\qquad\qquad\qquad\qquad\qquad$ (6.1)

$$M_j^* = K_j - a_{ji}(M_i^*)$$

where M_i^* is the observed number of members in organization type i, K_i is the number of potential members in the absence of competition from other organizations (the carrying capacity), and a's are the coefficients of competition between organization i and organization j.

The competition coefficients (a's) are the ratio of niche overlap to the organization's total niche volume. The competition coefficients measure the proportion of organization j's niche volume, which is contested by organization i. If the competition coefficient is at its maximum of 1.0, then organization j's niche volume is entirely inside that of organization i. All members of j are eligible for i. If it is at its minimum of 0.0, the two organizations' niches do not overlap at all. No members of j are eligible for i. The coefficients are not symmetric (a_{ij} does not necessarily equal a_{ji}) because the overlap may be a larger proportion of one organization's niche than the other's.

For example, the overlap between civic and business groups in Figure 6–1 is more than one-half the niche volume of civic groups ($84/144 = .58$), while it represents only about one-third of business/professional organizations' niche ($84/267 = .31$). Therefore, the coefficient ($a_{cb} = .58$) for the competition that business groups exert on civic groups is larger than the coefficient ($a_{bc} = .31$) showing how civic groups compete for business group members.[1] A business/professional group membership is less likely to take a member from the civic groups' social niche than vice versa.

Several points are important about this ecological competition. First, competition need not be conscious. If organizations i, j, and k recruit from the same segment of the social system at the same time, then they are in competition, even if members are totally unaware of the other organization. In particular, members need not feel any conflict between activities in the two groups. In fact, two competing groups may be cooperating in some strategic enterprise, may have formal alliances with one another, or have other institutionalized or informal relationships. If, however, they recruit from the same pool of potential members, they are in ecological competition.

Second, competition does not depend on activities inside the group or on any characteristic of the group other than group composition. Unions can compete with religious groups; business/professional groups may compete with youth-serving organizations. The functional requirements and goals of the organizations may be completely compatible (or unrelated). All that is required for competition is that limited resources (the time of a limited number of people) in a given social domain are sought by two or more types of organizations.

Finally, we must be clear that competition is ecological, not economic. There is not necessarily any bidding process for members, involving rational calculation of costs or benefits. The niche space in which organizations overlap could define a market in which economic competition for members occurs (such as in sustenance organizations), but economic competition is only a subset of the kind of ecological competition in this model.

When there are more than two organizations (or organization types) in the system, the two-equation model of (6.1) expands to matrix form:

$$K = AM^* \tag{6.2}$$

The K matrix is a vector of the carrying capacities of all r organizations, the A matrix is an $r \times r$ matrix of competition coefficients, and the M^* matrix is a vector of the observed sizes of the organizations. This system is the equilibrium form of the Lotka-Volterra competition equations (Hannan and Freeman 1977) and is derived from the model in McPherson (1983).

The K matrix tells us how many members there would be available for each type of organization if the organization were able to recruit from its niche without competition. It is a count of the number of people who have all the requisite characteristics for potential membership. The A matrix tells us which organizations compete with each other, and which do not. Large entries in the A matrix indicate that two organizational types have substantial overlap in their niche spaces, while small entries suggest that the two types are recruiting dissimilar people. In this sense, the A matrix is very much like a similarity matrix in multidimensional scaling, except that the matrix is a theoretically derived entity rather than simply a description of data.

Estimating Competition with Survey Data

The information needed for estimating the model is available in many social surveys of organizational participation, in the form of questions about voluntary affiliations. Such surveys are well suited to testing the model for several reasons. First, voluntary organizations engage in diverse activities; competition among them will illustrate the ecological, noneconomic nature of the process. Second, voluntary organizations are free to recruit members with few restrictions; there is usually less formal external control over voluntary organizations than businesses. Thus, differentiation among voluntary organizations is likely to reflect ecological competition in a clear, unambiguous manner. Third, voluntary organizations may be more likely than business organizations to meet the equilibrium assumption necessary to test the model (McPherson 1983: 525). They are less likely to undergo sudden shifts in resource base or competitive pressures as the result of business cycles, technological innovation, and the like. Finally, a traditional sociological interest in the social correlates and individual consequences of voluntary participation (see reviews in

Smith 1973 and Smith and Freeman 1972) has produced many high-quality representative surveys with data on voluntary organization membership and sociodemographic characteristics.

The ecological model was tested previously using survey data on voluntary organizations in a midwestern community system in the United States by McPherson (1983). The correlation between the observed carrying capacities (K) and the carrying capacities predicted by the model was .87, indicating very strong support for the model. Particularly impressive was the strength of the transformation that resulted when the membership vector (M) was multiplied by the competition matrix (A). Before this transformation, the K vector correlated only .06 with the M vector— meaning that one cannot predict the number of memberships in an organizational type from the number of people who fit the niche; one must take into account the amount of competition for those people from other organizations.

This chapter will use similar survey data from five national systems to test the model. Therefore, we will be able to examine whether or not the model can adequately describe the competition for members in the voluntary sector at a national level. By examining several systems, we also will be able to relate some aspects of the competitive system described by the model to more traditional measures of voluntary affiliation (such as the mean affiliation rate). Finally, we can use the competition matrices to compare the national voluntary systems in an interesting and novel way.

DATA

The cross-national data we use come from the Five Nation Study by Almond and Verba (1963, 1968). Probability samples of roughly 1,000 individuals were interviewed in 1959 and 1960 from each of five countries—the United States, the United Kingdom, Germany, Italy, and Mexico. Interviewers asked the number and types of organizations to which the respondents belonged, as well as standard demographic information and many political variables.

Resource Dimensions

Seven sociodemographic variables define the resource space for our analysis: work status, the length of residence in the present community, age, income, the size of community of current residence, sex, and education. Sex, education, and age were all important dimensions in the earlier study of a midwestern community. Income reflects some of the same attributes as occupational status (SES score), the fourth resource dimension in the earlier study. Work status of members has also proved important in studies of organizational size and composition (McPherson and Smith-Lovin 1982: 890, 1986: 73–74). The community variables are an attempt to tap the geographical dimensions that are clearly important in competition but typically impossible to measure in a sample survey of individuals. Town size will distinguish between types of organizations that feed in urban areas versus those that operate in small town or rural environments. Length of residence will contrast organizations that attract old-time, stable residents with those that are of interest to more recent migrants.

Organizational Types

The respondent in each of the five surveys was asked to indicate whether he or she then belonged to any of the following organizations: trade or labor unions, business organizations, social groups, professional or farm organizations, cooperatives, fraternal or veterans' groups, athletic clubs, political, charitable, civic, or religious organizations. In many cases, there were less than ten members of a given type in a given country. Because ten cases is a reasonable lower limit for reliable estimation of the niches, we were forced to combine types to form six standard categories for the analysis: (1) labor and trade unions, (2) business and professional organizations, (3) social and fraternal organizations, (4) religious groups, (5) civic and political organizations, and (6) veterans' groups. In the case of civic and political groups in Italy and veterans groups in Mexico, there were still less than ten cases, but reducing the number of types still further was judged inadvisable. In the case of Germany, as will be discussed below, we used more organizational types to test an hypothesis about omitted competitors.

Calculating Niche Breadths, Niche Volumes, and Carrying Capacities

The niche breadth for each organizational type is formed by constructing a 2.0 standard deviation window for each resource dimension, centered on the mean.[2] Because a niche consists of a (hyper) rectangular shape in n-dimensional space (seven-dimensional space, in this case), the volume of the niche is the simple product of each of the edges. The overlaps among the niches are also (hyper) rectangular shapes, whose volumes can be directly calculated in the same manner.[3] Competition coefficients are the ratio of the niche overlap to the niche volume.

The carrying capacity for the ith type of organization (K_i) is the number of potential members of the organization. For a sample survey, K's can be calculated directly by obtaining frequencies of sample respondents who are contained in the intersection of all niche breadths for a given organizational type. Similarly, the observed members in each organizational type are simply the frequencies on these variables.

RESULTS

Competitive Structure

The competition matrices for the five nations' study are shown in Table 6–1. Note that the matrices are not symmetric; as illustrated in Figure 6–1, an overlap is likely to constitute a larger proportion of one organization's niche volume than its competitor's. For example, in the United States the competition coefficient for unions with veterans groups is .48, while the corresponding coefficient for veterans groups' competition with unions is .22. This pattern indicates that almost half of the unions' recruitment area is overlapped by veterans groups—roughly half of union memberships will be a potential veterans group member. On the other hand, only about one-fifth of veterans groups members are potential members of unions—a union membership is less likely to compete with the veterans groups in an ecological sense.

In fact, one of the few major consistencies across the five competition matrices is the high competition of other types with unions (that is, the large values in the first column of each matrix). Unions typically have a relatively small niche volume; they are organizations specializing in a working, male, urban, low-income, low-education area of the social space. Other organizational types (in particular, religious and social/fraternal groups) compete heavily in this range. These types, however, are generalists. They have large niche volumes and recruit many members who would fall outside the unions' typical membership.

Another feature of the matrices that deserves comment is the extremely low competition of veterans' groups with other organizational types in Mexico. This lack of overlap is due to the fact that Mexican veterans' groups occupy a range on the age dimension overlapping almost no other organizational types; the niche breadth is from ages 57 to over 65. Only religious organizations, with a niche that extends up to include 58-year-olds, overlaps (and therefore competes with) the veterans.[4] In other countries, veterans have a much wider age range, typically extending down to age 38 (down to age 32 in the United Kingdom); they therefore compete with other organizational types to a much greater extent.

A more systematic way to compare the competitive structure in the five countries is to empirically measure their similarity to one another. A simple method of comparison is to correlate the thirty off-diagonal coefficients for countries. The top panel of table 6–2 shows the results. Clearly, the United States and the United Kingdom have strikingly similar competitive

Table 6–1. Competition Matrices and Carrying Capacities for Five Nations.

	Competition Matrices						Observed Members (M)	Estimated Carrying Capacities (K)	Observed Carrying Capacities (K)
	Unions	BusProf	SocFrat	Relig	CivPol	Veterans			
United States									
Unions	1.00	.07	.15	.16	.17	.22	135	234	198
BusProf	.06	1.00	.17	.12	.23	.16	80	181	200
SocFrat	.57	.45	1.00	.68	.85	.66	247	601	408
Relig	.50	.26	.56	1.00	.52	.58	176	489	432
CivPol	.39	.37	.51	.37	1.00	.34	97	390	442
Veterans	.48	.26	.39	.40	.33	1.00	60	344	298
United Kingdom									
Unions	1.00	.13	.19	.11	.10	.31	215	271	148
BusProf	.25	1.00	.23	.24	.26	.18	68	178	138
SocFrat	.73	.47	1.00	.56	.43	.67	137	387	558
Relig	.53	.63	.72	1.00	.52	.57	35	331	270
CivPol	.54	.77	.65	.61	1.00	.42	28	325	329
Veterans	.45	.14	.26	.17	.11	1.00	44	196	243
Italy									
Unions	1.00	.40	.27	.22	.09	.20	55	101	208
BusProf	.59	1.00	.56	.22	.13	.35	33	112	211
SocFrat	.27	.38	1.00	.13	.12	.28	25	75	238
Relig	.40	.28	.24	1.00	.11	.33	82	134	312
CivPol	.71	.67	.95	.46	1.00	.42	6	146	544
Veterans	.10	.12	.14	.09	.03	1.00	41	61	247

Mexico									
Unions	1.00	.10	.08	.08	.09	.00	102	113	191
BusProf	.52	1.00	.33	.10	.20	.00	19	94	162
SocFrat	.23	.19	1.00	.08	.23	.00	33	70	234
Relig	.47	.11	.14	1.00	.22	.03	55	115	435
CivPol	.58	.24	.48	.25	1.00	.00	23	116	298
Veterans	.00	.00	.00	.00	1.00	1.00	3	3	106
Germany									
Unions	1.00	.09	.20	.09	.11	.08	146	177	99
BusProf	.29	1.00	.25	.11	.07	.12	74	146	56
SocFrat	.64	.24	1.00	.21	.23	.24	92	219	181
Relig	.42	.16	.32	1.00	.30	.35	28	145	248
CivPol	.29	.06	.20	.17	1.00	.40	30	104	212
Veterans	.41	.17	.38	.36	.74	1.00	12	152	311

Legend:
Unions: trade or labor unions.
BusProf: business or professional organizations.
SocFrat: social or fraternal organizations.
Relig: religious organizations.
CivPol: civic or political organizations.
Veterans: veterans organizations.

Table 6–2. Interrelationships among Structural Features.

	United States	United Kingdom	Germany	Italy	Mexico
Correlations among competition matrices					
United States	1.00				
United Kingdom	.68	1.00			
Germany	.38	.14	1.00		
Italy	− .10	.39	− .17	1.00	
Mexico	.04	.32	.01	.71	1.00

	Mean a_{ij}	Mean Affiliation
Mean competition coefficients and mean affiliation rates		
United States	.24	1.17
United Kingdom	.26	.70
Germany	.16	.50
Italy	.18	.36
Mexico	.10	.23

Correlations between competition matrices and membership overlap matrices	
United States	.27
United Kingdom	.13
Germany	.28
Italy	− .02
Mexico	.01

structures (correlating .78). Italy and Mexico also have striking similarities, with little relation to the U.S./U.K. structure. Germany displays a somewhat individual pattern, not highly similar to any of the other four countries.

Several factors contribute to the pattern. The position of veterans groups and religious groups is different in the U.S./U.K. and Italy/Mexico structures. In the United States and United Kingdom, veterans groups compete heavily with other parts of the voluntary sector, in particular with religious, social/fraternal, and union groups. More than half of religious and social/fraternal memberships will be drawn from potential veterans members in the United States and the United Kingdom, while fewer than one-third will come from this domain in Italy and Mexico. Undoubtedly, the fact that the United States and United Kingdom experienced large (and successful) mobilization of men from across class structures in World War II contributes to the pattern: Middle and upper-middle class men (with a large niche breadth on age, income, and education) in these countries are drawn into veterans' memberships that compete with their other business, social, and civic affiliations.

Similarly, religious groups in Mexico and Italy compete heavily only with unions (and to a much lesser extent, civic/political groups). In the United States and United Kingdom, religious groups draw from a wide range of ages, incomes, and educational backgrounds; this fact leads these groups to compete widely with other generalists like social/fraternal groups and with specialists like unions and veterans groups. In Italy and Mexico, religious groups draw from a poorer, less-educated, more rural segment of social space and do not compete with generalist types to a significant extent.

A final distinctive difference that separates the U.K./U.S. pattern from the Italian and Mexican cases is the relationship between unions and business/professional groups. In the United States and United Kingdom, these types are very separate with little overlap. In Mexico and Italy, the distinction is less clear—business/professional groups draw heavily from potential union members, and in Italy unions attract a substantial proportion of their members from the business/professional niche. We suspect that the business groups are weighted toward professional and managerial organizations in the United States and United Kingdom—they are white-collar and do not recruit from the same domains as unions. In Italy and Mexico, business groups may be concentrated in trades, crafts, and smaller retail areas that are less socially distinct from unions. The analysis for Germany will be discussed below because there are significant omitted competitors there.

Relating Competition to Other Structures

The relations among the competitive structures in the voluntary sectors of the five nations suggest the interesting possibility that these patterns are linked to other macrolevel features. Analyses of this sort can be only suggestive: We, in effect, have only five cases for studying relationships between national-level structures. However, we hope to provide some leads for future work.

Links with Economic Development and Class Structure.   Our observations about the competitive positions of religious, union, and business/professional groups suggest that the class structure of nations might explain the considerable similiarity of the United States and United Kingdom versus Italy and Mexico. Nie, Powell, and Prewitt (1969a, 1969b) provided considerable background information on these topics. First, they measured economic development as (1) percentage of the labor force in service occupations, (2) gross national product (in U.S. dollars), and (3) literacy rates (Nie, Powell, and Prewitt, 1969a: app. C). On all of these measures, the United States and United Kingdom were clearly the most economically developed; on the first two (service employment and GNP), Italy was much closer to Mexico than it was to the United States or the United Kingdom.[5] Germany occupied an intermediate position on service employment and GNP. Nie, Powell, and Prewitt (1969b: table 6) also argued that development influenced class structure, with the United States, the United Kingdom, and Germany having a heavily middle-class, relatively "flat" class structure; Mexico and Italy had a substantially larger proportion (over half) of their population in the lower class, with a distinctly pyramidal class structure. Class and organizational participation were also more correlated in the United States and the United Kingdom— upper- and middle-class respondents were much more likely to belong to voluntary organizations than are lower class respondents. Historical attempts by political parties to mobilize the lower classes had lowered the correlation in other countries.

We suggest that the larger lower-class population, together with the systematic attempts to create an organizational structure in these strata, have produced the very different pattern that we see in Italy and Mexico. Here we find significant organizational types (religious, veterans, and, to some extent, civic/political groups) specializing in the low-education, low-income population. Conversely, the upper- and middle-class populations are not present in numbers to support a business/professional sector; therefore, this type reaches down in the class structure to compete with unions, religious, and civic/political groups. In the United States and United Kingdom, the lower-class population is smaller and does not participate to the same degree. Here, religious and civic/political groups are forced up into the middle- and upper-class strata, where they compete with many other types for members. Only unions continue to specialize in the lower-education, lower-income population.

Probably the pattern of unions illustrates the distinction that ecologists make between fundamental and realized niches (Morse 1980). A fundamental niche is the niche that could be exploited by a species if there were no competitors. In biology, this niche can only be changed through genetic mechanisms. The realized niche is the niche actually exploited in the environment containing competitors; it can change relatively quickly with the presence or absence of competing forms. Because we observe religious and civic/political organizations occupying rather different locations in social space across the countries (that is, varying realized niches), we know that their fundamental niche must include a wide range of the social resource dimensions. Unions, on the other hand, are confined to the low-education, working population in all countries we observed; the fundamental niche of this organizational form may be more restricted (although, of course, we cannot be sure because we observe only realized niches in a variety of competitive situations).

We have not discussed Germany's competitive patterns to any great extent. It stood alone in a position somewhat in between the U.S./U.K. pattern and the Italy/Mexico pattern; this is consistent with a link to economic development because it also fell between these two extremes on the service employment and GNP measures (Nie, Powell, and Prewitt, 1969a, 1969b). Its class structure was much more similar to the United Kingdom and United States than to less developed countries, while the correlation between social status and organizational participation was very low. Because of the social and political upheaval of the two world wars, it appears that Germans (especially educated, high-income Germans) did not participate in voluntary organizations to the extent that the level of development and class structure would lead one to expect (Almond and Verba 1963: 314–16). This was especially true of civic/political organizations and veterans' groups (the latter for obvious reasons). The main features of the competition matrix that distinguish Germany's voluntary sector from the United States and United Kingdom is the extent to which the veterans and civic/political groups do not compete in social space; they have little overlap with the religious, business/professional, and social/fraternal groups that feed in the middle- to upper-class populations.

Links to Other Affiliation Measures.   The overall mean of the competition coefficients in the competition matrix tells us how closely packed the organizational types are in the niche space (McPherson 1983: 526–27). Extremely high means suggest that the organizations are very similar to one another in composition and that the occupied part of the niche space is densely filled with competing organizations. Very low means suggest that the organizations are dissimilar in composition and that the space is not densely packed. Systems with very high competition coefficients would have a large number of organizational types competing for the same people. Such systems would have many organizations of quite similar composition, which might lead to similarities in other properties such as resources, power, and so forth. Systems with low coefficients will have diverse organizational populations and are likely to have organizations that are quite different in other ways, as well.

The most widely used measure in cross-system comparisons is the mean affiliation rate, which is the average number of organizations to which respondents belong (cf. Almond and Verba 1963: 319–22). This mean measures the richness of the resource environment for organizational support. The higher the mean affiliation, the greater the participation in the voluntary sector and the more (or larger) organizations can be supported.[6] Therefore, higher mean affiliation rates indicate greater productivity of resources in the habitat for organizations. We hypothesize that this greater

productivity leads to more "packing" of organizations in the niche space because the resources are greater. In a resource rich environment, many species can flourish within close proximity; in a poor system, species may need to be more differentiated to survive.

The second panel of Table 6–2 (columns 1 and 2) shows mean affiliations and mean competition coefficients for the five countries. The correlation between the two measures is .78 ($N = 5$). Thus, there is a strong relationship between mean affiliation and competition. Only Germany prevents a near-perfect relationship.

Another issue that relates the competition matrix to affiliation patterns is the issue of overlapping memberships. Researchers in the voluntary association literature have stressed the importance of individuals' multiple memberships in creating information and resource flows between organizations (McPherson and Smith-Lovin 1982, 1986). Joint memberships will create similarities in membership, but can we consider this to be competition in the ecological sense? In one way, yes: Given limited time and energy even two organizations that share a member compete for that member's attention, time, and resources. If one makes demands that are too heavy, it will either be dropped or will force out its competitor. In another sense, however, such organizations may have a mutualistic relationship rather than a competitive one. The joint membership may be an indicator that the organizations are mutually supportive, rather than competitive.

One way of assessing the extent of this mutualism is to relate the competition matrices to correlation matrices that measure the extent of overlapping memberships (such as the correlation of a business/professional membership with a religious group membership). Panel 3 of Table 6–2 displays the correlations of the thirty off-diagonal elements in the competition matrices with the corresponding off-diagonal elements in membership overlap matrices. Clearly, some of the competition represented in the A matrices *is* the result of overlapping memberships; this is especially true in the United States and Germany. But only one-fifth of the variance in the a's is explained by overlap even in the United States. Clearly, mutualism is not the major force operating in the voluntary sector. Most of the competition represented in the A matrices is not competition for an individual's time in an overlapping membership; it is ecological competition for members with similar characteristics.

Summary.   The above analyses are suggestive. With only five cases, we cannot be sure how structural and historical aspects of national systems relate to the competitive structure in the voluntary sector. However, we are encouraged that the structures that we obtain have reasonable interpretations. It is striking that the picture of the voluntary structure that emerges is quite consistent with the general interpretations that Almond and Verba (1963) give to national differences in *The Civic Culture*. The substantial differences that they find between political attitudes and behavior in the United States and United Kingdom as opposed to the other three countries is only roughly mapped onto the voluntary system by mean affiliation rates. The richness of our description of the voluntary structure would allow much more detailed analyses of the relations among class and demographic structure, voluntary affiliation, and the political system. For example, correlations among sociodemographic dimensions would collapse the niche space, simplify the environment, and define limits to the potential diversity or organizations. National systems with low correlations among resource dimensions would accommodate a wider variety of organizational types, with implications for both system-level and individual-level outcomes (such as political consensus or network ties). These extensions are beyond the scope of this chapter, however.

Testing the Model

Five Independent Tests.   Although five nations allow only limited opportunities for relating competitive structure to other aspects of the national systems, the data do provide enough information for five independent tests of the ecological model in cross-section. We do this by comparing the predicted carrying capacities to the values calculated directly from the survey data (the number of respondents who represent the intersection of all the characteristics defining the niche of the organizational type). The last three columns of Table 6–1 show these values: the observed memberships, the predicted carrying capacity, and the observed number of individuals in the niche base.[7]

As Figure 6–2 shows, there is an extremely strong correlation between the observed and predicted carrying capacities in the United States and the United Kingdom (.85 and .80, respectively). These values are very close to the results of the earlier test in a midwestern community system ($r = .87$ in McPherson 1983: 528), indicating that the model can work well at the national system level.

The model also works well in Italy and Mexico, with correlations of .67 and .65, respectively. The carrying capacities for union and business/professional organizations are underestimated somewhat. Significant omitted competitors of unions and business/professional groups (like work organizations) may lower the estimated value. (Notice that union and business/professional groups are underestimated in every analysis; see panels 1 through 5.) Alternatively, it is possible that some of these sustenance-related organizations have more competitive than mutualistic

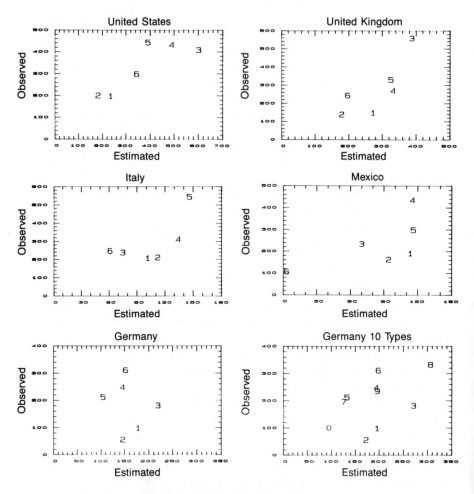

Source: Data from Almond and Verba (1963, 1968).

Key: 1 = unions, 2 = business/professional groups, 3 = civic/political groups, 4 = religious groups, 5 = social/fraternal groups, 6 = veterans groups, 7 = farm oriented organizations, 8 = charitable organizations, 9 = other organizations, and 10 = cooperatives.

Figure 6–2. Observed and Estimated Carrying Capacities for Organizational Types in Five Countries.

relations, such that the competition matrix is underestimating the conflict between them relative to the conflict among other types.

The striking failure of the model is in Germany (panel 5 of Figure 6–2). Here the predicted and observed carrying capacities are actually negatively correlated ($r = -.19$). Apart from assuring us that the relationship established in the other tests is not definitional, this finding is quite inter-esting. We suggest three possibilities for explaining the failure. First, the turmoil experienced by German society during and after the two world wars almost certainly caused dramatic changes in the voluntary sector. Perhaps the system had not yet reached equilibrium in 1959 when the Almond and Verba data were collected. Because equilibrium is necessary for testing the model in cross-section (McPherson 1983: 525), this could account for the negative results. A second possibility is a data problem. Although Germans reported a fairly high number of affiliations, they were more likely than members in other countries to be "passive" members—their participation tended to be formal in character and involve less indi-vidual commitment and activity (Almond and Verba 1963: 314–20). Perhaps German memberships are less reliable indicators of true competi-tion than those in the other surveys.

A third possibility is the existence of omitted competitors. Although we suspect that there are omitted competitors in all of the analyses (work organizations and families certainly compete for members' time), these omissions are not particularly problematic if they are spread fairly evenly throughout social space. They may cause the scale of predicted values to be off, but they will not disturb their ordering (McPherson 1983: 529). However, if omitted competitors focus only on limited parts of the volun-tary system, they will cause underestimates of the carrying capacity for those sectors.

The Impact of Omitted Competitors.   The third possibility is especially interesting because an empirical test is possible. The Almond and Verba data actually included ten types of voluntary organizations: the six types listed on Table 6–1, farm organizations, cooperatives, charity groups, and other groups (a residual category). These types were not used in the analyses reported above because they contained so few members for most nations (an average of less than fifteen members in the named types, which is quite small for reliable statistical analyses). After the failure of the model in Germany, we reexamined the organizational distribution and noticed that 29 percent of all German affiliations were in these groups (with an average size of thirty). Also, the residual "other" category formed a more coherent social category for Germany than for the other countries.

Table 6–3 shows a new competition matrix including the previously omitted competitors.[8] We see that all of the new types compete strongly with unions (as do all other types because unions are such specialists—see column 1 here and in Table 6–1). This is significant because unions' low predicted carrying capacity was an important factor in the model's lack of fit in Germany (see panel 5, Figure 6–2). Charitable organizations are generalists, competing heavily with almost all types (see row 8) but

Table 6–3. Revised Competition Matrix and Carrying Capacities for Germany: Ten Types of Organizations.

	Competition Matrix (A)										Observed Members (M*)	Estimated Carrying Capacity (K̂)	Observed Carrying Capacity (K)
	Unions	BusProf	SocFrat	Relig	CivPol	Veterans	Farm	Charit	Other	Coop			
Unions	1.00	.09	.20	.09	.11	.08	.20	.07	.06	.26	146	195	99
BusProf	.29	1.00	.25	.11	.07	.12	.12	.18	.17	.17	74	172	56
SocFrat	.64	.24	1.00	.21	.23	.24	.48	.18	.29	.48	92	271	181
Relig	.42	.16	.32	1.00	.30	.35	.38	.28	.30	.16	28	193	248
CivPol	.29	.06	.20	.17	1.00	.40	.42	.17	.06	.33	30	132	212
Veterans	.41	.17	.38	.36	.74	1.00	.62	.38	.13	.43	12	198	311
Farm	.29	.05	.21	.11	.22	.17	1.00	.09	.08	.43	34	126	196
Charit	.66	.50	.54	.54	.60	.70	.62	1.00	.38	.46	20	306	332
Other	.24	.20	.35	.24	.09	.10	.22	.16	1.00	.11	90	196	235
Coop	.28	.06	.16	.03	.13	.09	.32	.05	.03	1.00	14	95	101

Legend:
Unions: trade or labor unions.
BusProf: business or professional organizations.
SocFrat: social or fraternal organizations.
Relig: religious organizations.
CivPol: civic or political organizations.
Veterans: veterans organizations.
Farm: farmers' organizations
Charit: charitable organizations.
Other: residual category.
Coop: cooperative organizations.

suffering relatively little competition from them (column 8). Coop and farm organizations are specialists, recruiting from a low-education, rural, stable-resident sector of the population. As specialists (like unions), they experience a great deal of competition from others (columns 7 and 10) but exert little on others. They do, however, compete to some degree with each other, as specialists trying to feed in the same resource space.

Table 6–3 also gives the observed memberships and carrying capacities and the predicted carrying capacities for the new analysis with ten types in Germany. The relationship between observed and predicted carrying capacities—the test of the model—is shown in panel 6 of Figure 6–2. With the omitted competitors included in the analysis, the correlation in Germany jumps from –.19 to .50—a tremendous improvement. Although still not as good as our results for the other five countries, the data now offer substantial support for the model.

The fact that the model still does not work as well in Germany as in other countries could be explained by the other two factors noted above (disequilibrium from the war and nominal membership). For example, the veterans groups are still an anomaly for Germany: The type encompasses the second-largest niche base of any organizational type (exceeded only by charitable organizations); therefore, the observed carrying capacity is very large (311). Its predicted carrying capacity is lower, however, because the membership is quite low (12) and the level of competition is not high enough to raise this value significantly. Obviously, membership in veterans' groups is suppressed in Germany because of nation-specific historical factors that are not directly related to the ecology of voluntary organizations. (Note that the carrying capacity for veterans groups is also overestimated for Italy; see Figure 6–1, panel 4, point 6.) One would expect the system to move toward equilibrium based on current competitive structure as the time lag from recent disturbing events increases.

Summary.   In general, the ecological model is supported by data in these five cross-national surveys. Support is strongest in the countries where data quality is highest and where the systems have not undergone recent shocks. We believe that our results demonstrate that the model can be applied effectively to national-level systems using standard survey instruments collected for other purposes. The implications for future work are exciting. Competitive structures can be analyzed for any system that has been studied with a survey using probability sample of individuals (if it included questions on memberships and basic sociodemographic characteristics). Competitive structures can be compared across surveys of any system with these measures; the implications for studies of community are many. Finally, ecological competition can be linked to other system-level properties, as we have illustrated. We expect further theoretical advances in many areas of comparative research when these methods filter their way into the literature. We now turn to some areas where future comparative work with this model may be fruitful.

CONCLUDING REMARKS

One of the important conceptual advances of this model is the explicit way in which the system of organizations is modeled as a community. The ecological relationships between organizations are clearly evident in the extent to which they compete in the same area of social space. The similarities and differences among the organizations are powerfully represented in terms of the relevant resource dimensions, while the entire system is summarized by the competition matrix.

The corresponding theoretical advance is that, for the first time, it is possible to understand the relationship between the vast body of survey evidence on organizational affiliation and broad-scale macroevolutionary processes. The flow of individuals into and out of organizations over time can now be interpreted in community-level terms. Organizations that recruit the same type of individuals over time and lose some members through systematic processes of attrition will reach a stable internal demographic structure. These organizations will have stable niches. Organizational communities with a high proportion of such organizations will tend toward equilibrium; the flow of individuals into and out of organizations will produce stable organizational size, stable sociodemographic structure, and a stable niche structure. On the other hand, organizations whose mechanisms of recruitment or attrition are changing will be changing in size or composition or both. Systems characterized by such organizations will have unstable niche structures and will not be at equilibrium.

According to our model, instability in niche structure for a single organization can come from two sources. First, the population of individuals in the community system may change. The individual level demography of the system may change because of migration, mortality, fertility, or any combination of these. Of course, the ecological model at hand gives us a powerful representation of how individual demography relates to organizational demography, by modeling the mechanism through which individual-level resources are translated into organizational niches.

A second source of instability is the territorial encroachment of other organizations through the emergence of a new organizational form or through changes in the niche of another organization. New organizations can crowd out old forms or force them to change their realized niches. The model we have developed allows us to trace the consequences of such changes throughout the system. Given better data, particularly dynamic data, we can begin to trace the natural history of evolving communities of organizations in a systematic and quantitative way. One concept that promises to be very useful is the notion of the climax distribution.

In bioecology, entire communities of species will sometimes reach an equilibrium state in which growth and decline is relatively constant for all species. This equilibrium is called the climax stage and occurs when the distribution of resources has been stable long enough for the perturbations and oscillations in population sizes to decay. The climax stage is the end point in a sequence of succession of populations. In the climax stage, the introduction of new forms into the system causes little change in the distribution of species.

This climax stage in ecological communities depends on stability in the environment. Drastic changes in climate, resource distribution, or exogenous sources of disturbance such as disease can produce changes in the system. Traditionally, the climax state has been viewed as the inevitable end point of successive stages in the community (Clemments 1936; Shimwell 1971), although this view has moderated in the recent literature (Peet and Loucks 1977).

The obvious analogue to the climax community in organizational ecology would be an equilibrium distribution of organizational types in human systems. In this equilibrium distribution, organizational types would bear the same relationship to each other and to the resources on which they depend. In a sense, the climax hypothesis is a strong form of the axiom of isomorphism (Hannan and Freeman 1977: 939). This axiom asserts that variation in environments leads to variation in organizational forms. The climax hypothesis is a stronger statement in the sense that it predicts that organizational forms in systems with similar resource distributions will not only have similar relative frequencies but will bear basically the same structural relationships to one another. One particularly powerful way of looking at these structural relationships is to examine the competitive positions of different organizational forms *vis-à-vis* the resources in their systems. The climax hypothesis predicts that organizational forms in basically similar systems will have similar competitive structures. This comparison could be made using the tools that we have developed, if better data on communities of organizations were available.

For example, in our current analyses, do the organizational forms that appear so consistently in the United States and United Kingdom represent a climax distribution for industrialized capitalist states? Are the patterns in Mexico and Italy typical of developing capitalist countries? The model provides a mechanism for mapping the demographic and class changes that occur with development onto the organizational fields that create network environments for individuals and growth potentials for social groups. We believe that these new theoretical connections between demography and organizational ecology will provide new insights into the character of organizational fields in the near future.

NOTES

1. Note that the competition coefficients (a's) have no units; the dimensions used to define the social space in which organizations compete drop out when the overlaps are divided by niche volumes. Thus, the fact that the areas are in age times education units is not problematic because the units cancel out in the numerator and demoninator of the competition coefficient.

2. McPherson (1983: 525) used a 1.5 standard deviation window. Experiments with a variety of window widths (1.0, 1.5, 2.0, 2.5 and 3.0 standard deviations) suggested that a window of 2.0 produced a maximum discrimination between organizations for these data, while retaining a reasonable degree of overlap. Analyses with other window widths, while not as clear, still provide substantial support for the model tested below; therefore, we conclude that the analyses are not particularly sensitive to this aspect of specification.

3. The dichotomous variables (work status and sex) pose special problems. Here, we deal with proportions of an organizational type's membership that is working or male. The end points of the niche on a dichotomous variable are calculated as follows:

   Let P_i represent the proportion of individuals with characteristic i in the system population, while p_i represents the proportion of individuals with characteristic i in the organizational type, where $p_j = 1 - p_i$. Calculate the niche width:

   $$NW = 1 - abs(P_i - p_i)$$

   Partition the niche width into the sectors of the i and j populations that will be in the niche of the organizational type:

   $$NW_i = NW^*p_i$$

   $$NW_j = NW^* (1 - p_i)$$

   The end points of the niche breadth, used to calculate the niche volumes, can then be calculated:

   $$\text{Upper bound of niche breadth} = p_i + NW_i$$

   $$\text{Lower bound of niche breadth} = p_i + NW_j$$

   Notice that if the proportion of individuals in the organizational type with characteristic $i(p_i)$ matches that of the population (P_i), then the niche width includes the entire population, and the end points are 0.0 and 1.0. Conversely, if the organizational type includes *only* individuals with characteristic i, then the niche width is equal to the proportion of the population with that characteristic (p_i), and the end points are p_i and 1.0.

4. This situation is analogous to the position of elderly oriented organizations in the McPherson (1983: 526) analysis. These zero overlaps do not imply that no

veterans belong to any other type of organization. This interpretation would be correct only if the niche breadth were defined by the total range along the resource dimension. Likewise, the zero values do not prove that there are literally no competitors in this region of the niche space. Other organizational types simply do not compete heavily in this region of older members.

5. In literacy, Italy was substantially below the United States and other European countries in 1960 (87.5 percent compared with over 98 percent) but is closer to them than Mexico (with 50 percent literacy).

6. Of course, organizations could also draw on the nonparticipating sector by attempting to attract new members from those who have not before joined an organization. Here, organizations would presumably be competing with nonvoluntary sector activities like work or family. Although these aspects are currently not included in the ecological model, they could be (with detailed work information, for example). At any rate, the fact that the model fits as well as it does indicates that these ignored competitors are spread fairly evenly throughout the system. Otherwise, they would weaken our predictions, and the model would be rejected (see the case of Germany, below).

7. A much more detailed description of the calculation of the predicted values is provided in McPherson (1983: 528).

8. Analyses with all ten organizational types were also conducted for the other four countries. The results for the correlation of estimated and observed carrying capacities were as follows: .63 in the United States, .69 in the United Kingdom, .34 in Italy, and .52 in Mexico. The poorer results in general are due to outliers because of the limited number of cases on which the estimates of niche width are based. Obviously, erring too far in the direction of including organizational types for which there are limited data can undermine results.

7 ORGANIZING BUSINESS INTERESTS
Patterns of Trade Association Foundings, Transformations, and Deaths

Howard Aldrich and Udo H. Staber

Trade associations are organizations created to represent business interests within specific domains, mobilizing firms within their domain so that collective action can be taken on common problems. The extent to which trade associations succeed in their objectives has clear implications for the interests of firms in other industries, consumers, and the state. In a pluralist society, well-organized interests generally have an advantage over other interests, and business interests are especially privileged (Offe 1985). Whether trade associations can come together for collective action that cuts across the specific industries each represents is, however, problematic. To the extent that external conditions facilitate association survival and growth, we might expect joint action by coalitions of trade associations to succeed in defining a general business interest. This development, in turn, may change the balance of power in U.S. society, perhaps affecting the legislative and regulatory policies of the state.

Three complementary models are reviewed as possible explanations for changes in the population of trade associations. First, theories of increasing social differentiation in industrial societies imply a general

Comments from the following friends and colleagues helped immensely: Nicole Biggart, Glenn Carroll, Lee Clarke, Eric Leifer, Tim McKeown, Samuel Shapiro, and Jitendra Singh. We are indebted to the following people for research and clerical assistance in our research: Jan Bryant, Sharon Byrd, Jeanne Hurlbert, Mal-Soon Min, Jane Morrow, Maureen O'Connor, Jane Salk, Jane Scott, Leslie Wasson, and Cathy Zimmer.

increase in organizing activity in all societal sectors. Experience in organizing is spread via major institutions, and imitation leads to the diffusion and adoption of new organizational forms across industries. Second, niche theory and competitive isomorphism imply that increasing economic differentiation should lead to newly emerging industries creating their own trade association and to trade associations limiting themselves to industries where members are most easily recruited. Third, theories of government intervention in the economy imply that association formation and survival are partially a response to political problems faced by business and that association activity should increase (or decrease) in parallel with government activity. After reviewing the general characteristics of trade associations in the United States, we will outline each model and then discuss their empirical implications.

TRADE ASSOCIATIONS

Trade associations can be defined as business interest organizations that represent their members' political and economic preferences, although at times they also act as vehicles for governments to implement public policies.[1] They differ in several important respects from previously studied populations of organizations: They are voluntary associations that depend on the survival of their constituents for their own existence; they represent segments of the most politically privileged sector in capitalist countries; they strive for a monopoly position within their domain (like labor unions); and by making substantial investments in their claimed domains, they restrict their prospects of changing domains. The population of trade associations in the United States has expanded dramatically since the mid-nineteenth century, from about 100 national or interstate associations at the turn of the century to over 2,000 in the early 1980s. Our long-term research objective is to explain variation in the growth pattern of U.S. national trade associations.

The Organizational Characteristics
of Trade Associations

The publicly stated purpose of trade associations is to defend and promote the interests of business firms. Their internal function is to integrate the often incongruent preferences of their members, although smaller firms' preferences are usually subordinated to those of larger members (Staber 1982). Externally, their function is to propagate a collective interest vis-à-vis interests outside their domain, including state agencies, labor unions, and other business interest organizations (Offe and Wiesenthal 1979; Schmitter and Streeck 1981).

As interest associations, trade associations are subject to the collective rationality problem (Olson 1965). They resemble labor unions in that their survival depends not only on how well they represent membership interests but also on how effective they are in aggregating the parochial preferences of their members. Some associations represent a specific industry, whereas others cut across what are commonly thought of as "industry" boundaries, linking groups of firms horizontally or vertically in different product or service lines. The organizational problem is that, under certain circumstances, it may be rational for potential members to refrain from participation in association affairs. This implies that trade associations may not persist (or arise at all), despite favorable external conditions.

The Environment of Trade Associations in the United States

Perhaps more than in any other country, the American state has affected the development of business associations recently by its prominence and, during earlier periods, by its absence. Viewed historically and cross-nationally, the amounts of political activity by business appear to be disproportionately greater today in the United States than in many other advanced liberal democracies. Previous research has suggested that increases in the extent of state intervention in market processes are responsible for the general expansion of business interest associations in general and the trade association population in particular (Schmitter and Brand 1979).

The history of state intervention in market processes has not been a linear one. The relationship between polity and economy has historically been weaker in the United States than in other industrialized nations, with firms enjoying considerably more autonomy vis-à-vis the state and organized labor than in Western Europe and Japan (Vogel 1978). In contrast to the Continental European context and in spite of legislation such as the Sherman Act (1890), the American state remained a mere agency for industrial development until well after the turn of the twentieth century (Roy 1981). In the early period of U.S. economic development, rapid economic growth, the fierceness of competition, the large number of enterprises, and the continual discovery of new domestic markets inhibited the development of a strong central state.

In time, however, increased industrial concentration, the need to find and stabilize export markets, and other developments laid the seeds for an enlarged role of the state. State intervention and state power intensified during three major phases of policymaking: the Progressive Era (1900–16), World War I (1914–18), and the New Deal (1933–40). The "age of reform" (Hofstadter 1955) marked an impressive expansion of state functions and tasks, and the passage of antitrust legislation, the creation of the Federal

Trade Commission, and Department of Justice surveillance of business activities represented a challenge to business dominance in setting economic policies.

The National Recovery Act proved to be an important stimulus to trade association formation (Himmelberg 1976). Although the NRA was declared unconstitutional in 1935, resulting in the dissolution of many trade associations (TNEC 1941), the federal government continued to expand the scope of its tasks, particularly its social regulatory activity. Businesses played a major role in the shaping of regulation, much of which was sought by producers themselves to regulate economic competition. The period following World War II up to the late 1950s was characterized by much popular support for business and by public confidence in the promises of a free enterprise system. In that era of complacency (Wilson 1981) there was little need for business to enter the political process, and firms tended to be politically inactive, if not naive (Bauer, Pool, and Dexter 1963).

The political situation changed dramatically during the following decade. Since the 1960s the private business sector has been confronted with the emergence of independent consumer and environmental interest organizations that have enjoyed increased access to the political process. Moreover, in the 1970s business perceived itself challenged by a large number of increasingly sophisticated political agencies, staffed with public bureaucrats who were more sensitive to the demands of nonbusiness interest groups than ever before. In that climate of heightened political conflict and debate, the regulatory process became more politicized. Interest group activity in general has notably expanded since the 1960s, responding to the increased involvement of governments in economic and social affairs (Schlozman and Tierney 1983, 1986).

Business reacted to the challenge both individually and collectively, and its political engagement has also been well accepted (Wilson 1981). A 1981 survey of seventy-one national trade associations in the manufacturing sector showed that 73 percent of those interacting with legislators and government officials on a continuous basis claimed they were viewed as necessary and legitimate partners in the political process (Staber 1982). Only 11 percent of those surveyed reported no continuous political relationships. For a time, roughly between 1972 and 1978, business was on the defensive, but then the balance shifted back toward business again. The reduction of the capital gains tax in 1978 altered a long-standing status quo in business's favor, and in the post-1980 environment, business has made other advances.

Three Models of Association Foundings

The first explanation for the expansion of trade associations is derived from Weber's thesis of social differentiation. Weber described the development of capitalist society as the growth of a rational order. Rational calculation, according to Weber, is essential to efficient entrepreneurial activity, and it encourages the spread of bureaucratic specialization in all spheres of social life. Bureaucratic task specialization will survive as long as it is technically superior to any other organizational form of administration or, as Marx proposed, as long as it remains the most efficient means of expropriation and social control.

The historical development of the state may be viewed as a reflection of society's structural evolution. The expansion of the state apparatus is the result of an increasingly differentiated accomplishment of old tasks and the discovery of new functions. With an increase in social differentiation, more claims are brought to the state, each representing the parochial interests of differentiated categories that politicians and state bureaucrats seek to reconcile in the political process. Olson (1982) observed that there is evidently a cross-national tendency toward interest fragmentation, creating a fertile seedbed for organized activity.

The second model is drawn from theories of niche width and competitive isomorphism, and rests on the assumption that the association population expands with industrial growth. On the assumption that resources (such as money, members, personnel, and legitimacy) for organizing interests are limited, resources can be mobilized only at the expense of other existing or potential organizational forms. Which form survives in the long run is difficult to predict because environments, as sources of organizational legitimacy (DiMaggio and Powell 1983), change over time.

The process of competition among organizational forms is dynamic and is driven by isomorphic forces. The concept of isomorphism is derived from human ecology, and when applied to organizations refers to the process by which organizational characteristics tend to become increasingly compatible with environmental properties (Aldrich 1979; DiMaggio and Powell 1983). According to the principle of competitive exclusion, the diversity of organizational forms is, in the long run, limited by resource diversity. Diverse environments support diverse organizational populations, while homogeneous environmental demands generate similar organizational forms.

Our third model introduces explicitly political concerns into the analysis, under the assumption that association foundings and dissolutions are partly a function of governmental regulatory activity. Federal regulatory activity (as measured by the number of pages of the *Federal Register*) has increased dramatically since the late 1960s. In an earlier paper, we proposed that a general increase in the magnitude of federal regulation would encourage business to engage in associative political action (Aldrich and Staber 1983). We hypothesized that government regulation and competition for governmental protection (against imports, organized labor, and so forth) may not only stimulate the formation of associations but also add a constraint that facilitates organizational survival (Hannan and Freeman 1977). If associations are successful in stimulating government action on behalf of their industries, two benefits result: (1) Their membership may stabilize, at least to the extent that government action is sufficient to ensure business survival; and (2) to the extent that they are perceived by their members as successful interest representatives, their survival chances are enhanced.

Our source for trends in federal regulation is the *Federal Register*, which has been available only since 1937. We measured the level of regulatory activity in two ways. First, we followed conventional practice and counted the number of pages in the *Federal Register* from 1936 to 1983. This measure is thought to overstate regulatory intensity, as it includes items other than rules or proposed rules. Second, we counted the number of entries, from 1937 to 1983, devoted to rules and regulations for each industry defined at the three-digit SIC level. (As it happens, the correlation between the two is so high that they can be used interchangeably.) In Figure 7–1 we show the trend from 1937 to 1983 in the extent of federal regulation, showing both indicators.[2] Regulations issued by the federal government increased during World War II, dropped slightly, leveled off in the 1950s, and then began a slow upward climb in the 1960s. The trend accelerated dramatically in the 1970s, nearly tripling between the early and the late 1970s, before falling during the early Reagan years.

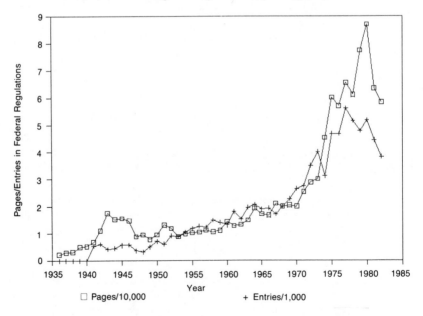

Figure 7–1.   Federal Regulations, 1937–83.

If the social differentiation thesis is correct, the population of trade associations should increase inexorably, regardless of government regulations, as organizational innovations and the accumulation of organizing experience facilitate the formation of new associations. Economic and social differentiation are usually seen as increasing linearly over time. If differentiation drives the establishment and maintenance of trade associations, then they, too, should develop linearly over time.

If the niche theory and competitive isomorphism arguments are correct, then the population of trade associations should expand at about the same pace as the economy. New associations should proliferate in emerging industries, and association foundings should diminish in aging industries. Note that this argument and the social differentiation model, drawn from Weber, make predictions that are very hard to distinguish from one another at the aggregate level. Distinguishing between them would require separate time series of economic indicators for each industry—a very difficult task, given the paucity of data over time at a consistently defined three- or four-digit SIC industry level—and we have not created such series yet. Thus, we are limited to some informed speculations in this paper.

If the model of governmental intervention is correct, then we would expect the growth in foundings and total association population size to follow the trends shown in Figure 7–1. If government regulation drives the process, then it should proceed less regularly, corresponding roughly to events and periods of intervention. For example, the large increase in regulation activity after 1970 should be mirrored in patterns of association founding.

THE STUDY

We distinguish trade associations from professional societies (such as the American Bar Association), from trade unions (such as the United Auto Workers), and various for-profit organizations that sometimes have *association* in their title.[3] We include only associations that are national in scope and that are engaged in the promotion or defense of business interests, although sixty-two regional associations that were predecessors to national associations, or that are otherwise linked to national associations, are included. Most of our sample is in the manufacturing sector, reflecting that sector's higher level of collective activities.

We aimed for an exhaustive listing of all associations created after 1942, as archival sources of information improved substantially in that year with the publication of Judkins (1942). We also collected information on all associations active after 1942, regardless of when they were born, and in the process obtained information on associations born before 1942. Finally, we discovered a number of useful sources giving founding dates of associations prior to 1942, and so our final sample covers over 100 years of association activity. However, the most reliable data is for 1942 to 1983, and so much of our analysis is restricted to that period.

Descriptive information about the associations was collected from two comprehensive listings of national trade associations, published annually since 1965 and intermittently in earlier years: *Encyclopedia of Associations* (various years) and Colgate (various years). A third source, Judkins (1942, 1949), proved very valuable for the 1940s. (Judkins also published a list of trade associations in 1956 for the Commerce Department, but the list did not contain founding dates or historical detail.) These sources typically include an association's year of formation, membership and staff size, budget, type of membership (individuals, firms, associations), and the type of product line represented, as well as the association's major activity areas.[4]

Information on the environmental conditions over the study period is being collected from a variety of sources. The U.S. Census of Business volumes provide economic data on associations' industries, although the match between an association's self-described domain and the Census Bureau's Standard Industrial Classification scheme is often poor. Because SIC definitions change with each census, sometimes radically, following industries over time is very difficult. Our integration of the various censuses into one time series is not complete, and so we have not used the economic indicators in our analysis.

RESULTS

Foundings and Deaths

Aggregate population change is produced by three processes: organizational foundings, deaths, and transformation. Transformations of trade associations—in which an association retains its name but changes its domain—are typically rare events (Aldrich and Auster 1986). Mergers between trade associations, however, are fairly frequent terminating events for associations, resulting in associations' covering more firms in an industry or firms in related industries. In this analysis, we focus on foundings and dissolutions, where many dissolutions involve mergers or acquisitions. Mergers and acquisitions result in a transformation of the association population, as associations enlarge their domains or integrate vertically by acquiring others. Their acquired or junior partner associations (in mergers) cease to exist, as far as our analysis is concerned.

A founding was recorded whenever an association name was discovered that had not appeared before in one of our sources, excluding associations that had merely changed their names. Name changes occurred more frequently than we had anticipated: 721 associations changed their name once, 184 twice, 37 three times, 13 four times, and 3 associations five times. Most associations began with no apparent predecessor, as only a few hundred (out of over 3,000) had previous organizational roots: 24 were created as spin-offs from other associations, 79 involved major transformations of existing organizations, and 162 were created by mergers between two or more associations that resulted in a totally new association.

Association deaths were more difficult to verify than foundings. We identified five types of association termination or disappearance: (1) 292 associations ceased operations and left no apparent organizational remnants; (2) 78 associations were transformed to such an extent that they became new associations, covering more products and services; (3) 545 associations merged into or were absorbed by another association; (4) 7 associations were absorbed as a division of another association; and (5) 85 associations stopped effective operations but we could not determine if they had actually ceased to exist. In addition, 222 associations were untraceable at some point after their founding.

Number of Foundings and Deaths.   Our information on association formation before 1942 is incomplete, as is our information on terminations. Therefore, our results for the years prior to World War II must be taken as suggestive, rather than definitive. In Figure 7–2 we show the numbers of association foundings and terminations plotted against year, for 1900 to 1983. The top line shows the number of foundings and the bottom line shows the number of terminations (of all types).

Prior to World War I, association formation fluctuated between ten and twenty new associations per year, with a sharp increase occurring during and immediately after the war. This increase no doubt reflects the efforts of the wartime Production Board and associated agencies. The next notable increase occurred in the 1930s, with the enactment of the NIRA. From the various accounts available of the NIRA's effects, we apparently missed quite a few formations.[5]

Association formation increased sporadically throughout the 1940s and 1950s, rising from about thirty-five a year to over sixty. It dropped in the 1960s, and climbed to a peak in the high sixties in the early 1970s, before dropping again in the late 1970s and into the 1980s.

Deaths and dissolutions, as shown in Figure 7–2, were rare events prior to 1940, partly because trade associations were still a relatively new form and partly because our data collection efforts were not as robust before 1940.[6] In the mid-1940s the number of recorded terminations began rising, gradually reaching a point in the late 1970s where they equaled or exceeded formations.

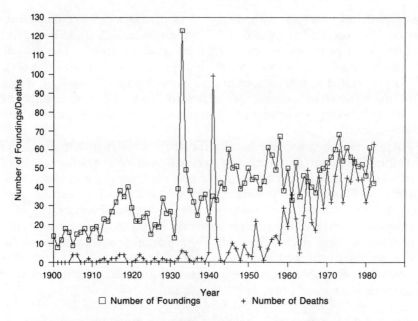

Figure 7–2. Number of Foundings and Dissolutions per Year, 1900–82.

Figure 7–2 shows quite a bit of activity within the trade association population, but absolute frequencies can be misleading unless the size of the base population is kept in mind. Thus we turn to a consideration of rates of formation and dissolution.

Rate of Foundings and Deaths. A better gauge of population dynamics than absolute foundings and dissolutions is the number of events relative to the base population. In the case of terminations, the base population is the population at risk of dissolving (ceasing operations, merging with another association, or otherwise disappearing as an independent entity). In Figure 7–3 we have plotted death rates as the number of terminations in a year divided by the number of associations alive in that year. Only data from 1942 to 1983 is presented because we have greater confidence in the information from this period than for earlier years.

In studying formations, one might use the total number of industries where associations might form as a base population for computing founding rates. Unfortunately, associations have not limited themselves to clearly defined industries, and their claimed domains often bear little resemblance to Census Bureau SIC codes. Instead, for purposes of this analysis, we frame the founding issue as a rate of addition to the existing population. In Figure 7–3

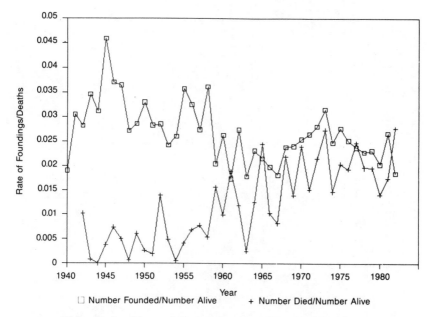

Figure 7–3. Rates of Association Foundings and Deaths, 1942–82.

we have plotted founding rates as the number of new associations formed in a year divided by the number alive in that year.[7]

Expressing foundings and dissolutions as rates rather than absolute numbers substantially clarifies population dynamics over the past forty years. Dissolution rates were extremely low in the 1940s and 1950s, usually below 1 percent of the population and never rising above 2 percent.[8] Beginning in the early 1960s, dissolution rates increased regularly until the mid-1970s, with the most recent rate at about 2 1/2 percent. Formation rates, by contrast, began much higher in the 1940s—between 3 and 5 percent—and gradually declined over the years. They rose once, in the late 1960s and early 1970s, but then declined again to around 2 percent.

Over the past forty years, founding and dissolution rates have converged to a point where they are now roughly in balance. For every association formed, another one dissolved, thus keeping the population at an equilibrium level. Many of the dissolutions were not complete disappearances but mergers.

Mergers. We classified dissolved associations by how they had ceased an independent existence and discovered that a high proportion had merged or been acquired by another association. In Figure 7–4 we show the proportion of association terminations that were mergers or absorptions, by year, for the period 1942 to 1983.

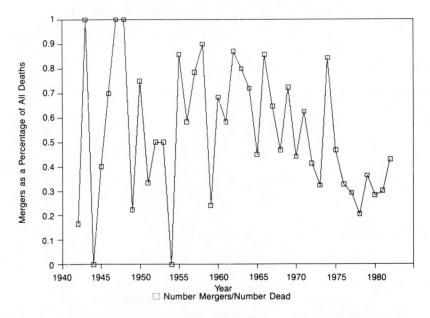

Figure 7–4. Mergers between Associations as a Proportion of All Deaths.

In the 1940s mergers and acquisitions accounted for all of the dissolutions in three years and remained a major source of dissolutions until the mid-1970s, when they dropped below 50 percent. Since 1975 mergers and acquisitions have accounted for between one-quarter and one-half of all terminations per year.

Figure 7–4 shows that most trade associations have not, in fact, died. Rather, if they have ended their independent existence, it has been through merger with or acquisition by another association. This pattern is similar to that for trade unions, which have gone through several cycles of mergers and absorptions (Freeman and Brittain 1977; Cornfield 1984). Only recently has a majority of associations completely disappeared on dissolution.

These findings have several implications. First, the organizational experience of most associations is not lost when they cease to exist but rather survives in a newer, more complex association. Second, although the matter bears closer examination, we surmise that association mergers and acquisitions have occurred for the same reasons as in the trade union population: (1) shrinking industries can no longer support their own associations, and (2) associations seeking increased economic and political power are searching for merger or acquisition targets. Third, if association size is correlated with potential political influence, then the stabilized population now includes more powerful associations than previously.

Population Growth

Foundings, dissolutions, and transformations in the twentieth century have produced a trade association population that grew rapidly from the turn of the century until the late 1950s. However, the gradual convergence of founding and dissolution rates after 1960 slowed population growth to the point where the number of associations has essentially been stable over the past decade at about 2100.[9] The number of associations alive each year is graphed in Figure 7–5.

The pattern shown in Figure 7–5 strongly suggests the relevance of two concepts from population ecology: an S-shaped logistic growth curve and a population that has reached the carrying capacity of its environment (Aldrich 1979). Early in this century, the environment for trade associations was underpopulated, with associative activity noticeable only in a relative handful of industries. As the new form of organization spread, helped along by favorable government treatment at several points, national associations formed in previously unorganized industries.[10]

By the 1960s few long-established industries were unorganized, and so new associations could form in only three ways: (1) as the first association in newly emerging industries, such as microelectronics, and various business services, such as photocopying shops; (2) by dividing an already organized industry into more homogeneous parts; and (3) through mergers and absorptions between associations in declining industries. (These

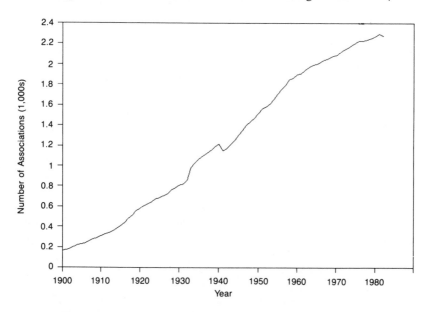

Figure 7–5. Number of Associations over Time, 1900–82.

speculations will be tested in subsequent analyses at the industry-specific level.) The combination of a rising termination rate (Figure 7–3) and declining merger rate (Figure 7–4) suggests that the carrying capacity has been reached. Some associations may be competing for members with other associations and many potential merger or absorption targets may be taken.

Federal Regulation

Association founding and termination rates were shown in Figure 7–3 and federal regulatory activity in Figure 7–1. Inspection of the two figures shows that there is no apparent relationship between trade association foundings or terminations and federal regulation. Indeed, during the 1970s, when regulations were increasing dramatically, founding and termination rates were stabilizing.

Between 1937 and 1983 the trade association population was growing independently of developments in federal regulatory efforts (at least at the aggregate level). Regulations are the product of a federal bureaucracy that is sensitive to short-term changes in the national political agenda, and successive administrations can have large effects on them. The population of trade associations, by contrast, reflects the level of industrial differentiation in the U.S. and organizational entrepreneurs' successes at stimulating collective action within an industry.

DISCUSSION

In this exploratory first report from our project, we examined the extent to which patterns of trade association foundings and dissolutions fit three complementary models. Our base-line social differentiation model, which posited an inexorable upward trend in the population, with incremental changes slowly cumulating, does quite well descriptively. A close rival, the model of associations responding to industry-level developments, with the population growing as the economy diversifies, also does well. However, the social differentiation model would not, we think, anticipate the leveling off in the association population observed in the past decade. No observers have concluded that U.S. society has ceased differentiating socially or politically or that bureaucratic administrative structures have been halted in their tracks. Equilibrium in the trade association population suggests that the carrying capacity for this form has been reached. Accordingly, the niche-width model deserves further investigation, and we suspect that a closer attention to industry-level forces might yield an explanation where the aggregate-level differentiation model fails.

A third model, that of association foundings sparked by federal regulatory activities, seems implausible because of the divergent paths taken by the time series we have reviewed. The population of associations has grown, regardless of the level of regulatory activity. Indeed, the population began stabilizing precisely when regulations soared in the late 1970s. Why have changes in federal intervention made so little difference? Several other developments must be taken into account. First, in the past few decades there has been an increase in cross-industry business interest associations, such as the Business Roundtable, and an expansion of activity of older peak associations, such as the Conference Board. Second, other vehicles for the articulation of collective business interests have sprung up, such as single-issue coalitions or business political action committees. These developments have taken some of the pressure off trade associations and allowed them to pursue the economic interests of their members.

A more plausible place to look for the effects of regulation is in the internal structural arrangements and policies of associations. New positions might have been created, new committees formed, dues raised, lobbyists hired, and other actions taken in response to industry-specific regulations. Such developments would not show up at the level of the analysis reported here.

CONCLUSION AND IMPLICATIONS

The usual explanation for the expansion of business interest associations has focused on a secular increase in the complexity of polity-economy relations. State expansion and an increasing number of entry points into the political process have been seen as providing more opportunities for business. However, at the level of aggregate federal regulation, increases in state activity do not seem to have provoked additional trade association foundings in the business community.

Another explanation for the growth of business interest associations has focused on changing patterns of industrial growth and decline. As economic differentiation increased in the first half of this century, new associations were formed to pursue the interests of specific segments of the business population. As available niches were filled, older associations have dissolved or been absorbed by newer associations. In our revised review of the social differentiation and niche-width models, we believe the diffusion of the trade association form across industries accounts for more population growth than the opening of new, unorganized niches. A diffusion model would fit the growth curves we have presented and would account for the rise of other, more recent forms of business interest organizations.

Testing the niche-width, competitive isomorphism model requires information on developments at the industry level. We are collecting information on trends in association foundings and dissolutions at the four-digit SIC level, and we are trying to construct time series data on the economic environments of industries at the three-digit SIC level. When these series are completed, we should be closer to a completely ecological analysis of trade association foundings and dissolutions than portrayed in this chapter.

NOTES

1. We define *trade associations* as business interest organizations, and we recognize the need to consider other ways by which business interests can be expressed. In this chapter, however, we focus only on trade associations, as a discussion of business PACS, peak associations, single-issue coalitions, and other forms of business interest articulation are beyond the scope of our research.

2. We will eventually conduct our analysis at the industry-specific level, linking regulation at the three digit SIC level to changes in association foundings and terminations. For the moment, data limitations force us to focus on the aggregate level.

3. In the sources we used, we discovered a number of for-profit associations that had apparently crept in because of misleading names or descriptions of purpose. Indeed, the two standard references on associations (*Encyclopedia of Associations* and Colgate) must be used with a great deal of caution.

4. Coding and processing this information in preparation for analysis has taken over two years, as it is a time-consuming and tedious task. Discrepancies between sources were investigated, and hundreds of letters were written to associations, asking them about their predecessors.

5. We were unable to locate any definitive lists of trade associations created via the NIRA with founding dates and industries covered. To the extent that such associations survived until 1942, they were undoubtedly picked up by Judkins (1942).

6. Accounts of association dissolution are extremely rare in the literature, with no one paying systematic attention to them until the Judkins, *Encyclopedia of Associations*, and Colgate volumes began publication.

7. Ideally, for death rates we should use as a denominator the average number alive in the year, and for founding rates the number alive at the beginning of the year. However, software limitations have prevented our computing these more sophisticated measures for the moment. Rest assured that any differences would be extremely slight.

8. Note that these rates are not age-standardized but are only a crude death rate. Other analyses, not reported here, show that age-dependence of death rates is quite low.

9. We know this result flies in the face of some recent claims about trade associations, but we believe our data are extremely reliable for the past decade, when equilibrium first became apparent. Claims about an increasing association population are undoubtedly valid if all types of associations, and not just trade associations, are counted. Also, existing associations have become increasingly active, perhaps giving the impression of an expanding trade association population.

10. Local and regional associations already existed for many industries, but they were not knitted together into a coherent and influential national unit.

8 ECOLOGICAL AND INSTITUTIONAL SOURCES OF CHANGE IN ORGANIZATIONAL POPULATIONS

David J. Tucker, Jitendra V. Singh, Agnes G. Meinhard, and Robert J. House

A central question in organizational ecology concerns the growth of organizational populations over time (Hannan and Freeman 1977). Most populations start with initially low rates of growth, which accelerate over time, reach a maximum rate, and then slowly decline until the population reaches a more or less stable size, the carrying capacity (Carroll 1984; Hannan and Freeman 1987). Ecological researchers have investigated population growth by studying both processes of organizational foundings and deaths over time (Brittain and Freeman 1980; Carroll and Delacroix 1982; Carroll 1983; Delacroix and Carroll 1983; Freeman, Carroll, and Hannan 1983; Freeman and Hannan 1983; Hannan and Freeman 1987; Carroll and Huo 1986; Singh, Tucker, and House 1986; Singh, House and Tucker 1986; Hannan 1986).

In this chapter, we use data from a population of voluntary social service organizations (VSSOs) to study founding and death processes. In particular, our research objective is to compare ecological and institutional

We are indebted to Glenn Carroll for his insightful suggestions on this paper and for his assistance in the developmental phase of our research on voluntary organizations in metropolitan Toronto. We also wish to acknowledge the important contributions Ralph Kramer, Howard Aldrich, and Paul DiMaggio have made to the development of our research program. This research was supported by grant number 410-84-0632 from the Social Sciences and Humanities Research Council, Ottawa, Canada, and grant number 4555-55-7 from the National Welfare Grants Directorate, Health and Welfare, Ottawa, Canada.

views (Meyer and Rowan 1977; DiMaggio and Powell 1983; Meyer and Scott 1983) about change in organizational populations. Ecological theory emphasizes the importance of intrapopulation processes of competition. On the other hand, institutional theory emphasizes changes in the legitimacy and institutional support afforded particular populations of organizations, particularly the role of the state, and its various agencies and programs. By examining foundings and deaths in the VSSO population as functions of both intrapopulation processes of competition and major institutional changes, we hope to compare the relative significance of ecological and institutional views of change in organizational populations. In that task, we also explore how institutional change affects intrapopulation competition processes—whether it simply raises or lowers the level of competitive activity or fundamentally alters the nature of the competitive process itself.

DENSITY-DEPENDENCE AND COMPETITION

Among the different population regulatory mechanisms discussed in the ecological literature (Krebs 1978: 295–96), competition clearly emerges as the single most significant one. Although difficult to observe directly, competition is defined as the occurrence of some form of mutual interference among population members in relation to the use of some common resource (Pianka 1976: 167). Its action as a controlling factor is governed by the density of the population controlled. When density is low relative to some fixed environmental carrying capacity, competition is minimal. It intensifies as the size of the population increases, resulting in reduced fitness on the part of some population members in relation to others. Decreasing birth rates and/or increasing death rates result, gradually causing the population's overall growth rate to decline and eventually equal zero.

These ideas concerning how density-dependence and competition enter into the regulation of population size have been applied to the study of organizational foundings and deaths by Delacroix and Carroll (1983), Hannan and Freeman (1987), and Hannan (1986). (See the chapter in this volume by Hannan and Freeman for an extensive theoretical discussion.) Delacroix and Carroll examined newspaper foundings in Ireland and Argentina in the period 1800 to 1925. They found curvilinear relationships between prior foundings and current foundings, and prior deaths and current foundings. They argued that organizational deaths increase organizational foundings because they instantly create free-floating resources that may easily be reassembled into new ventures. However, a continued increase in the number of deaths signals a noxious environment. Entrepreneurs respond to this signal by staying away from creating new organizations, and foundings decline.

Similarly, an initial increase in the creation of new organizations encourages the subsequent creation of others because it is interpreted as a signal of a supportive environment. However, unrestrained entrepreneurial activity results in a saturated and competitive market, suggesting that even higher founding levels restrict the frequency of subsequent foundings.

Hannan and Freeman (1987) explicitly invoked the classic ecological idea of density-dependence in explaining the cyclical patterns of foundings in populations of labor unions in the United States during the period 1836 to 1975. They argued that as the number of unions in existence grows, intraspecific competition for available resources increases, resulting in lowered founding rates and consequently the effective imposition of constraints on the growth in number of organizations. They tested this argument by estimating a number of stochastic models embodying different assumptions about the ecology of organizational foundings. The best-fitting models were those positing a nonmonotonic relationship between founding rate and population size, indicating support for the argument that density dependent competition regulates population growth by limiting foundings.

Hannan and Freeman also explored the effect of prior foundings on current foundings. The argument made, similar to Delacroix and Carroll (1983), posited a curvilinear effect, based on the operation of intraspecific imitation processes and the emergence of intraspecific competition. The findings showed that the effect of recent foundings on current foundings was monotonic in nature, indicating support only for the imitation aspect of the hypothesis.

Finally, Hannan (1986) examined the effect of both competitive and institutional processes on the founding and death rates of labor unions in the United States in the period 1836 to 1985. Hannan argued that increasing density, which is associated with increasing competition, regulates both founding and death processes. Initially, an increasing number of foundings increases the legitimacy of the organizational form, and increasing deaths decrease it, leading to an increase in foundings and a decrease in death rate. But as the number of foundings and deaths increase further, the effects become curvilinear due to the operation of competitive processes. Consequently, patterns of foundings and deaths are related in nonmonotonic ways to density. The empirical findings indicated strong support for this argument.

INSTITUTIONAL SOURCES OF POPULATION CHANGE

Despite the favorable empirical evidence, it is important to recognize that density-dependence arguments deal mainly with the effects of resource environments on population change. Changes in density vary the resource availability in a population. This creates variations in the intensity of the effect of competition on individual members and results in fluctuations in founding and/or death rates. However, the environments of organizations are more than "sources of resources for inputs, information and know-how for outputs, markets for outputs" (Scott 1983: 158). They also include institutionalized rules and beliefs about the creation and structuring of organizations as well as relational networks of other formal organizations (Meyer and Rowan 1977; Scott 1983). In short, organizations exist in and are affected by both institutional and resource environments (Scott 1983; Carroll and Huo 1986; Hannan 1986). Based on the above, it is interesting to ask how change in the institutional environment affects the intraspecific population processes generated by competition.

Recent studies (Carroll and Huo 1986; Hannan 1986) have examined the effects of institutional environments on the foundings and deaths of organizations. Carroll and Huo distinguished between task and institutional environments in studying changes in the structure of a local newspaper industry in California over a 125-year period. They analyzed relationships between environmental conditions, the foundings and deaths of newspapers, and performance levels. The findings showed that institutional variables, particularly political turmoil, affected foundings and deaths, but task environmental variables affected performance more. Thus, task environmental and institutional variables had differential impacts on the population studied.

Hannan (1986) studied populations of labor unions in the United States in the period 1836 to 1985. A central thesis of the paper was that ecological and institutional approaches to the study of organizations are complementary. Thus, theorists should "consider competition and institutionalization as processes that apply to all organizations in all social settings" (Hannan 1986: 2). The theoretical model proposed assumed that institutional processes, like competition, depend on population density. Two distinct institutional processes were identified. First, powerful actors in the system legitimate particular forms of organization by endorsing their claims in disputes. Second, certain organizational forms attain a "taken-for-granted" character in the sense that they come to be regarded as the "natural" way to effect some kind of collective action. For a number of reasons, both forms of legitimation increase with the prevalence of the particular organizational form in society. The resulting predictions were that, other things being equal, legitimation processes produce a positive relationship between density and founding rates and a negative relationship between density and death rates. The empirical findings provided strong support for these predictions.

Both of these studies clearly illustrate the importance of including institutional variables in studies of organizational foundings and deaths. However, neither study addressed the issue of how change in institutional environments may affect intrapopulation competition processes. We concentrate specifically on the role of the state, particularly as expressed through changes in government policy and programs. By how it allocates resources, adjusts tax laws, and selects between different mechanisms of benefit distribution, the modern state establishes conditions that can either stimulate organizational creation or death. This suggests that there are strong *a priori* reasons to expect that patterns of foundings and deaths of organizations may be influenced by the decisions and activities of the state and that, as a consequence, density-dependent processes of population regulation will themselves be affected by major institutional changes.

The Nature of VSSOs

The specific kind of organizations studied here, voluntary social service organizations (VSSOs), are defined as "organizations governed by a board of directors and that operate on a nonprofit basis and are concerned with changing, constraining and/or supporting human behavior" (Singh, Tucker, and House 1986: 175). As a population, VSSOs are similiar to other groups of human service organizations because they are quite diverse. Some are small and rely mostly on volunteer labor. Others are large, sophisticated organizations employing professional staff and using advanced computer technology. The services offered range from highly specialized legal, medical, and counseling services performed by professional staff to settlement and interpretation services provided by volunteers (Singh, Tucker, and House 1986: 175).

A significant feature of VSSOs is that they have somewhat indeterminate technologies (Tucker 1981: 605; Singh, Tucker, and House 1986: 174). Thus, their ability to demonstrate their effectiveness in terms of conventional output, efficiency or process criteria is very limited. Under these conditions, social criteria, like the satisfaction and the approval of external constituencies, are more likely to be used to judge effectiveness (Daft 1983: 107–08). This suggests that VSSOs are specifically vulnerable to conditions and constraints that have their origins in the institutional environment and that factors such as the acquisition of external institutional support significantly affect their survival chances (Singh, Tucker, and House 1986).

Change in the Institutional
Environment of VSSOs

Institutional environments can be conceptualized in terms of the decisions and activities of a few powerful institutional actors (Rowan 1982; Tolbert and Zucker 1983). In this study, the most significant actor in the institutional environment of VSSOs is the state, and its respective agencies and programs. Because of the state's control over the authoritative allocation of values and resources, a number of theorists (such as Aldrich 1979; Brown and Schneck 1979; Freeman 1979) maintain that the role of the state is the major factor accounting for patterns of population change. This seems particularly to be the case for the voluntary social services sector. Unlike the newspaper industries studied by Delacroix and Carroll (1983), which have traditions of independence from the state and records of resisting its influence, voluntary social services have historically had a close association with the state, frequently being regarded as complementary to, or in some circumstances an appendage of, state-operated service systems (Webb and Webb 1912; Wilensky and Lebeaux 1957; Splane 1965; Kramer 1981).

During the 1960s and the early 1970s the Canadian government introduced a number of programs that, in general terms, were intended to promote the increased involvement of selected citizen groups in dealing with social problems (Loney 1977). The most significant of these was the Opportunities for Youth program (OFY) that was launched in 1971 and terminated in 1976. We contend that the implementation of OFY elaborated an institutional rule that enhanced the legitimacy of dealing with social problems by creating new organizations. It also generated new resources supplied directly by the government. One implication is that the patterns of foundings and deaths of VSSOs may have been influenced by these changes in the institutional environment.

By 1970 youth had emerged as an important and visible object of political concern in Canada. This was in part a function of changes in the demographic characteristics of the Canadian population. Young people had become a significantly larger proportion of the population (Committee on Youth 1971). In Metro-Toronto, for example, Statistics Canada census data reveal that between 1961 and 1971 the proportion of the population ages 15 to 24 increased by over five percentage points—from 12.4 to 17.6 percent.

Associated with the demographic adjustments in the population was a more intangible but, in political terms, more significant change—an intense dissatisfaction with the status quo, particularly among youth. This manifested itself in a variety of ways, including the formation of public-interest and advocacy groups, sit-ins and demonstrations, the articulation and pursuit of alternate life styles, and the rejection of employment that was not seen as personally meaningful or socially relevant (Best 1974).

Within government circles, particularly at the federal level, there was great concern over the meaning, and the political and economic implications of disaffected youth (Committee on Youth 1971). Faced in 1970–71 with the additional problem of suddenly increasing unemployment among youth, the federal government resurrected the concept initially developed by the Company of Young Canadians of providing resources directly to local community groups to enable them to implement projects that were regarded as socially useful (Gwyn 1972). Specifically, it promoted the development of demonstration projects aimed at determining whether youth were capable of organizing, implementing, and operating their own projects. These demonstration projects were greeted with great enthusiasm and the OFY program was subsequently launched with a budget of just over $14 million. The response was both unexpected and overwhelming. As a result, the budget was increased by $10 million over the first summer. The following year in 1972 the national budget for the funding of youth-initiated projects was increased by 900 percent to $250 million and what has been called the great Ottawa grant boom was under way (Gwyn 1972).

Three plausible arguments may be made in support of the claim that the implementation of OFY constituted a major institutional change for the VSSO population. First, data on the initial funding sources of VSSOs show that of those born in the OFY period, most did not initially receive funds from OFY or from other similiar government programs. Moreover, in comparing VSSOs born in the OFY period with those born later, we find that a significantly larger number of those born in the non-OFY period received money in their first year of operation (28.5 percent as compared to 23.0 percent). A reasonable interpretation of these data is that the founding of VSSOs in the OFY period reflects the influence of symbolic considerations.

Second, it might normally be assumed that the introduction of a new government funding program, like OFY, would mainly be followed by expansion and diversification in the service delivery activities of existing organizations as opposed to the proliferation of new organizations. Because existing organizations are already in operation, their initial costs of organization have been met (Olson 1965: 47). Thus, compared to new organizations, existing organizations may be competitively advantaged in going after new funds. Although we cannot refute this argument unequivocally, two interrelated factors can be identified that make it somewhat implausible. First, the voluntary sector is characterized by ease of entry. The material and human resource requirements of setting up a VSSO are small. Most of the VSSOs in our population began without a budget or paid staff, and the median board size was only six people. The characteristics of the voluntary sector itself—highly dispersed, not regarded as economically significant, and constrained by government legislation from engaging in self-interested political lobbying—are not those usually associated with high barriers to entry (Pfeffer and Salancik 1976; Aldrich 1979). Second, OFY's selection criteria, although not formalized, clearly presented the expectation that the work performed would be controlled by project participants themselves and be innovative in nature—that is, differ from work being done by existing organizations (Best 1974: 144–60). For existing organizations to receive funds, these conditions suggested they had at least to incur the cost of appearing to have changed, such as by an adjustment in internal reporting relationships to accommodate a new, autonomous unit. Because there was an upper limit on the size of individual grants and no guarantee of future funding, this effectively lowered the value of the benefit to existing organizations while increasing the risks (Olson 1965). Based on the above arguments, it seems reasonable to suggest that OFY's endorsement of the legitimacy of local community groups engaging in independent organizational activity to achieve collective ends may have influenced the proliferation of VSSOs in Metro-Toronto.

Third, policy theorists assert that the policy outputs of government reflect political decisions not only about the ends of policy but also about the means of ensuring compliance with and/or social acceptance of the policy decisions (Lowi 1964, 1970, 1972; Salisbury and Heinz 1970; Sabatier 1975; Hayes 1981). One legitimate means of coercion available to government is the use of symbolism (Edelman 1967; Lowi 1970). By how a particular policy is presented, and the meaning ascribed to it, government may consciously attempt to evoke and reinforce particular behaviors in policy constituents (see also Piven and Cloward 1977). Best (1974), in a study of the origin and nature of youth policy in Canada, addressed the question of the symbolic significance of OFY. He noted that although OFY, by its nature and process, was a distributive policy (that is, resources were distributed in a highly disaggregated form to individual projects), its impact at an aggregate level was intended to be mainly "constituent or symbolic" (Best 1974: 160). Although government was concerned about the value of projects supported by OFY in helping solve social problems, it was more concerned with the symbolic impact of OFY in convincing youth that the government was responding to their demands for meaningful participation and socially relevant work (Best 1974: 162; see also Houston 1972 and Loney 1977). Thus, the founding of VSSOs in the OFY period may reflect the influence of pressure on constituents to act in conformity with government-initiated institutional rules that defined such behavior as socially legitimate.

There was some initial resistance to and criticism of the federal government's administration of OFY by established voluntary organizations and by other levels of government (Paris 1972; Best 1974; Loney 1977). Established organizations argued that they were the experts on the needs of their communities and should have been given priority for funds. Other levels of government expressed reservations that certain projects were too radical or that they might inherit future obligations for funding VSSOs. Nonetheless, conditions defining organizational responses to social problems as legitimate persisted until 1975 (Wharf and Carter 1972; Social

Planning Council of Metropolitan Toronto 1976). By the mid-1970s, however, some important changes were occurring. Concern with economic issues had replaced concern with social issues. Inflation in Canada was at record levels, and the view was emerging that if it was to be controlled and economic recovery nurtured, governments were going to have to restrain and redirect their spending. The consequence was actions by the federal government, and by the Ontario provincial government, that undermined the support of local community groups in seeking organizational solutions to alleviate social problems.

The federal government terminated OFY and replaced it, beginning in 1976, with a series of programs explicitly emphasizing the appropriateness, in efficiency terms, of using established organizations, government agencies, and corporations as employment sites for youth and others (Economic Council of Canada 1976, 1977). The orientation of these programs was mainly economic. They were to prepare persons for entry into the labor market and at the same time support the productivity of the host organization (Economic Council of Canada 1977). The message was clear that the federal government was no longer specifically oriented toward legitimating the development and maintenance of nonprofit organizations, like VSSOs, that were controlled by project participants and mainly concerned with solving social problems.

Under the Canadian constitution, provincial governments are formally responsible for planning and implementing public policy pertaining to social services and social welfare. In this regard, the government of Ontario, in its 1975 budget (McKeough 1975), noted the importance of restraining government expenditures. The following year a comprehensive expenditure restraint program was introduced (McKeough 1976). Social expenditures were a particular object of restraint, with most social services being limited to a 5.5 percent increase in funding for fiscal year 1976–77 (Puckett and Tucker 1976). Considering that the annual rate of inflation at the time was in the vicinity of 11 percent, this represented an actual reduction in levels of expenditure. In the same way that the introduction of OFY seemed to legitimate the founding of VSSOs and create opportunities and incentives favoring their creation, the introduction of the Ontario government's Restraint Program seemed to reduce legitimacy, limit opportunities, and be a disincentive to creating organizations.

METHOD

Data Collection

Sources of data used to identify and characterize the VSSO population, and establish founding dates, are mainly archival (Singh, Tucker, and House

1986; Singh, House, and Tucker 1986). They include (1) files, documents, and indexes maintained by the federal, provincial, and municipal levels of government; (2) files, lists, and documents made available by local planning, coordinating, and funding agencies (such as the United Way, the Community Information Centre); and (3) the annual reports of individual VSSOs.

The process of identifying the study population was an exhaustive one and was implemented in two phases, the first in 1981 and a second in 1983. Identical procedures were used in both phases. We began by compiling a comprehensive list of all the distinct voluntary associations and collectives that came into existence in Metro-Toronto in the period 1970 to 1982. This list was compared to the *Provincial Index of Incorporated Non-share Organizations*, and all associations and collectives without incorporation numbers were eliminated. This left a list of 681 organizations. Archival data were then reviewed to determine if each organization on the list was an independent operating unit and conformed to our definition of a VSSO. Two hundred thirty organizations were subsequently eliminated leaving a study population of 451.[1]

Measurement

Foundings.   We define *organizational founding* as the date of formal incorporation. Our assumption is that incorporation reflects a clear signal from the founders that there is a commitment to ensuring that the collectivity being established will persist over time (Singh, Tucker, and House 1986: 176). The founding frequency of VSSOs is operationalized as the number founded by quarter (that is, every three months) from January 1970 to December 1982.

Deaths.   In this chapter, an organization is counted as dead when it ceases to exist as a distinct legal entity. The death frequency for VSSOs is operationalized here as the number that died by quarter from January 1970 to December 1982.

Death Rate.   The death rate of a VSSO is described by the hazard function $h(t)$, which gives the instantaneous rate of death at each instant of a VSSO's life.

Major Institutional Change.   We define *major institutional change* in terms of the occurrence of two historical events, the Opportunities for Youth period (OFY), lasting from 1971 to 1975, and the Provincial Restraint period (RES), lasting from 1976 to 1981. OFY corresponds to a period when involvement in the creation of new VSSOs was accepted as a preferred way of contending with social problems (Houston 1972; Wharf and Carter 1972; Best 1974; Loney 1977). RES corresponds to a period characterized by fiscal restraint (McKeough 1975, 1976; Puckett and Tucker 1976; Miller 1980), with more emphasis on increasing the productivity of existing organizations than on legitimating the creation of new ones (Economic Council of Canada 1976, 1977). OFY and RES are treated as dummy variables coded 1 when present and 0 otherwise.

ANALYSIS AND RESULTS

Founding Patterns of VSSOs

Figure 8-1 shows the quarterly number of foundings in the VSSO population during the period 1970 to 1982. Although the pattern showed cyclical fluctuations, the broad trend was an increase in the number of foundings from the beginning of 1970 to a high during 1975–76. Subsequently, there was a declining trend, except for a surge during 1981, to the end of 1982.

In order to test the empirical validity of the ecological and institutional arguments outlined earlier, we regressed the time series of the quarterly number of foundings in the VSSO population on the ecological and institutional variables. The data were analyzed using SHAZAM, an econometric package that can be used for time series analysis. We first estimated the model using ordinary least squares (OLS) procedures and then tested for the presence of autocorrelation, a frequent problem with time series data. If the results showed evidence of significant autocorrelation, we reestimated the model with generalized least squares (GLS) methods, using the iterative Cochrane-Orcutt procedure. Although the

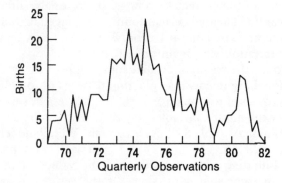

Figure 8-1. Births of VSSOs by Quarters, 1970–82.

presence of autocorrelation does not bias the OLS estimates, it significantly understates the standard errors of estimates. Thus, the usual tests of significance are no longer valid, and the significance of the coefficients is overstated.

Table 8–1 summarizes the regression results for how the ecological and institutional variables affect the patterns of organizational foundings. All independent variables were lagged one time period. We first modeled the impact of the ecological variables. The first column of Table 8–1 reports the curvilinear effects of lagged foundings and lagged deaths on current foundings. Although the overall regression was significant (F-ratio = 11.45, p <.01) and explained 45.5 percent of the variance in foundings, only the coefficient for previous foundings was significant. Because it was positive, this suggested there was an imitation effect operating in the VSSO population, but, unlike results from other populations (Delacroix and Carroll 1983), internal self-regulation was not supported by the data. Further, the presence of significant autocorrelation was indicated because the calculated Durbin-Watson statistic was lower than the upper bound of the appropriate criterion value at the 5 percent level of significance, a commonly accepted test for first-order autocorrelation (Johnston 1972: ch. 8).

The results for the curvilinear effects of lagged density on current foundings are reported in the second column of Table 8–1. The overall model was again significant (F-ratio = 4.025, p < .01), although the explained variance was dramatically lower (10.8 percent). However, lagged density had significant curvilinear effects on current foundings, with foundings increasing with density initially but declining at higher density levels, suggesting the possibility of competitive dynamics. The Durbin-Watson statistic again indicated the presence of significant first-order autocorrelation.[2]

Next, we modeled the impact of the institutional variables. The results are shown in the third column of Table 8–1. As expected, the overall model was significant (F-ratio = 12.675, p < .01) and explained 31.8 percent of the variance in the current foundings. Interestingly, although lagged OFY significantly increased current foundings, lagged RES did not affect founding patterns. Based on the Durbin-Watson statistic, significant first-order autocorrelation was again present.

To this point, the results indicated some support for both ecological and institutional arguments in explaining patterns of foundings. To rule out problems of specification error in the models tested, we next modeled both sets of explanatory variables together. The results are reported in the fourth column of Table 8–1. As before, the overall model was significant (F-ratio = 8.653, p < .01) and explained 55.1 percent of the variance in foundings. However, the specific values of the parameter estimates were somewhat surprising. Of the ecological variables, the previously significant curvilinear effects of lagged density were eliminated,

Table 8–1. Least Squares Estimates: Ecological and Institutional Effects on Foundings.

Independent Variables	Dependent Variable: Foundings_t							
	OLS	OLS	OLS	OLS	GLS¹	GLS¹	GLS²	GLS²
Constant	2.448	−1.169	6.444ᵇ	3.074	1.211	8.623ᵃ	4.891ᵃ	3.324ᵃ
	(1.735)	(4.998)	(1.048)	(3.603)	(1.261)	(4.618)	(2.579)	(1.980)
Foundings$_{t-1}$	0.715ᵃ			.571	0.895ᵇ			1.141ᵇ
	(0.349)			(0.351)	(0.271)			(0.187)
Foundings²$_{t-1}$	−0.004			−0.009	−0.003			−0.019ᵃ
	(0.016)			(0.015)	(0.012)			(0.009)
Deaths$_{t-1}$	1.020			2.851ᵃ	0.508			2.079ᵇ
	(0.979)			(1.182)	(0.632)			(0.488)
Deaths²$_{t-1}$	−0.220			−0.340ᵃ	−0.132			−0.226ᵇ
	(1.735)			(0.179)	(0.115)			(0.072)
Density$_{t-1}$		0.057ᵇ		0.0005		0.019		−0.009
		(0.022)		(0.019)		(0.019)		(0.010)
Density²$_{t-1}$		−0.00007ᵇ		−0.000007		0.00004		0.000002
		(0.00002)		(0.00002)		(0.00003)		(0.00001)
OFY$_{t-1}$			6.732ᵇ	3.305ᵃ			3.019	1.124ᵃ
			(1.504)	(1.686)			(1.995)	(0.604)
RES$_{t-1}$			0.181	−2.970			−5.384ᵇ	−2.905ᵇ
			(1.528)	(1.874)			(2.083)	(0.789)
Adjusted R^2	0.455	0.108	0.318	0.551	0.543	0.546	0.621	0.712
F-ratio	11.45	4.025	12.675	8.653	15.868	31.109	41.988	16.808
p-level	<.01	<.01	<.01	<.01	<.01	<.01	<.01	<.01
Durbin-Watson Statistic	2.504	0.811	0.927	2.501				
	d<d$_{u,.05}$	d<d$_{u,.05}$	d<d$_{u,.05}$	d<d$_{u,.05}$				

Note: Standard errors in parentheses.
[a] $p < .05$.
[b] $p < .01$.
1. Second-order autocorrelation.
2. Fourth-order autocorrelation.

and, instead, lagged deaths had a significant curvilinear effect on foundings. As may have been expected, density is most likely correlated with deaths and foundings and, evidently, the inclusion of all the variables altered the previous results. The significant effect of lagged foundings obtained earlier was eliminated. Lagged OFY continued to have a significant positive effect on current foundings. Lagged RES did not have a significant effect. However, the parameter estimate was negative, as may have been expected.

The results from the most fully specified model above supported the earlier conclusion of partial support for both ecological and institutional arguments. An important qualification to the analysis concerns the presence of autocorrelation. Its presence is indicated in each regression and can be interpreted to mean that the OLS results are incorrect. In order to rule out this possibility, we reestimated all the above models using GLS methods. To begin with, a first-order autocorrelation process was specified, such that,

$$U_t = \rho U_{t-1} + e_t,$$

where

$$| \rho | < 1, \text{ and } E(e_t) = 0, \text{ E } (e_t e_s) = 0, \text{ for } s \neq t,$$

and

$$E(e_t \, e_s) = \sigma^2, \text{ for } s = t$$

Rho is the autocorrelation parameter, and unlike U_t, the autoregressive error term, the error term e_t satisfies the usual OLS assumptions. Maximum likelihood methods were then used to estimate the value of rho and to obtain the parameter estimates and their standard errors. In most cases, we found through exploratory data analysis that the residuals from a first-order autocorrelation were still autoregressive. Consequently, we estimated parameters for models with higher-order autocorrelations and chose the best models based on the significance of the estimates of the autocorrelation coefficients and the minimum sum of squared residuals. These results for the models with the appropriate autocorrelation process are shown beginning in column five of Table 8–1.

The results for the curvilinear effects of lagged foundings and lagged deaths on current foundings are shown in column six of Table 8–1. Other than the higher explained variance compared to the earlier OLS results (adjusted $R^2 = 0.543$), the overall results are quite similiar. The only significant parameter was that for previous foundings, again supporting the operation of imitation effects in this population. The results for the curvilinear effets of lagged density on current foundings are shown in column five of Table 8–1. Interestingly, lagged density no longer had significant effects on current foundings, an important departure from the earlier findings, although the regression was still significant (F-ratio = 31.109, $p < .01$) and the explained variance was 54.6 percent. The pattern of effects for the institutional change variables, lagged OFY and lagged RES, shown in column seven of Table 8–1, also changed significantly. Lagged

OFY, which earlier had a significant positive effect on current foundings, was no longer significant, and lagged RES, which was earlier unrelated to foundings, now had a significant effect. The overall regression was still significant (F-ratio $= 41.988, p < .01$), and the explained variance was 62.1 percent. Finally, we modeled the effects of all the ecological and institutional variables using GLS. The results are reported in column eight of Table 8–1. They show that lagged foundings and lagged deaths both had significant curvilinear effects on current foundings, but density did not have any effect. Further, lagged RES had a significant negative effect on current foundings, and lagged OFY had a significant positive effect. Again, the overall model was significant (F-ratio $= 16.808, p < .01$), and the explained variance was 71.2 percent.

Interaction of Institutional Changes and Ecological Processes

The next substantive question addressed concerned how the occurrence of major institutional changes affected the ongoing ecological processes in the VSSO population. Did the occurrence of OFY and RES simply raise or lower the level of the ecological processes, or did it change their nature fundamentally? We answered this question by introducing the dummy variables for OFY and RES into both the intercept and slope terms of the regression models estimated earlier. However, due to problems of muticollinearity between variables, we had to estimate the effects of OFY and RES separately on models with the curvilinear effects of lagged foundings and lagged deaths. For the model with the curvilinear effects of lagged density, we were able to model OFY and RES together.

The OLS model for the interactive effects of lagged OFY with the curvilinear effects of lagged foundings and lagged deaths was significant overall (F-ratio $= 9.49, p < .01$) and had an adjusted R^2 of 0.605. The Durbin-Watson statistic for this model ($d = 2.408$) indicated the presence of first order autocorrelation. Despite this, we were unable to obtain results for a model with first-order autocorrelation, and a fourth-order process provided the best-fitting model. The estimated regression equation for this model was (a. $p < .05$; b. $p < .01$; standard errors in parentheses):

Foundings$_t$

$$= 1.931^b - 0.638 \text{ foundings}_{t-1} + 0.005 \text{ foundings}^2_{t-1} - 0.029 \text{ deaths}_{t-1}$$
$$(1.337) \quad (0.425) \qquad\qquad (0.024) \qquad\qquad (0.479)$$

$$- 0.004 \text{ deaths}^2_{t-1} + 0.215 \text{ OFY}_{t-1} + 0.298 \text{ OFY}_{t-1} \times \text{foundings}_{t-1}$$
$$(0.088) \qquad\qquad (4.285) \qquad\quad (0.852)$$

$$- 0.032 \text{ OFY}_{t-1} \times \text{foundings}^2_{t-1} + 1.875 \text{ OFY}_{t-1} \times \text{deaths}_{t-1}$$
$$(0.0035) \qquad\qquad\qquad (2.847)$$

$$+ 0.971 \text{ OFY}_{t-1} \times \text{deaths}^2_{t-1}$$
$$(1.285)$$

Despite the significance of the overall model (F-ratio $= 13.580, p < .01$; adjusted $R^2 = 0.694$), none of the coefficients was significant, suggesting that OFY did not have an impact on this aspect of the ecological dynamics in this population.

Using OLS again, we modeled the impact of lagged RES on the model for the curvilinear aspects of lagged foundings and lagged deaths. The overallmodel was significant (F-ratio $= 6.145, p < .01$) and the adjusted R^2 was 0.481. As in the case of the previous model, the Durbin-Watson statistic indicated significant first-order autocorrelation, but we were unable to obtain results due to nonconvergence of the procedure. Examination of models with higher-order autocorrelation revealed that a fourth-order process was significant overall (F-ratio $= 9.011, p < .01$; adjusted $R^2 = 0.590$) and the parameter estimates (and standard errors in parentheses) were given by:

Foundings$_t$

$$
\begin{aligned}
= \; & 0.147 + 1.116^b \text{ foundings }_{t-1} - 0.011 \text{ foundings}^2_{t-1} + 0.401 \text{ deaths}_{t-1} \\
& (1.277) \quad (0.307) \qquad\qquad\quad (0.013) \qquad\qquad\qquad (1.405) \\[4pt]
& - 0.063 \text{ deaths}^2_{t-1} + 2.988 \text{ RES}_{t-1} - 0.473 \text{ RES}_{t-1} \times \text{foundings}_{t-1} \\
& \;\;(0.434) \qquad\qquad (11.243) \qquad (1.079) \\[4pt]
& - 0.051 \text{ RES}_{t-1} \times \text{foundings}^2_{t-1} - 2.874 \text{ RES}_{t-1} \times \text{deaths}_{t-1} \\
& \;\;(0.069) \qquad\qquad\qquad\qquad (4.537) \\[4pt]
& + 0.254 \text{ RES}_{t-1} \times \text{deaths}^2_{t-1} \\
& \;\;(0.660)
\end{aligned}
$$

Similiar to the previous model, there was again no significant interaction effect of lagged RES with the ecological dynamics of lagged foundings and lagged deaths, although lagged foundings were themselves significantly related to current foundings.

Finally, we modeled the interactions of lagged OFY and lagged RES, using OLS, with the curvilinear effects of lagged density. The overall model was significant (F-ratio $= 9.74, p < .01$) and had an adjusted R^2 of 0.578. The Durbin-Watson statistic for this model ($\hat{d} = 1.860$) was not significant, suggesting that autocorrelation was not a problem in this case. Thus, we did not have to reestimate the model using GLS procedures. The estimated regression equation was (standard errors in parentheses):

Foundings$_t$

$$
\begin{aligned}
= \; & 1.328 + 0.018 \text{ density}_{t-1} - 0.00001 \text{ density}^2_{t-1} - 164.59^a \text{ OFY }_{t-1} \\
& (2.508) \;\; (0.014) \qquad\qquad (0.00002) \qquad\qquad (83.50) \\[4pt]
& + 0.685^a \text{ OFY}_{t-1} \times \text{density }_{t-1} - 0.0007^a \text{ OFY}_{t-1} \times \text{density}^2_{t-1} - 592.3 \text{ RES}_{t-1} \\
& \;\;(0.368) \qquad\qquad\qquad\quad (0.0004) \qquad\qquad\qquad\qquad (1649.7) \\[4pt]
& + 2.087 \text{ RES}_{t-1} \times \text{density}_{t-1} - 0.002 \text{ RES}_{t-1} \times \text{density}^2_{t-1} \\
& \;\;(5.369) \qquad\qquad\qquad\qquad (0.004)
\end{aligned}
$$

These results were dramatically different compared to the two previous models. The most interesting result was the significant interaction of lagged OFY with lagged density in affecting current foundings. In fact, when the main effects of ecological and institutional variables were modeled alone (see column four, Table 8–1), only lagged deaths had curvilinear effects on current foundings, and lagged density had no effects. However, the introduction of OFY fundamentally changed the nature of the ecological dynamics in the VSSO population by altering the slopes of the density effects.

One surprising aspect of the results is the significant negative coefficient of lagged OFY. The theoretical arguments we had made earlier had anticipated a significant positive effect, or possibly no effect. But the results suggest that the intercept changed negatively due to OFY. It is important to have a substantively correct interpretation of the negative intercept term of lagged OFY. As has been seen, all the terms that did not involve lagged OFY were not statistically significant—that is, statistically not different from zero. Further, *during OFY*—that is, when the OFY_{t-1} is unity—there was a curvilinear density dependence of foundings given by:

$$\text{Foundings}_t = -164.59^a + 0.685^a \, \text{density}_{t-1} - 0.0007^a \, \text{density}^2_{t-1}$$

Thus, the intercept term is the number of births when the density level is zero. Because, during the study period, density varied between 359 and 668, the intercept term was not within the observed range of density, and the result was, therefore, not substantively meaningful. This reduced our concern about the negative effect of OFY.

However, there was a significant interaction between lagged OFY and the curvilinear effects of lagged density. The interpretation is that during OFY, the curvilinear density dependence operated, but not otherwise. Lagged OFY had a significant positive impact on the slope of lagged density, and a significant negative impact on lagged density squared. Put another way, OFY enhanced both the facilitating and the competitive aspects of the density dependence of foundings.

Another interesting aspect of these results is that, during OFY, foundings reached their maximum value for a lagged density value of approximately 489, which was within the observed range of density.[3] Thus, the competitive dynamic was in operation during the OFY period—that is, when density increased beyond 489—it began to influence foundings negatively.

Death Patterns of VSSOs

Figure 8–2 shows the annual number of deaths in the VSSO population during the period 1970 to 1982. The study population here was comprised of 389 organizations compared to the 451 studied for the analysis of

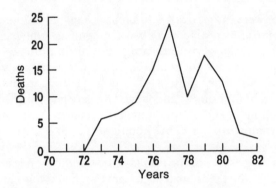

Figure 8.2   Annual Deaths of VSSOS, 1970–1982.

founding patterns. This smaller population of 389 VSSOs was the number born during the period 1970 to 1980. Death data for organizations founded during 1981–82 are currently unavailable. The death pattern showed that there were no organizational deaths in the first three years. After that, the number of deaths increased each year, reaching a high in 1977, and then declining steadily to 1980. The methodology used to analyze the deaths data is event history analysis (Tuma, Hannan, and Groeneveld 1979; Carroll and Delacroix 1982).

Similiar to earlier studies of death rates in this population (Singh, Tucker, and House 1986; Singh, House, and Tucker 1986), we estimated parametric models of the death rate using Makeham-Gompertz models. However, unlike other studies (Carroll and Delacroix 1982; Freeman, Carroll, and Hannan 1983; Singh, Tucker, and House 1986), our primary emphasis here was on the effects of ecological and institutional variables on death rates, rather than the age-dependence of death rates. Therefore, we thought it appropriate to use as a baseline model a two-time period model that best fitted the death rate data in this population (Singh, House, and Tucker 1986). This model was of the form

$$h(t) = \exp \{\beta_o (p)\} \exp \{\yen_o (p)\}t, \quad p = 1,2 \qquad (8.1)$$

To test the empirical validity of the ecological and institutional arguments made earlier, we entered the appropriate time-varying covariates into the above model. Further, because we used multiple spells models with yearly spells, it seemed equally meaningful to model the covariates in either the β or $\yen$ vectors because, in such models, the substantive interpretations of the two vectors are not very different (Singh, House, and Tucker 1986). Unfortunately, all the models we estimated using the baseline model in equation (8.1) ran into severe convergence problems, and we were forced to change the baseline model in order to obtain results. We chose a simple Gompertz model that was not period dependent

$$h(t) = \exp (\beta_o) \exp (\yen_o)t \qquad (8.2)$$

Time varying covariates were entered into the β and $\yen$ vectors of the multiple spells models like equation (8.2). These were of the form

$$h(t) = \exp \{\beta_o + \sum_i \beta_i X_i(\tau)\} \exp (\yen_o)t \qquad (8.3)$$

and

$$h(t) = \exp \beta_o \exp \{\yen_o + \sum_i \yen_i X_i(\tau)\}t \qquad (8.4)$$

where the X_is are the time varying ecological and institutional covariates. Table 8–2 presents the maximum likelihood estimates and standard errors for the parameters of the Gompertz models using RATE (Tuma 1980).

We first modeled the curvilinear effects of density on the instantaneous rate of death in order to investigate the validity of ecological arguments.[4] The results are shown in the first and second rows of Table 8–2. When the effects of density were modeled in the β vector (row 1), the overall model was strongly significant compared to a constant rate model, based on a *chi*-square likelihood ratio-test ($\chi^2_{3\,d.f.} = 25.23, p = 1.32 \times 10^{-5}$). There was also a significant curvilinear effect of density. However, our findings contradicted findings in other populations (see the Hannan and Freeman chapter in this volume) because death rates initially increased with density, but as density increased even further, they began to decline. This does not support arguments that suggest that for low levels of density, increases in density enhance the legitimacy of the organizational form, thereby decreasing the death rate. As density increases even further, however, the effects of competition take over and death rates increase. Further, in our population, density has a maximum impact on the death rate when it is approximately 524, which was during the year 1975–76.[5] Because density during the period of observation ranged between 359 and 668, the declining death rate at higher levels of density is within the observed range of density and occurred in this population. Another surprising finding is the positive and significant value of the $\yen_0$ parameter, because this does not support the well-accepted ideas of liability of newness.

When these density effects were modeled in the $\yen$ vector, the results were more or less identical. The overall model was significant compared to a constant rate model ($\chi^2_{3\,d.f.} = 41.93, p = 4.15 \times 10^{-9}$), and density again had strong curvilinear effects. But now the $\yen_0$ parameter was significant and negative, suggesting that the previous significant and positive value of $\yen_0$ may be an artifact of the modeling. In any case, because the primary focus here was not on $\yen_0$, we did not pursue this question any further.

Next, we modeled the impact of major institutional changes on the death rates of VSSOs (rows 3 and 4 of Table 8–2). When OFY and RES were modeled in the β term, the overall model was significant compared to a constant rate model ($\chi^2_{3\,d.f.} = 48.22, p = 1.92 \times 10^{-10}$). Both OFY

Table 8–2. Maximum Likelihood Estimates: Ecological and Institutional Effects on Death Rate. (multiple spells models)

Covariates in β or ¥ vector	β_o	$¥_o$	Density	Density^2	OFY	RES	χ^2	d.f.	p-level
1. β	−29.12[b] (6.658)	0.159[b] (0.044)	0.099[b] (0.025)	−0.00009[b] (0.00002)			25.33	3	1.32×10^{-5}
2. ¥	−3.977[b] (0.221)	−5.980[b] (2.024)	0.025[b] (0.007)	−0.00002[b] (0.000006)			41.93	3	4.15×10^{-9}
3. β	−6.139[b] (0.556)	0.182[b] (0.042)			2.447[b] (0.549)	2.387[b] (0.476)	48.22	3	1.92×10^{-10}
4. ¥	−3.871[b] (0.209)	−0.111[a] (0.068)			0.384[b] (0.100)	0.310[b] (0.065)	46.10	3	5.41×10^{-10}
5. β	−16.95[b] (6.959)	0.215[b] (0.046)	0.049[a] (0.027)	−0.00005[a] (0.00003)	1.435[a] (0.785)	2.016[b] (0.505)	52.56	5	4.13×10^{-10}
6. ¥	−4.073[b] (0.027)	−1.483 (2.245)	0.009 (0.008)	−0.00001 (0.000007)	0.067 (0.170)	0.202[b] (0.071)	58.46	5	2.53×10^{-11}

Note: Standard errors in parentheses.
[a] $p < .05$.
[b] $p < .01$ (one-tail test).

and RES had significant effects on death rates. Whereas the positive effects of RES were as expected, the positive effect of OFY was surprising. Contrary to our expectations, OFY significantly increased death rates of VSSOs. The results were similiar when OFY and RES were modeled in the ¥ vector, with both OFY and RES significantly increasing the death rate.

We next modeled the impact of both the ecological and institutional variables together, in order to rule out problems of specification error. Row 5 of Table 8–2 presents the results for all covariates modeled in the β vector. As before, the overall model was significant compared to a constant rate model ($\chi^2_{5\ d.f.} = 52.56$, $p = 4.13 \times 10^{-10}$), and all the variables continued to show the previous pattern of results. However, when all the covariates were modeled in the ¥ vector (row 6 of Table 8–2), with the exception of RES, the earlier results were eliminated, even though the overall model was highly significant. Generally, the broad pattern of results showed some evidence that the ecological and institutional affects were still present.

Interaction of Institutional Changes and Ecological Processes

Despite the unexpected effects of density and OFY, the evidence suggested that ecological processes of competition and institutional changes both significantly affected death rates. Next, we asked whether the institutional changes influenced the nature of the ecological process itself. We answered this question by introducing dummy variables for OFY and RES separately into the models in equations (8.3) and (8.4). Because more complex models did not converge, we had to introduce OFY and RES separately into both the constant terms and coefficients of the density variables. None of these models converged, despite raising the number of iterations to 100. However, the intermediate solution for a model specifying the interaction of OFY with the curvilinear effects of density provided interpretable results. The overall model fitted the data well ($\chi^2_{6\ d.f.} = 33.79$, $p = 7.39 \times 10^{-6}$), although the fit was worse compared to the models without interaction effects in Table 8–2. There was no significant interaction effect, although density still had a curvilinear relationship with death rate. Thus, the available evidence seemed to indicate that the institutional changes did not significantly alter the nature of the ecological processes of competition because the addition of interaction effects either produced worse fitting models or models that did not converge.

DISCUSSION

The broad pattern of results from this study was quite intriguing. In addition to supporting some of our expectations based on theory, they also contain some unanticipated surprises. The analysis of patterns of founding provided partial support for ecological arguments because we found results that showed significant curvilinear effects for lagged foundings and lagged deaths (see Table 8–1, column 8). The curvilinear effects of lagged foundings had their maximum impact on current foundings at a lagged foundings level of about 30 ($1.141/2 \times 0.019 = 30.02$), which was not in the observed range of foundings. Thus, in this population, only the initiation part of the foundings dynamics operated during the period of observation. The curvilinear effect of lagged deaths, however, reached a maximum at a level between 4 and 5, which was within the observed range ($2.029/2 \times 0.226 = 4.6$). Thus, lagged deaths first enhanced and then decreased births, and this occurred during the year 1976–77.

Regarding the institutional variables, lagged OFY significantly increased foundings, and lagged RES significantly decreased foundings. When we modeled the interaction of lagged OFY with the curvilinear effects of lagged density, the main effect of lagged OFY, surprisingly, became significant and negative. Further, the interactions with lagged density were significant, suggesting that ecological competition was enhanced during the OFY period. However, because the main effect of lagged OFY is the number of foundings when density is zero, it was clear that the intercept term was not within the observed range of density. Thus, we concluded that OFY had completely changed the nature of the ecological processes—making the effects of density more positive (that is, enhancing the legitimacy of the organizational form) and making the effects of density squared more negative (that is, increasing the effects of competition in the population).

On the other hand, the pattern of results for deaths was somewhat more unexpected. The results strongly supported a curvilinear effect of density on death rate, although the shape was the opposite of what we had expected. Instead of increases in density reducing the death rate, presumably by enhancing the legitimacy of the organizational form, the death rate increased with density, lending more support to the notion that competition increases with density in this population. The effect of density squared was negative instead of being positive. Although we do not currently have a precise explanation for this latter finding, two possibilities seem likely: (1) Unlike Hannan and Freeman's labor union population, density seems to generate stronger competition effects at relatively low levels, perhaps because the population is closer to its carrying capacity; and (2) the effect of density at even higher levels to reduce death rates is consistent with a threshold view of how density may affect legitimacy, such that these effects occur only above a fairly high threshold level of density. Of course, this is only an informed guess at this point and needs to be investigated further.

The effects of institutional variables on the death rate showed that, as expected, RES significantly increased the death rate. Surprisingly, OFY also increased the death rate, the opposite of what would have been expected. Two possible explanations of this result that incorporate the impact of OFY on founding patterns seem plausible. First, it is possible that OFY increased foundings beyond the point where the competitive effects of increased density begin to occur, thereby increasing deaths in the population. As discussed earlier when patterns of foundings were analyzed, this effect occurred when lagged density exceeded about 489. The density data clearly showed that this occurred during the year 1974–75, when density went from 457 to 517. This was the last year of OFY, and it seems clear that OFY raised births to the level where overcrowding led to greater competition for resources among organizations. Beginning in 1975–76, the level of foundings began to decline.

The second explanation is one we plan to investigate further in the future. It suggests that the impact of OFY may have been more selective in that it specifically led to the founding of more unfit VSSOs, which had lower survival rates and raised the death rate for the whole population.

One major difference in the results for death rates compared to the founding patterns was that we were unable to find a significant interaction effect between the institutional changes and ecological processes. Most of the models we estimated did not converge, and the only results we obtained did not show any evidence of significant interaction effects. Thus, in this population both the ecological and institutional variables had significant effects on deaths, some of which were unexpected, but the institutional variables did not alter the nature of the ecological competitive processes. This suggested that the institutional variables had a greater impact on the pattern of foundings than they did on the death rate. The impact of institutional changes on the death rate was indirect and seemed to operate through excessive increases in foundings.

The complex interplay between the founding and death patterns may also help explain why RES did not have a significant impact on foundings and the strange effects of density on death rates. As discussed earlier, foundings reached their maximum level when lagged density was about 489. Because density reached this level during 1974–75, the foundings began to decline the next year during 1975–76, which happened to coincide with the introduction of RES. Thus, it seems plausible that the negative effect of density may have overshadowed the negative effect of RES. Further, death rates reached their maximum when the density level was 524, which also occurred during 1975–76. This was the same year in which foundings began to decline, and this would have led to an easing of competitive pressures in the population, making deaths decline as density increased even further.

Although this possibility is interesting by itself, the general implications are even more fundamentally important. Most research has either tended to study founding and death processes independently, or as interdependent in simple ways. The arguments outlined above underscore the possibility of complex and intimate relationships between processes of founding and death, and point to the need to develop more complex models of founding and death processes.

The results of this study have elaborated the findings of related studies on similar questions. Our results are somewhat different than Carroll and Huo 1986), who found that task environmental and institutional variables had differential impacts on a newspaper population. Whereas the institutional environment explained entries and exits from the population better, the task environment, which included competition effects, had stronger effects on performance of newspapers. The findings here show greater complementarity between the effects of institutional and ecological arguments on foundings and deaths in the population. However, it is important to point out that Carroll and Huo concentrated on macroeconomic indicators and years of political turmoil or presidential elections, whereas this study has placed greater emphasis on the role of the state and, most particularly, on changes in its policies and programs.

There are also both similarities to and differences with Hannan and Freeman's research on labor unions. Our results for patterns of foundings are generally similar to their findings. But this study deals more explicitly with the effects of the institutional environment, and demonstrates how major institutional changes can dramatically alter the ecological dynamics of founding in a population. Our results for deaths are quite different and suggest that, in general, the birth and death processes need not be symmetric in their relationships with density. In fact, the evidence seems to suggest that founding processes can mediate the density dependence of death in quite intricate ways.

Finally, at a broader level, this study has two implications that warrant further thought, both of which are related to the state in its role as a policymaker in modern societies. One, the intentions of policies may be quite loosely coupled to their consequences. This is suggested by how OFY effects the competitive dynamics of the VSSO population. Ironically, the success of OFY resulted in some perplexing and apparently unanticipated consequences. The evidence seems to suggest that OFY led to the founding of so many organizations that it also increased the death rate in the population. This study suggests that increased knowledge of the complex ecological and institutional dynamics involved may be of help in more informed policy formulation. Two, critics of the ecological paradigm (Perrow 1985, 1986: ch. 6) have pointed out that the power of organizations and institutions must play an important role in ecological dynamics but has not been incorporated in ecological studies. Because the state is potentially the most powerful actor in modern societies, this study deals directly with Perrow's observation, demonstrating that it is meaningful and possible to study the interplay of the state as a dominant institutional actor and the dynamics of ecological processes as complementary approaches.

NOTES

1. The number of organizations studied here, the 451 born during the 1970–1982 period, differs from the 389 studied in analyses of death rates (Singh, Tucker, and House 1986; Singh, House, and Tucker 1986). The 389 VSSOs studied in the analysis of the differential death rates were the number born during the 1970 to 1980 period. Updated death data are presently not available for VSSOs born during 1981 and 1982.

2. Although the quadratic effects of lagged births and lagged deaths and the quadratic lagged density effects have frequently been treated as generally equivalent in the literature, it is appropriate to point out that the quadratic terms for lagged births and deaths seem to capture information about change in density rather than density itself. Thus, the two are related but not identical. This is because we know

$$density_t = density_{t-1} + (births_{t-1} \sim deaths_{t-1})$$

or, Δ density $= (births_{t-1} \sim deaths_{t-1})$,

or, Δ density^2 $= births^2_{t-1} + deaths^2_{t-1} - 2births_{t-1} deaths_{t-1}$,

$\therefore$ Δ density $+$ Δ density^2 $= births_{t-1} + births^2_{t-1} - deaths_{t-1} + deaths^2_{t-1}$
$$- 2births_{t-1} deaths_{t-1}$$

3. Since none of the other terms is significant, during OFY,

$$F_t = -164.59^a + 0.685^a density_{t-1} - 0.0007^a density^2_{t-1}$$

For a maxima, the first derivative with respect to density must be zero, thus

$$\frac{df_t}{d\ density_{t-1}} = 0.685 - 0.0007\ density_{t-1} \times 2$$

or, $density^a_{t-1} = 0.685/2 \times 0.0007 \approx 489$

4. We modeled the effects of density in the current year rather than lagged density because we had only thirteen years of data. A one-year lag would have led to the loss of one year of data, which we considered to be excessive. Lagged births and deaths were not modeled for the same reason, nor were the lagged institutional variables.

5. Elementary differential calculus shows that this is the case because for a maxima, the first derivative of $h(t)$ with respect to density must be zero.

$$h(t) = \exp (\beta_o + \beta_1 d + \beta_2 d^2) \exp (¥_o t)$$

for a maxima, $\frac{\partial h}{\partial d} = 0 = (\beta_1 + 2\beta_2 d) h(t)$, and, thus, $d^* = -\beta_1/2\beta_2$

9 SUPPRESSION AND FAILURE IN THE POLITICAL PRESS
Government Control, Party Affiliation, and Organizational Life Chances

Terry L. Amburgey, Marjo-Riitta Lehtisalo, and Dawn Kelly

Most research dealing with the effects of sociocultural environments on organizational change has focused on organizational transformations—that is, the process wherein organizations change one or more attributes in response to normative requirements (Tolbert and Zucker 1983; Rowan 1982). On the other hand, most of the research on the differential replacement aspect of organizational change has focused on the technical or resource requirements of organizations (Carroll 1985; Freeman and Hannan 1983; see, however, Carroll and Huo 1986). In this chapter, we explore the impact of social and cultural factors on differential replacement in an organizational population.

Two aspects of the institutional environment are investigated. The first is the state. Institutional theorists all seem to agree that the state is the dominant element in the institutional environment of modern organizations (Scott and Meyer 1983; DiMaggio and Powell 1983; Zucker 1983). As Scott and Meyer (1983) note, an important assumption of their work is that contemporary societies increasingly exhibit functionally differentiated sectors whose structures are vertically connected with lines stretching up to the central nation-state. These vertical connections are more consequential than horizontal connections between organizations so that actions by the state comprise the most important normative demands placed on organizations.

The second aspect of the institutional environment examined here concerns political parties and their espoused political issues. Because of the focus on vertical connections, the empirical work of the institutionalists generally assumes that all important pressures or demands are channeled through the apparatus of the state. We explore here the possibility that political movements and issues have a direct effect on organizational life chances.

The organizational population we examined consists of all newspapers published in Finland between 1771 and 1963. The relationship between the state and the press has long been a topic of great interest in western societies. Most of the recent work on political development uses "freedom of the press" as an indicator of political liberty; the level of government sanctions against the press, such as censorship or closures, are taken as an empirical measure of a society's political structure (Timberlake and Williams 1984; Bollen 1979, 1980).

Political parties have also had a long, intimate relationship with the press. In its earliest period, the press was dominated by explicitly political papers in many countries such as the United States, Great Britain, France, and Norway (Williams 1978; Hoyer, Hadenius, and Weibull 1975; Bleyer 1927). The issues that dominate discussion in a polity have important consequences for newspapers since they are frequently a "raw material" as well as an occasion for policy choices (Lester 1980). The choice of positions on political issues and affiliation with political parties affects not only the institutional position of a newspaper but also its internal processes (Lester 1980; Hoyer, Hadenius, and Weibull 1975).

Although a complete treatment of differential replacement involves an examination of both foundings and failures, this study examines only the cessation of publication. Our focus is the effects of government control and political affiliation on the likelihood of failure, suppression, and voluntary suspension of publication. From an ecological point of view, organizational failure is the most important event. Our interest in suppression by the state and suspension stems from the belief that they contribute to the probability of failure. Institutional models predict a positive relationship between sanctions from the state and failure. We propose that voluntary suspension is an avoidance mechanism used to stave off impending failure or suppression. If suspension is a response to impending failure, suspension would be an indication of organizational morbidity.

ECONOMIC MODELS OF PRESS DEVELOPMENT

Models of the development of the press typically concentrate on economic factors and the rise of the general newspaper oriented toward the mass market (for example, see Bucklin, Caves, and Lo 1985; Rosse, Owen, and Dertouzos 1975; Hoyer, Hadenius, and Weibull 1975). When so viewed, newspaper industries in many western societies apparently evolve by similar phases—introduction, expansion, and consolidation (Høyer, Hadenius, and Weibull 1975). In the introductory period, the number of newspapers grows slowly. Most of the growth occurs in the larger urban areas where the primary audience is the upper class. Expansion occurs both geographically and socially. Geographically, the press extends into smaller cities and towns, although growth in the number of places in which a newspaper is published is slower than growth in the number of newspapers (Høyer, Hadenius, and Weibull 1975). Socially, expansion occurs by incorporating the middle and working classes. Political and social differences, however, make it increasingly difficult to balance the diverse interests of readers as the market expands. An audience-maximizing strategy requires the relinquishment of special ties or contents that may alienate some potential readers. Consequently, content material shifts toward news and entertainment and away from political and social issues (Høyer, Hadenius, and Weibull 1975). In the consolidation phase, coverage extends to small communities. Advertising fees replace subscription as the primary source of income; newspapers are sold at prices lower than the cost of production. The high capitalization required to obtain economies of scale serves as an entry barrier and few new daily newspapers are founded. Intense competition for the mass market (necessary to obtain advertising fees) increases the failure rate. As the founding rate decreases and the failure rate increases, the net population of newspapers declines.

The three-phase economic model of press development is not consistent with the historical development of the Finnish press. Figure 9–1 provides the annual number of newspapers published in Finland between 1771 and 1963. The earliest period of the Finnish press is consistent with the introduction phase of the economic model. There is very slow growth, and the growth is concentrated in larger cities such as Turku and Helsinki. From 1860 to 1890 geographic expansion occurred. During the 1870s there was a rapid increase in the number of post offices, and in 1880 networks of subscription agents were put into place. However, social expansion did not take place. Political cleavages based on ethnicity and language prevented a shift toward noncontroversial content. Attempts to maintain a neutral attitude were not well received by the readership (Kurian 1982). In 1890 a mail delivery system for the countryside was established, which presumably would begin the last phase of consolidation. But as Figure 9–1 shows, there was no decline in the number of newspapers. In fact, the number of newspapers rises monotonically until World War II. We propose that the lack of social expansion during the late nineteenth century and the complete absence of a consolidation phase are due to political and social factors not included in the economic model.

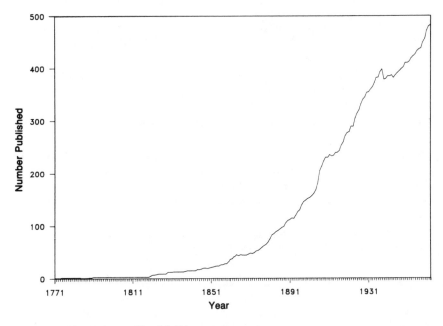

Figure 9-1. Finnish Newspapers.

POLITICAL MODELS OF PRESS DEVELOPMENT

The purely economic view of press development neglects the role of the state and the role of sociocultural movements. Economic models tend to assume the *a priori* existence of a stable state that passively allows the "invisible hand" of market forces to mold the press. However, states do not spring into existence *de novo*; they develop over time. The process of state formation involves social mobilization intimately connected with communications media. Political theorists frequently assume that widespread access to newspapers and other mass media heightens awareness of national political processes (Bollen 1983). The political functions of the press have not been lost on those individuals and organizations in the apparatus of the state. The history of the press is checkered with periods of close state control.

A variety of methods have been used by states to exercise control of the press. The most obvious is prepublication censorship and the outright suppression of dissenting newspapers. States also attempt to control access to resources. One extremely important resource is information. In some cases the flow of information across political boundaries is controlled through censorship of foreign news. Another popular method is the steering of administrative information to favored or official newspapers. States sometimes control access to material resources such as newsprint or printing presses. States attempt to control the founding of newspapers by requiring licences or patents for publication and by setting minimum qualifications for publishers and journalists. The judicial system is used as a control mechanism through prosecutions for seditious libel or the libel of government officials. Finally, economic measures are sometimes used such as control of advertising, subsidies, or bribery.

As it develops, the press seems to pass through several stages that are intimately related to the process of state formation. Stein Rokkan (1975) has proposed four phases in the process of state formation: initial state building, incorporation of the masses, participation of the masses, and expansion of the administrative apparatus. During the initial period of state formation (or after a political revolution) the position of the state is precarious and newspapers are subject to stringent control. The full panoply of measures are utilized as necessary. Newspapers either function to support the state or are vigorously suppressed (Curran 1978).

Once the state is more securely established, less formal methods are preferred and the use of coercive controls is restricted to dissenting, politically oriented newspapers. Supportive or official newspapers act as channels for direct contact between the central elite and parochial populations of the peripheries and are used to generate widespread feelings of identity with the political system (Rokkan 1975). Once the position of the state is secure (as in phases 3 and 4), only the most dangerous of political newspapers are coercively controlled. Control of other newspapers is left to market mechanisms and professional norms (Curran 1978).

Economic models not only neglect the role of the state, they also neglect the role of ideology. Viewing newspapers as profit-maximizing firms ignores the ideological passions of activists who are intensely concerned with the resolution of social issues and who use the press as an organizing and propagandizing tool. Viewing the contents of newspapers as value-neutral information where "quality is determined solely by monetary expenditures on reporting, editorial staff, etc." (Bucklin, Caves, and Lo 1985: 2) ignores the same passions in the general populace. The structure of the polity and sociopolitical movements have profound influences on the development of the press.

An important prediction of the economic model of press development is that newspapers consistently shift to a strategy of audience-maximization through the adoption of generalized content materials. The extent to which this shift can take place is a function of the degree of polarization and segmentation in the reading audience. The party-structure model of Høyer, Hadenius, and Weibull (1975) predicts that in a fragmented multiparty system, party loyalties and political passions limit the possibility of expansion to many market segments. When social issues produce cleavage and polarization among sociopolitical groups, a strategy of content homogenization is difficult to implement. The lower level of fragmentation inherent in a two-party political system makes audience-maximization a more feasible strategy than in a multiparty system.

The party-structure model is also consistent with the resource partitioning process among newspapers described by Carroll (1985). In the resource partitioning model, the viability of generalist and specialist strategies depends on the existence of a common denominator in the readership, such as language and ethnicity. If no common denominator exists, specialist strategies targeted to different segments are optimal. Furthermore, if newspapers attempt to "move to the center" with generalized content, resources in the peripheral segments are abandoned to specialist papers. These resources are monopolized by segment specialists that then enjoy enhanced life chances. Both the party-structure model and the resource partitioning model propose a survival premium for specialist newspapers in segmented, polarized polities.

Political models of press development propose several modifications to the developmental process described by the economic model. The state apparatus relies on market mechanisms and professional norms as control mechanisms only when it is secure. When the state is endangered (during initial formation or when facing internal political threats, for example), it utilizes direct intervention. The severity and scope of direct intervention vary according to the level of the threat: When the threat is strong, there are more kinds of intervention and a greater proportion of the press is controlled; when the threat is less severe, there are fewer kinds of intervention and it is directed toward particular segments of the press.

Intervention by the state, in turn, affects organizational life chances by limiting access to resources. In some cases, intervention results in increased costs to newspapers. In other cases, intervention results in a complete loss of a resource. In either case, the life chances of newspapers will be degraded. When intervention is comprehensive, the entire population of newspapers will be affected. When intervention is targeted, there will be a differential effect, and the composition of the population will change accordingly.

The structure of the polity will also affect the life chances of newspapers. In a relatively homogenous polity, generalist newspapers will be selectively favored in the fashion described by the economic model. In a fragmented polity, however, affiliation with a particular segment (such as political party and ethnic group) will provide improved life chances. This "specialist premium" operates through subsidization and assured audiences. Subsidization can occur through the provision of capital or labor, but in either case, it improves life chances. Similarly, an assured or "built in" audience provides a steady cash flow that improves life chances. Although all specialist newspapers should receive some specialist premium in a fragmented polity, some segments will provide a greater premium than others. In particular, those segments that are large, well organized, and with high levels of fervor among their members will provide the largest premium. Consequently, the structure of the polity will affect the composition of the population not only in terms of the relative proportions of specialists and generalists, but also in terms of particular types of specialist newspapers.

PROPOSITIONS

We argue that there will be both direct and indirect effects of different political regimes on newspapers in Finland. The direct effects occur through explicit interventions by a regime into the operations of the press. In the history of the Finnish newspaper industry, three types of intervention occurred. First, there were two periods where the state controlled publication of foreign news (1809–40 and 1892–1918). Second, there were three periods where the state exercised *a priori* censorship (1829–55, 1867–1905 and 1939–46). Finally, there was a period (1850–62) when the Tsarist regime restricted publication in Suomi, the Finnish language.

Control of foreign news should increase the failure rate of newspapers by limiting access to an important resource. Many newspapers rely heavily on foreign news items. Nineteenth-century newspapers in Great Britain and the United States placed a strong emphasis on foreign news (Palmer 1978; Bleyer 1927). Finnish newspapers emphasize foreign news much more than their European counterparts. Control of foreign news should also increase the suppression rate of newspapers. As foreign news becomes less available, domestic content materials will increase. Some of the increase will go to politically innocuous areas. To the extent that coverage of politically sensitive topics (such as nationalism) increases, the risk of suppression increases. Because crime, sex, and other scandals are shunned by Finnish newspapers (Kurian 1982) and they display a penchant for political discourse, it seems very likely that publication of sensitive items would increase as foreign news becomes scarce.

Proposition 1. Control of foreign news increases the rate of failure, suppression, and suspension.

A priori censorship should increase the failure rate by adding costs and reducing revenues. These effects will be incurred both by compliance and noncompliance with regulations. Compliance required the free delivery of papers to the state, and more important, the loss of lucrative but prohibited advertising revenues. Advertisements for patent medicines and lotteries were important sources of revenue for many nineteenth century newspapers, but they were prohibited by Tsarist regulations (Rothenberg 1946; Rogers 1919). Noncompliance meant additional costs, such as court fines and salaries for "jail editors" (responsible editors whose primary function was the provision of a warm body to go to jail when necessary). Furthermore, noncompliance drastically limits circulation.

A *priori* censorship should also increase the suppression rate. The requirement that newspapers provide free copies to central authorities shifts "search" costs from the state to the newspapers. Assuming that the amount of search is inversely related to cost, more material gets read under an *a priori* system. Greater exposure to intervention by censors should increase the likelihood of suppression.

Proposition 2. A priori censorship increases the rates of failure, suppression and suspension.

Prohibiting the publication of noncommercial and nonreligious text in Suomi (Finnish) should increase the failure rate. Finnish nationalism was a strong cultural force, and Suomi played an important role in the nationalist movement. The prohibition of Finnish text increases resource scarcity by limiting access to a very important segment of the readership. Language prohibitions should also increase the suppression rate. By prohibiting the publication of certain kinds of text, the Tsarist regime increased the possible grounds for intervention by the state. If the definition of objectionable material is expanded, the number of suppressions should increase.

Proposition 3. Language prohibitions increase the rates of failure, suppression, and suspension.

Different state regimes can influence organizational life chances independently of specific legislation. Enforcement of statutes can vary with the succession of elites or with changes in the priorities of existing elites. Ideally, regime would be categorized by leadership succession or by major changes in military, political, or economic circumstances. In an exploratory effort, we divide the political history of Finland into three regimes: the Swedish (1771–1809) and Russian (1809–1918) empires and the independent republic (1919–63). The Swedish period is used as a baseline to evaluate the Tsarist and Republican regimes.

The Tsarist regime should have the highest failure rate. The Tsarist regime had broader concerns and broader criteria for intervention than the republic. In many ways, the position of the Tsars in Finland was more insecure than that of the republic. The Tsarist regime was threatened by the entire populace, whereas the republic was threatened by only one segment of the polity. The Tsarist regime also had broader authority. As an absolutist state, the Tsarist regime could take actions that the constitutional heritage of the republic ruled out. The oppressive nature of the Tsars should produce higher costs to newspapers and thereby increase the failure rate.

Because of its broad concerns, the Tsarist regime should also exhibit the highest suppression rate. During the Republican regime, the "excluded" portion of the political spectrum is at greatest risk. During the Tsarist regime, the entire political spectrum is suspect because of the consensus on nationalism. Because more types of newspapers are at risk of suppression, the rate should be higher.

> **Proposition 4. The Tsarist regime will exhibit higher rates of failure, suppression, and suspension independently of the effects of direct intervention.**

We also propose that social and political fragmentation in Finnish society will affect organizational life chances among newspapers, both directly and indirectly. Association with a segment of the polity will produce a "specialist premium" for survival through an assured or built-in audience and through subsidization. Specializing to a particular political segment will also affect life chances indirectly through differential rates of suppression. Newspapers that are affiliated with political segments excluded from the dominant coalition, or otherwise viewed as threatening, will be at greater risk of suppression and their life chances should suffer accordingly.

Political affiliation has three basic categories: nonpolitical, independent political, and party affiliated. The party affiliated category is further subdivided into three groups along the political spectrum: left wing, center, and right wing. Nonpolitical newspapers (those devoted to local news, announcements, religious or commercial activity, and so forth) may publish text with political import, but political discourse is not a central concern. Nonpolitical newspapers are used as a baseline to evaluate the effects of membership in one of the other affiliation categories.

Independent political newspapers have political discourse as their primary content area. Independent papers may act as a forum open to all political views, or they may adopt a partisan stance, but in both cases they lack formal affiliation with a party organization. Independents are more specialized (vis-à-vis content) than nonpolitical newspapers but less specialized than party-affiliated newspapers. Consequently, independent political newspapers should be less likely to fail than nonpolitical papers but more likely to fail than party-affiliated newspapers.

Proposition 5. Independent political newspapers will have a lower failure rate than nonpolitical newspapers but a higher failure rate than party-affiliated newspapers.

The reverse pattern should hold for the suppression rate. The higher level of political content increases the likelihood that independent political newspapers will attract intervention from the state. Independent political newspapers should also be less likely to be suppressed than party-affiliated newspapers. Party-affiliated newspapers have a formal connection with an organization engaged in a wide variety of political activities. A publication is more threatening as part of a coordinated set of activities.

Proposition 6. Independent political newspapers will have a higher suppression rate than nonpolitical newspapers but a lower suppression rate than party-affiliated newspapers.

Political parties in Finland can be grouped into three broad categories: left, center, and right. Left-wing parties represent the industrial and agrarian working class and endorse socialist policies. Centrist parties represent the middle and upper classes of both linguistic groups and most agrarian interests. The centrist parties endorse liberal and moderate policies. Right-wing parties represent segments of the Finnish (as opposed to Swedish) middle and upper classes and the independent peasantry in Ostrobothnia. The right-wing parties endorse conservative or, in some cases, fascist policies.

Newspapers affiliated with left-wing parties should have the lowest failure rates. Social Democratic newspapers received both financial subsidization and editorial freedom (Salmelin 1968). The Social Democrats had a more close-knit organization than other parties, a mass party structure, and a set of constituency organizations such as local workers associations. Left-wing parties also had high levels of internal cohesion and political fervor due to the continued exclusion of the left-wing pluralities from governing coalitions. All of these factors should operate to increase the suppression rate. Continued opposition to the governing coalitions and extreme political fervor enhances the threat posed to central authorities by left-wing newspapers.

Proposition 7. Newspapers affiliated with left-wing parties will have the lowest failure rate and the highest suppression rate.

Newspapers affiliated with center parties should have failure rates larger than left-wing newspapers but smaller than right-wing newspapers. Political fervor is lowest among the moderate parties of the center and the party organizations of centrist parties was based on election cadres rather than mass participation. Both these factors should reduce the assured audience available to newspapers affiliated with parties of the center. However, center parties were usually included in governing coalitions. Political inclusion, along with low levels of political fervor, should make centrist newspapers less likely to be suppressed.

> **Proposition 8. Newspapers affiliated with center parties will have the highest failure rates and lowest suppression rates of party-affiliated newspapers.**

Right-wing newspapers should exhibit failure rates lower than the centrist papers but higher than left-wing newspapers. The right-wing parties had very high levels of political fervor, which should provide more of an assured audience than that available to centrist newspapers. However, only the conservative Old Finns and their descendant, the National Coalition Party, had an effective party structure and it was an election cadre rather than mass based. Furthermore, the extremist parties were geographically restricted to Ostrobothnia. These factors should produce less of an assured audience than that available to left-wing newspapers.

> **Proposition 9. Newspapers affiliated with right-wing parties will have a higher failure rate than left-wing newspapers but a lower failure rate than centrist newspapers.**

Newspapers affiliated with right-wing parties should be less likely to be suppressed than left-wing newspapers but more likely to be suppressed than centrist newspapers. The Old Finns and National Coalition Party were frequently included in governing coalitions, so only the extremist groupings were politically isolated. On the other hand, the political fervor of the fascist parties made them dangerous.

> **Proposition 10. Newspapers affiliated with right-wing parties will have a lower suppression rate than left-wing newspapers but a higher suppression rate than centrist newspapers.**

Although a party's position on the political spectrum may be a reasonable indicator of the assured audience that is accessible to an affiliated newspaper, we would argue that a measure more closely tied to party size and loyalty is preferable. Because we lack data on party membership, we use electoral support as an indicator of party support. If party affiliation has an advantage above and beyond financial subsidization (through an assured audience), then the size of electoral support should affect the failure rate. Parties with broad support should be less likely to fail than other parties with the same position on the political spectrum but smaller support.

High levels of electoral support should also decrease the likelihood of suppression. The state is likely to alienate a larger portion of the polity if it suppresses newspapers affiliated with parties that have broad support. However, the effect will be moderated by political fervor—a large and militant segment of the polity is likely to be viewed as particularly dangerous by the state.

> **Proposition 11. Newspapers affiliated with political parties that have large electoral support will have lower rates of failure, suppression, and suspension than those affiliated with parties that have lower levels of electoral support.**

DATA AND METHODS

We collected data on all newspapers published in Finland between 1771 and 1963. The *Bibliography of the Finnish Newspapers 1771–1963* (Kaarna and Winter 1965) published by the University of Helsinki Library was the primary source of information used to construct the sample. To our knowledge, the *Bibliography* is the most comprehensive listing of Finnish newspapers in existence—the only periodicals excluded from the list were those containing little or no news, such as advertising sheets or trade journals.

The *Bibliography* contains comprehensive information on name, location, political affiliation, content materials, language, publication layout, frequency of publication, publisher, editor-in-chief, responsible editor, coverage (general or local), market (rural or urban), suspensions, government suppressions, mergers, and the times of founding and failure. The timing of any changes in these characteristics (a change of editor-in-chief for example) was recorded in the *Bibliography*; timing was always recorded at least as to year and month and in the vast majority of cases to the day. The information contained in the *Bibliography* was used to construct event histories for each of the 1,014 newspapers in the sample. Twelve types of events were included in the event histories, but for the purposes of this study only failure, suppression, and suspension were analyzed as dependent events.

Information from the *Bibliography* was also used to construct two types of covariates. The first type consisted of the values of the newspaper's attributes at the time of an event—that is, its frequency of publication, political affiliation, and so forth. The other covariates were constructed by calculating the prior number of events of all types at the time of an event. In other words, at the time of each event, the numbers of prior content changes, name changes, and so forth were recorded and included as covariates.

Two of these "cumulative event" covariates were retained for analysis in this study: the number of prior suppressions and the number of prior suspensions. These covariates were used in two ways. First, they allow testing for interdependence between suppression, suspension, and failure (Amburgey 1986a). If, as we hypothesize, suppression, and suspension increase the likelihood of failure then the number of prior events of this type should be positively related to the failure rate. Second, they were used as control variables. Prior research indicates that the rate of occurrence of an event is sometimes related to the number of prior events of the same type (Amburgey 1986a; Amburgey and Kelly 1985). Inclusion of these variables allows the estimation of any reinforcement processes.

The political environment was measured in two ways. The three regimes were included with two dummy variables (Tsarist and Republic) and an excluded baseline category (Swedish). Variations in government control were included with three dummy variables: control of foreign news, a priori censorship, and language prohibition. Those periods of time when foreign news was controlled received ones, the remainder received zeros. A priori censorship and language prohibition were coded in a similar fashion.

Political affiliation was also coded as a set of dummy variables. Newspapers without significant political content (as judged by the authors of the Bibliography) comprised the excluded category and was used as a baseline for evaluating the other categories. Newspapers with political content but without a party affiliation were coded as independent political papers. Newspapers that were affiliated with political parties were grouped along the political spectrum into three categories: left wing, center, and right wing. These groupings are based upon a factor analysis of party platforms (Borg 1966), a study of voting strength (Sankiaho 1970), and a study of cabinet coalitions (Tornudd 1969).

Electoral support was included by coding the percentage of total votes received by the parties in the parliamentary and presidential elections (Rantala 1969: 96–101). Although members of the Diet of Estates were frequently associated with political movements, the political parties did not submit candidates for election to the Diet. Consequently, Diet elections were excluded from the analysis. The parliamentary period (1907–63) does not include the Swedish regime nor the period of language prohibition so these variables were dropped from the analysis when electoral support was used as a covariate. In the case of language prohibition, the variable was simply dropped from the equation when electoral support was included. In the case of the regime variables, the Tsarist regime dummy variable was retained and the Republican period was excluded and used as the baseline category.

Several control variables were used in the analysis. Age was included as a control variable because most studies of organizational failure have shown that the risk of failure decreases with age (Carroll and Delacroix 1982; Freeman, Carroll, and Hannan 1983). Furthermore, prior research on newspapers indicates that the likelihood of organizational tactics such as voluntary suspension of publication declines with age (Amburgey and Kelly 1985).

The other control variables are product characteristics of the newspapers: language of publication, number of content areas, scope of geographic coverage, and frequency of publication. Finnish-language papers should have decreasing death rates as Suomi becomes legitimized through the nationalist movement. Finnish-language papers should also exhibit a higher suppression rate. During the Tsarist period, language legislation and the Russification campaign puts Finnish papers at higher risk. During the Republic, Swedish papers were usually affiliated with the ruling coalition, while radical papers were usually published in Finnish.

Scope of coverage and the number of content areas are indicators of niche width. Both the resource partitioning model and the polity fragmentation model predict that generalists will have higher failure rates, so these variables provide an additional test for a specialist premium. We would also anticipate a higher suspension rate for generalists because of their greater resource requirements. Frequency of publication is also likely to affect resource requirements. More frequent publication requires not only more physical resources but also more content material and a more differentiated work force (Smith 1978).

Failure, suppression, and suspension were modeled as competing risks, such as at any point in time during its existence a newspaper was at risk for any of the three events. Both suppression and suspension are repeatable point events so a multivariate point process model was used to analyze the competing risks (Amburgey 1986a). The rate of occurrence of each of the three events was specified as a loglinear function of the covariates and a set of parameters. Maximum likelihood estimates of the covariate parameters, standard errors, and associated F ratios were obtained using Tuma's RATE (1980) program.

FINDINGS

Table 9–1 provides some selected frequency distributions of organizational characteristics at the time of founding and of the different events.

Table 9–1. Selected Frequency Distributions.

Political Affiliation			*Births*	
Nonpolitical	– 656		Swedish regime	– 4
Independent political	– 72		Tsarist regime	– 486
Left wing	– 135		Republic	– 524
Center	– 86			
Right wing	– 65		*Failures*	
			Swedish regime	– 1
Language			Tsarist regime	– 230
Finnish	– 806		Republic	– 298
Swedish	– 162			
Other	– 46		*Suppression*	
			Swedish regime	– 0
Coverage			Tsarist regime	– 105
General	– 373		Republic	– 40
Local	– 641			
			Suspensions	
Contents			Swedish regime	– 2
Multiple contents	– 64		Tsarist regime	– 62
Single content	– 950		Republic	– 76
Frequency of Publication				
Daily	– 45			
Triweekly	– 48			
Biweekly	– 66			
Weekly	– 329			
Bimonthly	– 30			
Monthly	– 15			
Quarterly	– 3			
Irregular	– 478			

Although the majority of Finnish newspapers were nonpolitical approximately one-third were political in nature. The number of newspapers is almost evenly divided between the Tsarist period and the Republican period. Because the Tsarist period is almost twice as long as the Republican period, the republic had a much greater founding rate of newspapers. The vast majority of newspapers were published in Finnish and contained a single content area. Most of the papers were local in nature but approximately one-third covered a broader geographic area. Almost half of the papers were published irregularly with most of the remainder published weekly or more frequently.

Slightly more than half of the newspapers failed, with the remainder still in existence in 1963. The vast majority of the newspaper failures occurred during the parliamentary period. There were 145 cases of suppression by the state, with the majority occurring during the Tsarist period.

There were 140 cases of voluntary suspension of publication, most of which occurred during the Republican period.

Table 9–2 provides the estimated parameter values for the three events. For each event, the first row consists of values for the entire observation period, while the second row covers only the parliamentary period. The two top rows in table 9–2 provide the parameter values for the failure rate. Of the state intervention variables only control of foreign news has a significant effect for the total observation period. During the parliamentary period both control of foreign news and *a priori* censorship significantly increase the likelihood of failure. There is no significant difference between the failure rates of the various regimes for the total observation period, but during the parliamentary period the Tsarist regime has a significantly lower failure rate.

Independent political newspapers exhibit a failure rate similar to nonpolitical papers, but newspapers affiliated with political parties are significantly less likely to fail. The specialist premium is smaller during the parliamentary period however and disappears for right-wing newspapers. Electoral support has no significant effect on the failure rate.

The number of prior suppressions increases the probability of failure for the total observation but has no significant effect during the parliamentary period. In neither case is the number of prior suspensions related to the probability of failure. The probability of failure declines with age, both overall and during the parliamentary period. Although the effects of age appear small, the basic unit of time used in the study is the day: consequently, the value of the parameter indicates the effect of a single day of further survival. Of the product characteristics, only geographic coverage has a significant effect; newspapers with general coverage have a higher failure rate than local newspapers.

The next two rows in Table 9–2 provide the estimated parameter values for the suppression rate. Overall, control of foreign news and *a priori* censorship increase the probability of suppression although the effect of censorship disappears during the parliamentary period. Language legislation again has no effect. There are no significant effects of regime on the suppression rate.

The effects of political content and party affiliation are to generally increase the risk of suppression. Left-wing newspapers are more likely to be suppressed, and right-wing newspapers are less likely to be suppressed for the entire period. However, during the parliamentary period all political papers are more likely to be suppressed except right-wing papers that lose their buffer versus suppression. Electoral support significantly decreases the likelihood of suppression by the state.

A history of prior suppressions and suspensions operates to significantly increase the likelihood of suppression for the total period. Only prior suppression has an effect during the parliamentary period. The likelihood of suppression significantly declines with age for the entire period but not during the parliamentary period. During the later period older papers are just as likely to be suppressed as young papers.

Only frequency of publication has an effect on suppression for the entire period; the other product characteristics do not alter the suppression rate. The picture is much different during the parliamentary period—all of the product variables have significant effects. Publishing in Finnish and multiple contents increase the risk of suppression, while general coverage and frequent publication decrease the risk of suppression.

Table 9–2 also provides the effects of covariates on the suspension rate. Control of foreign news and *a priori* censorship significantly increase the likelihood of suspension both in the total period and during the parliamentary period. Language prohibitions have no effect. The Tsarist regime consistently decreases the likelihood of suspension.

The effects of political content and affiliation differ between the two periods. Independent political status has an effect by significantly decreasing the suspension rate for the entire period. Newspapers affiliated with political parties are no different from nonpolitical papers. During the parliamentary period the effects are reversed, all of the party-affiliated papers are significantly less likely to suspend publication, while independent political papers have the same risk as nonpolitical papers. Electoral support has a small but positive effect on the likelihood of suspension.

The number of prior suspensions consistently increases the probability of suspension, while age consistently decreases the likelihood of suspension. The number of prior suppressions has no effect on the suspension rate. Of the product characteristics, only general coverage has a consistent effect. Both overall and during the parliamentary period general newspapers are more likely to suspend operations. Frequency of publication slightly decreases the suspension rate for the total observation period but not for the parliamentary period. None of the other product attributes has any effect.

DISCUSSION

Government control generally has effects of the sort we predicted. Control of foreign news consistently has detrimental effects on newspapers. *A priori* censorship has less robust effects across the two time periods, but nonetheless they are systematically detrimental. The fact that statutes limiting publication exhibit no effects may be due to wording and timing— too little and too late as it were. The statutes allowed text aimed at economic benefit and religious text to be published in Finnish. It may be that newspapers could circumvent the statutes by including some commercial and religious content. The timing of the statutes may also be a factor. The

Table 9–2. Effects of Covariates on Failure, Suppression, and Suspension Rates.

Event	State Intervention			Regime		Political Affiliation				
	Foreign News	A Priori Censorship	Language Law	Tsarist Regime	Republic	Independent	Left Wing	Center	Right Wing	Electoral Support
Failure	1.309[a] (0.162)	0.168 (0.107)	0.157 (0.260)	0.423 (1.021)	1.564 (1.007)	0.007 (0.195)	−1.103[a] (0.214)	−0.910[a] (0.168)	−0.618[a] (0.188)	NA
Failure	1.052[a] (0.219)	0.343[a] (0.145)	NA	−0.856[a] (0.226)	NA	0.049 (0.210)	−0.913[a] (0.303)	−0.524[a] (0.198)	−0.315 (0.266)	−0.001 (0.008)
Suppression	1.309[a] (0.337)	1.026[a] (0.194)	−11.070 (99.000)	11.050 (50.300)	10.940 (50.300)	−.0526 (0.465)	1.111[a] (0.375)	−0.213 (0.263)	−2.170[a] (0.737)	NA
Suppression	2.967[a] (0.665)	−10.160 (110.300)	NA	−0.155 (0.516)	NA	1.364[a] (0.614)	5.088[a] (0.633)	1.703[a] (0.534)	0.555 (1.902)	−0.121[a] (0.017)
Suspension	1.508[a] (0.303)	0.567[a] (0.205)	0.805 (0.493)	−2.381[a] (0.810)	−0.656 (0.745)	−0.883[a] (0.383)	0.260 (0.348)	0.005 (0.287)	0.001 (0.368)	NA
Suspension	1.583[a] (0.326)	0.803[a] (0.254)	NA	−2.176[a] (0.372)	NA	−0.566 (0.405)	−2.100[a] (0.753)	−0.905[a] (0.425)	−1.014[a] (0.497)	0.060[a] (0.018)

	Prior History			Product Characteristics			
	Cumulative Suppressions	Cumulative Suspensions	Age	Finnish Language	General Coverage	Multiple Contents	Frequency of Publication
Failure	0.189[a] (0.008)	0.111 (0.008)	−0.001[a] (0.000)	0.054 (0.125)	0.470[a] (0.109)	0.327 (0.225)	0.001 (0.001)
Failure	0.154 (0.100)	0.120 (0.086)	−0.001[a] (0.000)	−0.124 (0.169)	0.389[a] (0.137)	0.273 (0.230)	−0.0001 (0.005)
Suppression	0.406[a] (0.033)	0.187[a] (0.083)	−0.0001[a] (0.000)	−0.188 (0.233)	0.403 (0.227)	0.603 (0.397)	−0.002[a] (0.001)
Suppression	0.233[a] (0.067)	0.183 (0.132)	0.000 (0.000)	1.794[a] (0.682)	−1.115[a] (0.447)	1.839[a] (0.469)	−0.004[a] (0.001)
Suspension	−0.042 (0.103)	0.494[a] (0.057)	−0.0002[a] (0.000)	0.355 (0.253)	0.925[a] (0.219)	0.355 (0.375)	−0.003[a] (0.001)
Suspension	0.111 (0.106)	0.459[a] (0.063)	−0.0002[a] (0.000)	−0.251 (0.292)	0.716[a] (0.264)	0.765 (0.402)	−0.0004 (0.001)

Note: Standard errors in parentheses.
[a]Significant at $p < .05$.

statutes were imposed after the Finnish language had taken hold as an important aspect of nationalism and during a period of growth in the newspaper population. The bulk of the new newspapers were printed in Finnish. It is possible that the increased volume may have temporarily exceeded the capacity of the Tsarist censors. Furthermore, the statutes may have been laxly enforced during the relatively liberal reign of Alexander II.

Although the regime variables have some significant effects, they are not consistent with our predictions. The life chances of newspapers are generally much worse during the independent Republic than under the Tsarist regime. The failure rate is either the same under the two regimes or, in the case of the parliamentary period, higher during the Republic.

The political environment appears to be much harsher during the Republic than during the Tsarist regime. In almost all cases, the effects of state intervention are stronger during the parliamentary period (which consists largely of the Republic). The same holds true for the effects of political affiliation. During the parliamentary period the "specialist premium" of political affiliation on the failure rate is smaller, and the effects of political content and affiliation on the suppression rate is larger. It may be that the newness of the independent state and the internal political turmoil that resulted from the civil war led to a much greater perception of threat on the part of the state apparatus during the Republic than that perceived by the Tsars.

With some important exceptions, political affiliation shapes the press in the ways we expected. In the Finnish press, party-affiliated newspapers are either less likely to fail or, at worst, no more likely to fail than nonpolitical or independent political newspapers. The survival premium found among newspapers affiliated with a political party seems to stem from a subsidization of resources rather than an assured audience from the party membership of sympathetic voters; there is no independent effect for size of electoral support. Furthermore, the size of electoral support is positively related to the likelihood of suspension. This suggests that large segments of the polity engender higher levels of competition among political newspapers attempting to base a readership in that segment. All in all, whether or not a newspaper has an affiliation is more consequential than the identity of the partner.

Political newspapers are more likely to be suppressed by the state than their counterparts, with the exception of right-wing newspapers. And, as we predicted, size of electoral support is negatively related to the probability of suppression. The suspension rate is significantly smaller for party-affiliated newspapers. This suggests that it is not used as a means of avoiding suppression by the state.

In general, our findings highlight the importance of the sociocultural environment in analyzing population processes among organizations.

Models of the development of the press that neglect the role of the state do so at their own peril. In Finland, attempts at control by the state operated as a strong selection mechanism both directly on the failure rate and indirectly through the suppression rate. The effects of political affiliation are contrary to the predictions of the economic model of press development. The economic model predicts a greater risk of failure for newspapers that reflect party loyalty rather than adopting a strategy of audience-maximization through noncontroversial content. Our results are supportive of the resource partitioning/party structure models. The effects of political affiliation also highlight the importance of examining aspects of the institutional environment other than the state. In Finland, position on political issues and relationships with other organizations in the political environment had an important impact on the life chances of newspapers.

10 ORGANIZATIONAL AND ELECTORAL PARADOXES OF THE KNIGHTS OF LABOR

Glenn R. Carroll and Yangchung Paul Huo

Labor historians and others have traditionally analyzed the Knights of Labor—that strange but popular reform organization of the late nineteenth century—within the context of national events and developments, especially those of the national labor movement. For instance, the Knights of Labor is generally acknowledged to be "the first organization to unify large sections of the working class and present a solid front against oppressors" (Foner 1955:170). The Knights are also credited with successfully introducing into the labor movement a number of progressive social innovations such as equal treatment for women and black workers (Beard 1930; Foner 1955; Grob 1961). And, perhaps most important, the experiences of the class-based, reform-minded Knights are frequently discussed in explanations of the subsequent pragmatic character of U.S. labor unions (Perlman 1918; Ware 1929; Grob 1961; Ulman 1961).

One major consequence of these scholarly efforts is the depiction—either explicitly through description or implicitly through assumption—of the Knights of Labor as a single, unified, national organizational entity.

This research was supported in part by the Institute of Industrial Relations, University of California, Berkeley (George Strauss, director), and by the Max-Planck-Institut für Bildungsforschung, Berlin (Karl Ulrich Mayer, executive director). We are grateful to Brian Rowan for bringing the data used here to our attention and for several stimulating conversations about the Knights of Labor. For helpful comments on an earlier draft, we wish to thank Jacques Delacroix, Mike Hannan, Judy Salamon, and George Strauss.

The typical depiction (Beard 1930; Foner 1947, 1955) describes the Knights of Labor in terms of its total national membership, its national leaders, and the policies of its national office. As an actor in the national labor movement, the Knights of Labor is usually analyzed in relation to its national competitors, the trade unions (Grob 1958; Ulman 1961). By the standard historical treatment (Perlman 1918; Ware 1929), even the rise and fall of the union itself is accounted for in terms of several national clashes between the Knights' leader, Terrence V. Powderly, and the nine-teenth-century monopolist, Jay Gould.

Although useful for analyzing the Knights' overall relationship with the U.S. labor movement, the unified organizational characterization is both incomplete and misleading. This failing is most clearly evident in the enigmatic quality of the union's life cycle as presented by the standard national history. Although founded in 1869, the Knights of Labor emerges on the national scene in the mid-1880s. It quickly becomes the largest labor union the country has ever known (by some accounts, with over a million members), but it collapses even more quickly than it emerged. Such an unlikely history begs the question: How did such a large organi-zation, representing interests so contrary to those of the dominant class, rise and fall so quickly in a time when long-distance communication and travel were still problematic? Are we to believe that, in a period when the local community and its social, intellectual, and political orientation reigned supreme, national events can account for the Knights' rapid rise and demise? Or is it possible that the perspective itself generates the or-ganizational history that seems so hard to explain?

We contend that the problem lies with the perspective. In our opinion, conventional analyses of the Knights of Labor generally overlook the union's real organizational dimensions and instead use idealized organizational assumptions that square neatly with the national level of analysis.[1] These highly questionable assumptions include a strong and effective centralized structure of authority; structural homogeneity among the subunits of the organization; tight coupling of the fates of the subunits; and a greater dependence of the subunits for resources on the national office than on the local environment. The net result is that "the national focus presents from the outset a circumscribed view of . . . the life of local assemblies, the heart of the Knights organization" (Fink 1983: 19).

Following Garlock (1974), Fink (1983), and Conell and Voss (1982), we argue that to understand the Knights of Labor as an organizational entity, to understand its social dynamics, its rise and fall, one must ana-lyze the union's basic organizational unit—the local assembly. As Garlock has demonstrated, focusing on the local assemblies yields a very different organizational image. The character of the Knights seems different: Evi-dently, more local assemblies were organized along conventional trade union lines than along the lines of the celebrated mixed trade union. The Knights of Labor also appears larger and more stable, and its period of influence is apparently much longer—in part because the decline occurs much more slowly. Consider that, in 1894, by which time the Knights have disappeared from most national-level analyses, 562 local assemblies, representing over 60,000 members were still in operation (Garlock 1974: 38, 230). What is perhaps even more startling, approximately 3,000 new local assemblies had been established since the alleged collapse of the Knights in 1888 (Garlock 1974: 36).

Despite these breakthroughs, we believe that the surface has barely been scratched for an organizationally informed interpretation of the Knights. In particular, we believe that the relationship between the local assembly and its local setting has yet to be investigated thoroughly. Consequently, we have undertaken, and report here the findings of, a systematic empirical study of over 11,000 local assemblies of the Knights of Labor. Our focus is on the longevity of the local assembly. We concentrate on the effects of various general organizational and political strategies of the local assembly. In regard to organizing strategies, we examine the consequences of organizational niche width (breadth of membership base) and local reorganization. In regard to political strategies, we examine the consequences of location near formal political bodies and of active, organized involvement in the local electoral process.

Obviously, the analysis should interest those concerned substantively with the Knights of Labor and the early U.S. labor movement. By focusing on the mortality rates of organizations in different environmental settings and with different organizational strategies, the study also falls squarely within the domain of organizational ecology (Hannan and Freeman 1977, 1984; Carroll 1984). In this respect the study has important theoretical implications: The findings reported here show, in answer to many critics (Perrow 1979), that arguments positing an environmental selection process can be invoked without resorting to concepts of effectiveness or efficiency. Indeed, we will focus explicitly on political criteria of selection and, in so doing, demonstrate that political success at the local level—which no doubt caused much jubilation among contemporaries—in fact ultimately led to failure at the organizational level.

ORGANIZATIONAL STRATEGIES

From its beginning in 1869, the Noble and Holy Order of the Knights of Labor of America was conceived to be broad in membership base and reformist in purpose. The membership base was defined to include all workers—unskilled as well as skilled—except for politicians, physicians, lawyers, and those engaged in the production or sale of liquor (politicians and physicians were later allowed; bankers, stockbrokers, and professional gamblers were later excluded). The goals of the organization were radical: the abolition of the wage system, the demonopolization of capital, and the establishment of a cooperative society of worker-producers. These transformations were to be achieved with moderate, nonconfrontational tactics. Strikes and other hostile work actions were not acceptable. Instead, the Knights were to rely on good-natured reform to be achieved through the secret organization of workers and the education of the public.

In principle, any person who did not hold one of the excluded occupations could join the Knights of Labor. Local assemblies were required only to have at least ten members, three-fourths of whom had to be employed workers. Membership records show that many nonworkers, especially small producers, did indeed join (Foner 1955: 55). However, they could not join any particular local assembly, neither could any given worker. Openness was a fundamental variable in local organizing strategies.

Local assemblies of the Knights adopted one of two different basic organizing strategies, referred to commonly as trade and mixed local assemblies. The trade local assembly was composed of workers from a single trade, usually involved in skilled or semiskilled work. Members of the trade local might be employed by one or several local employers, and, as would be expected under such conditions, their purposes in organizing tended to be pragmatic. They viewed the local assembly's main function as collective bargaining and consequently used it primarily to push for issues such as higher wages and an eight-hour work day. Dealing primarily with such job-related issues, the trade locals operated much as any trade union might, which means they were regularly forced to resort to strikes.

Because of their pragmatic orientation and confrontational tactics, the trade locals were treated ambivalently by the reform-minded national leaders of the Knights. As applicants for new assemblies, trade groups usually did in fact receive authorization. However, the motivation was not sympathy for their goals but simply the desire to bring more workers into the Order. Once admitted, the trade locals were frequently discriminated against (for example, by exclusion from the General Executive Board). Often, pressure was exerted to move the local trade closer to the mixed model. This ambivalent treatment, the lack of national support for their tactics, and the lack of a unified national base severely inhibited the effective operation of the trade locals within the Knights of Labor (Foner 1955; Grob 1961).

The mixed local presented a real contrast. It recruited workers from a broad cross-section of occupations and industries, including both skilled and unskilled workers. Such a diverse group probably had so few common practical problems that it is doubtful whether they could have effectively organized around such issues even if they had wanted to (Grob 1958:

177). But they rarely wanted to. The mixed locals typically embodied the reformist spirit of the national organization. Their goal was to abolish the wage system through the organization and education of workers, and the establishment of cooperative enterprises. As a consequence, the mixed local was favored by the national leaders of the Knights, the General Executive Board, and even the General Assembly.

Of course, in some areas, especially rural ones, there were so few skilled workers of a single trade that there was no choice but to organize as a mixed assembly. But as Garlock (1974) has shown, the mixed assembly also flourished in urban areas where organizing along trade lines was a viable option. Nevertheless, for most of the history of the Knights, the trade form still dominated both in numbers and in weight of members. Trade assemblies flourished first among miners and then later among manufacturing workers. Their habitat was the city: 44 percent were in metropolitan areas with populations of over 90,000; another 28 percent were located in cities with 8,000 to 90,000 persons. Although the mixed assembly was more popular in the rural areas, its presence in the cities was far from insignificant: 11 percent were located in the metropolitan areas, 22 percent in cities between 8,000 and 90,000 persons. In the overall make-up of the Knights, the two organizational forms of the local assembly alternate in prevalence: first the trade form dominates, then the mixed form, and finally the trade form again.

Niche Width

It is useful to conceptualize the differences between the trade and mixed local assemblies in terms of organizational niche width (Freeman and Hannan 1983; Carroll 1985). Specialist organizations, such as the trade local assemblies, rely on a narrow set of resources for membership and sustenance. By contrast, generalist organizations, like the mixed local assemblies, draw from a diverse set of resources. Given an area with a sufficient number of workers in a particular trade, one might expect specialist local assemblies to be easier to organize and maintain because of their common identities and problems. Communication with and within such a homogeneous group would probably be easier as well. However, the specialist local assembly also presented an easily identifiable and vulnerable target—a single employer could often wipe it out. In the late nineteenth century such considerations were important because employers would resort to almost any means in fighting organized workers.

Conversely, the generalist local assembly, being less homogeneous, lacked a strong common basis of appeal to potential members, especially given the precedents of solidarity among the working class at the time. It is thus likely that the generalist local assembly, in comparison to the specialist form, had greater ideological and practical problems in establishing and maintaining itself. However, at the same time, the generalist local assembly must have been less vulnerable and must have offered greater security against employers—to attack it meant to attack a wide section of the working-class community.

So depicted, there existed an organizational tension in the tradeoffs between the two forms: those factors that facilitated solidarity and internal cohesion led to external vulnerability and, conversely, those factors that facilitated external hardiness made it difficult to maintain internal solidarity and cohesion. Because the consequences of such tradeoffs are not understood at all, we undertook the empirical analysis without prior expectations as to which of these opposing effects would be stronger. However, we did realize that it was not necessary to posit a single monotonic effect across the entire life of the local assembly. In fact, it seemed quite likely that internal cohesion would be more important at some stages of the organizational life cycle, while external invulnerability would be more important at other times.

Reorganization

One other potentially important organizational factor, which to our knowledge has not been analyzed before, concerns the difference between local assemblies that were "pioneers" in their locations and those that were established in places where a similar assembly had existed before but had subsequently lapsed. A substantial number of reorganized versions of previously established local assemblies are identified by Garlock (1973). It is likely that the experiences of these units differed from those of the pioneers for a number of reasons. First, the reorganized locals were no longer innovations in their areas as their earlier counterparts had been. Because such locals could draw on the experience of at least some of the previous members, and because the legitimacy of the organizational form was more likely to be already established, the reorganized locals may have had fewer "liabilities of newness" (Stinchcombe 1965). It is also possible that the original organization left behind physical resources that did not have to be mobilized again. Second, reorganized local assemblies could rely on the institutional memory of the local community to avoid mistakes made by the prior assemblies. They could also take advantage of previously established beneficial network linkages. Third, a reorganized local assembly may have been able to reap immediately the benefits of in-roads made by the earlier units—in-roads that may have cost them their lives, as for example, might have happened in a bloody strike.

When combined, these arguments suggest that the reorganized local assemblies may have had substantial institutional advantages over their pioneering predecessors. Economists sometimes use a similar argument, known as the "infant industry argument" to account for the fragility of the first firms in a new industry (see Krueger and Tuncer 1982). We shall see below whether it holds any weight in explaining the longevities of the local assemblies of the Knights of Labor.

POLITICAL STRATEGIES

The inconsistency of the national policies of the Knights is nowhere better illustrated than in the political realm. Powderly and the 1884 Constitution unequivocally pointed out the need to use political action rather than strikes to accomplish the Order's goals (Foner 1955: 81). Yet, at the same time, Powderly was regularly ruling that political action must not be discussed in the local assemblies and that local assemblies must not engage in political activity. The reason, he maintained, was that the Knights of Labor was "higher and grander than party" (quoted in Foner 1955: 81). It is not surprising, then, that "political action (of the Knights of Labor) *as an integrated whole* was negligible" (Foner 1955: 82, emphasis added).

In many areas of the country, the local political experiences of the Knights completely contradicted the national experience: Political action was not only significant but central to the purpose of many local assemblies. Fink (1983) has shown that between 1885 and 1888 the Knights of Labor organized third-party labor tickets and entered elections in 189 towns and cities, located in thirty-four of the then total of thirty-eight states. He writes that "beginning with the early spring municipal elections and symbolically sanctioned by the special General Assembly in June 1886, the Knights flexed their political muscle virtually everywhere they were established" (Fink 1983: 26).

What prompted the Knights to enter local elections given their avowed disdain of everything political? Rarely was the motivation linked to class-related legislation, or to some other such strategy involving positive use of state power. The Knights' agendas were usually quite sparse, promising mainly to return the government to the people by putting clean men with good hearts into office.

In an extremely insightful analysis into the political action of the Knights, Fink (1983) has identified two primary reasons for the involvement of the Knights in local elections. First, politics was often simply a "spillover effect" of the organization of the working class. By bringing together for the first time diverse workers with common grievances directed not (as in the past) against a single employer but against many employers, the Knights' organizations facilitated the workers' identification of politics as their most effective mode of action. The local assembly also provided a ready-made organizational base from which any political plan that might develop could be easily implemented. Second, the local assemblies used politics to curtail outside interference and state repression. After defeat in a strike, politics emerged as a way "to punish your enemies" and to protect yourself from punishment by them.

Political Effects

Both of Fink's reasons suggest that those local assemblies that engaged in organized politics were probably stronger than those that did not. Only an organization with strength in numbers, or strength in solidarity, would experience a complete organizational spillover effect into politics. Only an organization with a strong community base of support would dare to challenge its enemies in a public election. And only an organization with the strength to protect its members could assemble a third-party ticket of reformists with a platform advocating the fundamental transformation of the economic system on which the elites depended. For these reasons, those local assemblies that organized labor party electoral tickets are likely to have lasted longer than those that did not.

Being utopian and reformist, the Knights organizations probably also experienced indirect political effects. Symbolizing the working class and advocating sweeping social reforms surely infused individual Knights with social responsibility and moral righteousness. The effects of such inspirations were probably greater in some areas than others. In rural areas, for instance, the local assembly was probably viewed in isolation from the larger social context. It likely survived only as long as its members believed in its purposes, in its leaders, and in the support of the national organization. It is unlikely that members of such locals considered their personal involvement, or even their local assembly, as either important or particularly symbolic.

State Capitals

Membership and the local assembly probably did take on greater symbolic importance in the state capitals. Here the proximity to the legislature, the governor and other state elites likely gave the members of the local assembly a greater sense of self-importance (after all, they were representing the whole working class to the established elites) and a deeper motivation to maintain the local assembly for symbolic reasons, even if the costs were great. Practical matters, such as the ease of lobbying, may also have been related, but because the Knights' goals were generally not pragmatic, symbolic moral issues probably took priority. If so, then Knights' organizations located in capital cities should have lived longer than those in other places.

Historical evidence (Fink 1983) shows that the capital cities were certainly different. Of the thirty-eight capital cities, thirteen saw labor party tickets develop; two more labor tickets developed in the counties of capital cities. In the 3,500 cities with populations of 1,000 or more at the time, only 176 witnessed labor party tickets. Thus the percentage of capitals with labor party tickets was much greater than the percentage for all cities—34 compared to 5. Labor parties in the capital cities were also more likely to experience electoral victory—the probability being .39 compared to .32 for the noncapitals.

DATA

The data we use here were collected by Garlock (1973) and provide information on every Knights of Labor local assembly leaving any record of its existence in any of numerous primary sources. For each local assembly, Garlock has recorded the dates of founding and dissolution, along with a code indicating the type of source.[2] He has also flagged those assemblies for which one or other of the dates are not known (referred to in the statistical literature as 'censored' cases). Systematic information is also included concerning the organizing strategy of the local assembly (trade or mixed), whether the local is new or reorganized, and the population size of the city in which the assembly is located.

Our interest here is with the longevity of the local assembly. To construct this variable, we subtracted the recorded last date of the assembly from the recorded first date. Cases where the last date was not known were classified as censored. Cases where the first date was not known were dropped from the analysis. From the remaining data, we calculated age-specific death rates using the life-table method (which takes censoring into account). These estimates simply calculate the number dying at a certain age over the number entering the age initially. Previous research on organizational mortality (see Carroll 1983) led us to expect a declining age-dependence in the age-specific mortality estimates, reflecting what Stinchcombe (1965) has called "the liability of newness."

Figure 10–1 shows a plot of the age-specific death rates of the local assemblies. Surprisingly, they show a nonmonotonic pattern of age-dependence: The death rates begin very low, increase sharply, decline again, and then later rise once more. Without the low first year, the pattern might be statistically indiscernible from the usual case of declining age-dependence. Such an observation leads us to suspect that the nonmonotonic pattern may be the consequence of some sort of bureaucratic reporting rule embedded in Garlock's sources. However, it may also be real. Aldrich and Staber (1983) and Tucker, Singh, and House (1984) both report periods of increasing age-dependence in rates of organizational mortality.

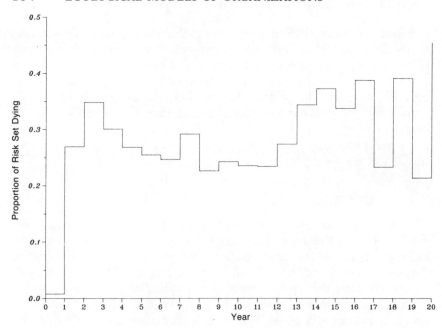

Figure 10-1. Proportion of Local Assemblies Dying at Each Age.

What their data have in common with these data is that they both concern nonbusiness, nonmarket organizations. Aldrich and Staber (1983) studied business interest associations. Tucker, Singh, and House (1984) studied voluntary social service organizations. It could be that such nonprofit organizations escape severe selection pressures in their first several years of existence. Because we regard this as a plausible hypothesis, we tentatively accept the nonmonotonic pattern as real and model it accordingly.

As discussed above, we are primarily concerned with the effects of four independent variables: the two organizing strategy variables of niche width and reorganization; the two political variables of capital city location and organized third-party electoral involvement. To measure niche width and reorganization status, we used information in Garlock's data. We defined as specialist organizations all those local assemblies that were organized on a single trade basis; all others we regarded as generalists. We compared specialist local assemblies with generalist ones by using a dummy variable that takes the value of one for single-trade local assemblies and zero for all others. For reorganization status, we relied directly on Garlock's coding and used an integer variable that indicates the number of times the local assembly was previously organized.

For the two political variables, we used other sources. To identify capital cities and their counties, we consulted historical census materials (some capitals have moved). To identify those places where the local assemblies organized labor party election tickets, we used the information listed in Fink (1983: 28–29), which was compiled using a variety of primary sources. For both pieces of political information, we again constructed dummy variables for use in the analysis.

MODELS

One way of examining the effects of these independent variables on the longevity of the local assemblies might be regressing longevity, or perhaps its logarithm, on the other variables. Despite its intuitive appeal, this method is fraught with serious problems. Specifically, such a regression cannot adequately treat the censored cases, does not plausibly specify the disturbance term, constrains each independent variable to have a single effect across the entire lifetime of the local assembly, and cannot model properly the functional form of age-dependence in the death rates (an issue of concern here). Individually, each of these problems has potentially serious consequences; together they are almost certain to generate biased estimates. Therefore, we adopt event-history methods and use the instantaneous rate of death as the dependent variable. Rate models have the advantage of being flexible in specification, and they are relatively insensitive to the censoring problem when properly estimated (Tuma and Hannan 1984). On an intuitive level, one can think of them as inversely predicting the longevity of an organization: The higher the rate, the lower the expected lifetime, and vice versa.

Modern analysts frequently use a rate model known as Makeham's Law to study organizational mortality (see, for example, Carroll and Delacroix 1982; Freeman, Carroll, and Hannan 1983). Makeham's Law captures well the common phenomenon of declining age-dependence and can be used to estimate the effects of covariates from within such a context. We have seen above, however, that data on the local assemblies of the Knights of Labor do not display the usual form of age-dependence—or for that matter, any apparent form of monotonic age-dependence. For this reason, we do not use Makeham's Law or any other parametric form of the rate that assumes monotonic age-dependence (as almost all do). Instead, we use a model that allows the rate to vary freely—up or down—in consecutive age periods but that constrains the rate to be constant within any single age period. This model, which might be described as a constant rate model with time-period effects, has the advantage of not prespecifying the nature of age dependence. Instead, it allows the effects of covariates to vary across age periods. Although it is more general than Makeham's Law, it also has more parameters.

Because any number of age periods can be specified for this model, our first task was to develop a baseline model for the pattern of age-dependence shown in Figure 10–1. Our goal was to find the most parsimonious model (meaning fewest parameters and therefore fewest age periods) that could be used to examine the effects of the independent variables. We began with a twenty-one-period model, where each age from ages 1 to 20 was defined as a separate period. We tried numerous other specifications, including an eleven-period model where each age from ages 1 to 10 was defined as a separate period. We also tried specifications with fewer time periods. The models were estimated with Tuma's (1980) RATE computer program. Because alternative specifications were always hierarchically nested within other models, we used the *Chi* square likelihood ratio test to compare the various models. After extensive searching, we concluded that the best baseline model was one that included seven time periods defined around the ages 0 to 1 year; 1 to 2 years; 2 to 3 years; 3 to 6 years; 6 to 7 years; 7 to 10 years; and over 10 years. We will use this framework to examine the effects of the independent variables in the analysis below.

ANALYSIS

Table 10–1 presents estimates of the effects of the four organizing and political strategy variables on the rates of death of local assemblies. It is worth noting at the outset that the statistically significant effects of these variables are more common in the early ages than in the later ones. This pattern supports the argument advanced by Carroll and Delacroix (1982) that

Table 10–1. Maximum Likelihood Estimates of Effects of Organizing and Political Strategy Variables on Rates of Death of Local Assemblies (standard errors shown in parentheses).[a]

Independent Variables	Age in Years						
	0–1	1–2	2–3	3–6	6–7	7–10	>10
Constant	−1.66[b]	−.904[b]	−1.04[b]	−1.33[b]	−1.32[b]	−1.33[b]	−.976[b]
	(.040)	(.036)	(.050)	(.046)	(.107)	(.086)	(.104)
Specialist	.273[b]	−.196[b]	−.175[b]	.029	.141	−.142	−.263[b]
	(.048)	(.047)	(.063)	(.056)	(.126)	(.105)	(.123)
Reorganized	.025	.0001	.171[b]	−.066	.297[b]	.058	−.197
	(.058)	(.068)	(.085)	(.079)	(.151)	(.151)	(.171)
Capital city	−.190[b]	.113	.028	.124	.182	.346	−.203
	(.092)	(.082)	(.177)	(.095)	(.222)	(.190)	(.277)
Labor party	−.190[b]	−.133[b]	−.220[b]	−.074	−.122	−.131	−.090
	(.048)	(.049)	(.065)	(.054)	(.120)	(.104)	(.119)

[a]Overall *Chi*^{2} value of this model relative to a single-period constant rate model is 429.9 with 34 degress of freedom. N = 11,851.

[b]$p \leq 0.5$.

selection pressures operate with greatest force on new and young organizations. It also supports the covariate specification of Makeham's Law advocated by Freeman, Carroll, and Hannan (1983) for the study of organizational mortality.

Based on the previous research of Freeman and Hannan (1983) and Carroll (1985), we had expected that the niche width variable indicating specialism would show directionally consistent (although not necessarily monotonic) effects across the age periods. The syncopating pattern of effects found here is thus apparently paradoxical—although, we believe, plausible. Remember that these effects are estimated relative to the generalist organizational form. The estimates, therefore, imply that specialist local assemblies have higher initial death rates in the first year, then lower rates in the next two years. After the third year, no significant differences are observed until after ten years of age. At a general theoretical level, this finding is important because it shows, for the first time (at least to our knowledge), that an organizational strategy that has beneficial consequences during one phase of the organizational life cycle may also have negative consequences at a later phase. For the local assemblies of the Knights of Labor, these effects can be explained by drawing on our earlier discussion regarding the advantages and disadvantages of specialism. Recall that we argued that specialist local assemblies are particularly vulnerable to hostile forces but that they are also likely to generate high internal solidarity. The vulnerablity is apparently greatest in the first year, which makes a great deal of sense for at least two reasons. First, solidarity takes time to build, and one year may not be a sufficiently long period in many situations. Second, employers often attempt to squash new unions immediately after they are established by firing all the involved employees. The establishment of the union may also be associated with risky and daring labor actions. In such situations, internal solidarity is undoubtedly important, but it is probably not the decisive factor. If, however, the trade union survives this precarious first year and establishes its right of existence, then its fate is likely to depend on its internal cohesiveness. The mixed trade local, in contrast, usually poses no initial threat to anyone, although its diversity may create solidarity problems. The enthusiasm surrounding its founding probably holds it together for the first year—or at least prevents it from dying as fast as trade locals are being squashed—but then its diversity begets faster dissolution than in the specialist local.

The findings for the reorganized locals also differ from our expectations. We argued earlier that the institutional changes created by previously established local assemblies would likely increase the life chances of subsequently reorganized local assemblies. The estimates show the reverse to be true: Reorganized local assemblies show higher death rates than initially established ones—but only in two later age groups. One plausible explanation for this pattern is that those areas where local assemblies are reestablished are also areas hostile to the Knights. In more receptive areas, the original local assemblies thrive and never need to be reestablished. In the hostile areas, the reestablished locals may live longer than their previously established counterparts; however, both may, on the average, live less long than initial assemblies in more receptive areas. Another possible explanation for these findings, suggested by Hannan and Freeman (1984), recognizes that the hazards of reorganization may be as great, if not greater than, the initial liability of newness. Mediation between the two alternative explanations would require more detailed data on the degree of continuity between the initial and reorganized local assemblies.

Capital city location of the local assembly shows the expected negative effect on the rate of death. However, because this effect is significant only in the first year of existence, our earlier argument concerning the symbolic behavior of capital-city Knights seems less plausible—we would expect that attempts to make a symbolic statement would involve later periods as well. Instead, this finding suggests that local assemblies in capital cities were somehow protected in their first year of existence. If our earlier statement about employers attempting to squash local assemblies in the first year is accurate, then it may be that, because of the presence of governmental and executive officials who work and reside in capital cities, and because the legitimacy of the government depends on the appearance of propriety when such officials are present, employers refrain—or are restrained from—taking the strong measures that they might exercise elsewhere. In short, the radical tactics used elsewhere against new local assemblies were probably less likely to be used in the capital cities where authorities would be forced to take an unpopular stand.

The other political variable, indicating the presence of a labor party in the county, also shows a significant negative effect. Moreover, this effect persists through the first three years of existence and thus strongly supports our earlier argument that those local assemblies that organized local political parties would show greater longevity. Of course, the question of cause and effect remains open. It could be that only strong local assemblies organize labor parties and the association is, in a sense, spurious (this interpretation is implied Fink's spillover effect argument). Or it could be that, once organized, the labor party provides protection to the local assembly (this interpretation is implied by Fink's protection argument). With the available data, direct discrimination between the two interpretations is not possible. However, an indirect test may be conducted using additional information available in Fink concerning which labor parties experienced electoral victories. If the labor party provided protection to the local assembly, then we might expect its position to be even further enhanced when the labor party assumes the local political apparatus.

On the other hand, if the labor party was simply the consequence of the organizational strength of the local assembly, then taking over the local regime may have few additional benefits. In any event, looking at the effects of labor party victory on the longevity of the local assembly should further our understanding of the political dynamics of the local Knights of Labor.

Table 10–2 presents estimates of the model with a dummy variable for electoral victory included. First, note that inclusion of this variable strengthens the effects of the labor party variable: It shows five significant coefficients here as compared to three before, and the absolute value of each of the significant coefficients is greater here. The victory variable shows significant effects in three separate time periods. Its effects are always positive. The absolute values of its significant coefficients are always larger than those of the corresponding coefficients of the labor party variable. Moreover, the absolute value of the combined effect of all of its significant coefficients is greater than the same total for the labor party variable.[3] That is, the disadvantageous effects of winning the election more than override the advantageous effects of organizing the labor party in the first place. Or, stated differently, losing the election has better consequences for the longevity of the local assembly than does winning. In fact, then, the local assemblies are actually losing by winning.

Table 10–2. Maximum Likelihood Estimates of Effects of Electoral Victory on Rates of Death of Local Assemblies (standard errors shown in parentheses).[a]

Independent Variables	Age in Years						
	0–1	1–2	2–3	3–6	6–7	7–10	>10
Constant	−1.68[b]	−.905[b]	−1.05[b]	−1.34[b]	−1.31[b]	−1.36[b]	−.979[b]
	(.041)	(.036)	(.050)	(.046)	(.107)	(.087)	(.105)
Specialist	.295[b]	−.193[b]	−.166[b]	.046	.130	−.088	−.258[b]
	(.048)	(.048)	(.064)	(.056)	(.127)	(.106)	(.126)
Reorganized	.026	.001	.172[b]	−.062	.297	.062	−.186
	(.058)	(.068)	(.085)	(.080)	(.151)	(.151)	(.171)
Capital city	−.181[b]	.113	.029	.128	.179	.327	−.203
	(.092)	(.082)	(.177)	(.095)	(.222)	(.190)	(.277)
Labor party	−.324[b]	−.143[b]	−.253[b]	−.123[b]	−.095	−.263[b]	−.098
	(.055)	(.054)	(.072)	(.059)	(.127)	(.115)	(.124)
Victory	.458[b]	.040	.133	.290[b]	−.148	.537[b]	.057
	(.081)	(.090)	(.119)	(.095)	(.246)	(.174)	(.249)

[a]Overall Chi^2 value of this model relative to a single-period constant rate model is 475.3 with 41 degress of freedom. N = 11,851.

[b]$p \leq 0.5$.

What is behind such an apparent paradox? Can it be believed? We contend that not only is this finding plausible but that it is the result of entirely rational social processes. As Fink (1983) has insightfully observed, control of the local government could in no way solve the self-defined social problem around which the Knights organized—namely, monopoly capital. Moreover, the Knights' disdain for conventional politics led them to organize and behave as though they were above the political process (even when they were becoming most political). Their primary motivation for entering the political arena was "to rescue society from the depredations of politics" (quoted in Fink 1983: 32). Their primary goal was to "send men 'untrammelled' and 'closely identified with the struggling masses' into office to clean things up" (quoted in Fink 1983: 33). The devastating consequence of such utopian positions was that the elected labor party had no workable platform, had few realistic goals, had no experienced politicians, and had few men capable of administering local municipal services. Threatening as it was to the elites, the new working-class regime also led the previously divided opponents to organize and coalesce in hitherto unprecedented ways. The strength of the inexperienced Knights was usually no match at all for these newly consolidated elites. Consequently, the effectiveness and legitimacy of the labor regime—and with it that of the local Knights of Labor as well—was quickly undermined. In short, by winning the election, local Knights were asked to deliver the goods they had promised— something they were ill-equipped to do but that they probably could not have done anyway given the nature of the promises and the power of the opponents. Sociologically speaking, one might say that the outcome of their organizational strength could not be transformed into a strong organizational outcome.

DISCUSSION

We began by arguing for an analysis of the Knights of Labor that focused not on the national organization and its leaders—as so many previous analyses have done—but, instead, on the basic organizational unit, the local assembly. One major premise of our argument held that the local assemblies, being heterogeneous and existing in heterogeneous environments, would show systematic variations in longevity. Understanding such variations in the rise and fall of the Knights' organizational structure, we argued, would yield new insights into the dynamics of the nineteenth-century labor movement.

The empirical findings presented above show that our arguments were well founded. We have seen that organizational death rates differ greatly between specialist and generalist local assemblies and between politically active and politically passive local assemblies. We also found some weaker evidence of differences between pioneer and reorganized local assemblies, and between those located in capital cities and other areas. Despite numerous analyses of the Knights at the national level, to our knowledge, not one of these findings has been demonstrated convincingly before. Yet each is clearly helpful in understanding the rise and fall of the Knights of Labor.

At a more abstract level, the findings reported here have several important theoretical implications. Theories of organizational strategy typically posit a single directional effect for any given organizational strategy in a given set of environmental conditions (although, of course, the direction usually varies depending on the specific conditions). The potentially paradoxical finding unearthed here, that a strategy such as specialism can have opposing effects at different stages of the organizational life cycle, shows that the conventional way of thinking about organizational strategy is unduly restrictive. Such thinking has evolved most probably because strategy analysts have focused on interactions between organizational form and environmental conditions to the exclusion of life-cycle phenomena. Clearly, we see now that it is important for both types of factors to be considered.

Our findings here also speak to the critics of organizational ecology, who have alleged that a selection perspective must rely on post hoc arguments of efficiency or effectiveness (Perrow 1979). Organizational ecology has also been criticized for allegedly assuming that organizations only react to their environments and do not proactively participate in them. We have seen here that these criticisms are not necessarily warranted. Few things could be more proactive than organizing a local political party and running in an election. Victorious parties, in fact, transformed the local environment so much that one might say that they became their own local political environments. Moreover, the environmental selection mechanisms at work in these processes were political and organizational, not economic.[4] Indeed, thinking about the local assemblies in terms of efficiency seems ridiculous. Effectiveness entails an even worse problem: It leads to the wrong conclusions; for we have seen that those local assemblies that were most "effective" politically signed, in reality, their own death warrants. This dilemma, which we have described as an apparent paradox, is to our knowledge the first organizational demonstration of how selection pressures at different levels of analysis can work at cross-purposes. When locals succeeded politically, the national organization began losing viability.

Deeper substantive insight into the apparent paradox of electoral success can be gained by studying the cases presented in Fink (1983). For each of six cities, Fink presents detailed analyses of the Knights' political activities, including their platforms, leaders, supporters, and performance in office. He also describes the reactions and activities of their opponents.

Because he chooses for study only cities where the labor parties are victorious, Fink could not compare the effects of victory and defeat on the local assemblies. Consequently, he fails to recognize the greater longevity of the local assemblies in areas where the labor parties were electorally unsuccessful. For this reason, he generally attributes the collapse of the labor parties in these areas to a prior decline in the local popularity of the Knights. Although this depiction correctly associates the political involvement of the Knights with their demise, it fails to see the prior reverse causal connection between local party rise and assembly fall—a connection that could be surmised only in a comparative perspective. Nonetheless, Fink's cases are highly instructive because they clearly show some of the different reasons that the Knights' electoral successes undermined the Order's legitimacy: These include

1. The lack of a pragmatic and implementable platform;
2. The political inexperience of the elected Knights;
3. The inability of the political coalition to accommodate the demands of its various diverse constituents;
4. The increased organization and scale of action of local employer opponents;
5. The corruption and goal displacement of elected leaders.

As Fink argues convincingly, not all this was for naught—in many locations the Knights fundamentally transformed local politics. Before their involvement, local politics was an elitist activity; local social and economic elites coincided with local political elites. After the Knights' participation, local politics shifted toward the masses, whose leaders were elected regularly. Despite these changes, local ex-leaders of the Knights must have looked back on the lost promise of the Gilded Age and sadly recalled the words of Friedrich Nietzsche, "Success has always been a great liar."

NOTES

1. We will not review here the standard historical accounts of the Knights of Labor. A detailed review and critique can be found in Carroll and Huo (1985). A general historical overview can be drawn from a variety of sources including Beard (1930), Buhle (1978), Cassity (1979), Dunham (1886), Foner (1947, 1955), Garlock (1974), Grob (1958, 1961), Kemmerer and Wichersham (1950), Meyers (1940), Perlman (1918), Ulman (1961), Ware (1929), and Wright (1887).

2. There are, of course, always questions concerning the reliability and validity of data taken from such old archival sources. Garlock appears to have taken great care in assembling and scrutinizing his data, although he is also careful to acknowledge its potential problems. These include the possible omission of some short-lived local assemblies and possible measurement error in the recorded dates of organizational founding and death. Given the large number of short-lived local

assemblies present in the data, we doubt that the extent of the omission is serious, if not totally negligible. For possible measurement error in the time variables, we are consoled by the apparent insensitivity of the methods we use to such problems (see the Monte Carlo studies reported in Tuma and Hannan 1984). Finally, we are optimistic about the general quality of the data because its collection constituted part of Garlock's dissertation in history at the University of Rochester, a fact implying that the effort was approved and monitored by a committee of professional historians.

3. Given the temporal and geographical patterns of diffusion of the Knights' organizations, we were concerned that our estimates might be confounded with differences in city size, national region, and date of establishment. We report in Carroll and Huo (1985) reestimates of the model including control variables for city size, region, and founding cohort. Although these variables do show statistically significant effects, the findings for the substantive variables of interest here remain basically the same.

4. For other examples of selection by political criteria and an initial development of a general ecological argument about political environments, see Carroll, Delacroix, and Goodstein (1988).

11 COMPETITION AND COEXISTENCE IN ORGANIZATIONAL COMMUNITIES
Population Dynamics in Electronic Components Manufacturing

Jack W. Brittain and Douglas R. Wholey

Competition and cooperation are generally cast as opposites, the presence of one excluding the other. "Competitive vs. cooperative" is used in organization theory to classify interorganizational relationships (Thompson 1967; Pfeffer and Salancik 1978), a characterization that has proven useful for understanding how different forms of interaction impact structural variables. This usage is of limited value when the form of the interaction is the dependent variable, however, because it does not capture (1) the asymmetries that can exist in organizational interactions (Hannan and Freeman 1977) and (2) the competitive evolution that accompanies technological development and market expansion (Brittain and Freeman 1980; Carroll and Delacroix 1982; Freeman 1982). These are major concerns in strategy research (Miles and Snow 1978; Porter 1980) and are basic to understanding the role organizations play in social structure (Aldrich 1979; Carroll 1984).

The difficulty inherent in the competitive/cooperative classification scheme is the implicit assumption that organizational interactions are symmetric, an assumption that is inconsistent with what is known about other types of social relationships. For instance, relational asymmetries are taken

The data used in this paper were collected with the support of the National Science Foundation (SES79-12315). The University Research Institute at the University of Texas provided partial support for this project.

for granted in buyer/seller interactions and are fundamental to theories that incorporate relative power, whether they concern monopolists and victimized consumers or film moguls and naive starlets. Competitive and cooperative strategic asymmetries are more difficult to observe because they do not involve explicit exchanges. Nevertheless, they are important where organizations depend on common market and knowledge resources but have different levels of control over resource acquisition.

Competitive asymmetries are also generated over time as organizations respond to environmental variations. Asymmetries develop because the strategic positions organizations occupy relative to unfolding events differ, and as a result they face different competitive problems. The dynamics of this process are clear in the following example. A few years ago, one of the authors and another driver were pulled over by a California Highway Patrol officer for "racing." The author involved correctly discerned that the California legislature frowns on racing—the citation given to the other driver—and so admitted the speeding violation but suggested the officer reconsider the racing allegation. The author was observed speeding before the other vehicle gave chase and continued at the same rate of speed, while the second driver was clearly attempting to gain ground by weaving through traffic and varying his speed. The logic is straightforward and was accepted by the CHP officer: The other driver's behavior indicated he was racing, whereas the author was simply speeding.

There is little difference between this speeder/racer competition and the strategic competition in high-technology industries (Tilton 1971; Wilson, Ashton, and Egan 1980). As with innovation leaders and late entrants (Brittain and Freeman 1980), the speeder sometimes makes it easier for the racer to succeed by clearing traffic and identifying productive paths. In other instances the speeder's lead is so great that the racer is merely absorbing the risk and consequences of failure. Both situations are "competitive" as defined by conventional usage in organization theory, but the organizations involved face different strategic problems.[1]

Although it is conceptually clear that competitive and cooperative relationships may be asymmetric, the implications for industrial development and strategic diversity are not obvious. We explore this further with an analysis of the electronic components industry. The rate of technical change in this industry has compressed dramatic processes of strategic succession into a relatively brief historical period, making it easier to observe how market changes and innovation impact competitive structure. Furthermore, electronic components have historically moved quickly from innovative design to commodity product, accelerating competitive processes that take decades to unfold for other types of organizations (Carroll and Delacroix 1982; Delacroix and Carroll 1983). We use an ecological framework to characterize competition in the industry and a modeling technique developed by Carroll (1981) to analyze the dynamics of the industry's competitive structure.

COMPETITION AND COMPETITIVE STRUCTURE

Organization and management theory are curiously ambivalent in their treatment of competition. Although theoretical discussions invariably include some competitive survival imperative (Thompson 1967; Child 1972; Pfeffer and Salancik 1978; Aldrich 1979), competition's effects are largely unexplored.[2] In part this is because the meaning of *competition* is not always clear, and existing theoretical treatments are amorphous. In some cases potential competitors and substitutable goods are included in the competitive set (Porter 1980), while in other discussions competition is equivalent to a zero-sum game among interchangeable players (Carroll 1985).

Direct competition is downplayed in organization theory (Perrow 1979; Scott 1981), especially competition that is "red of tooth and claw." Such aggressive competitive confrontations certainly occur, as evidenced by the highly charged battles involving Coke vs. Pepsi, McDonald's vs. Burger King, and IBM vs. Digital Equipment. However, it is unclear whether these reflect basic structural relationships, or ineffective management and poor strategic choices (Porter 1980). The evidence from industrial economics indicates that elaborate collusive schemes designed to circumvent market mechanisms occur frequently (Scherer 1980), and organizations researchers have documented numerous interfirm coordinating structures that are legally used to limit competitive pressures (Pfeffer and Salancik 1978). Management efforts to avoid direct competition are not successful in every industry and market sector, but current research does indicate a potential for avoidance that is realized frequently enough to appear as a general phenomenon.

Although organization theorists are somewhat skeptical about the operational importance of direct competition, indirect competition's impact on organizational actions is taken for granted. Indirect competition is pivotal in entrepreneurial theories of industrial development (Schumpeter 1934; Nelson and Winter 1982), ecological approaches to industrial evolution (Brittain and Freeman 1980; Carroll and Delacroix 1982; Carroll 1985), and strategic choice research on relative performance levels (Miles and Snow 1978; Snow and Hrebiniak 1980). In addition, indirect competition is widely recognized as a core issue in strategy formation as a result of Porter's work (1980), which provides a detailed analysis of the sources of indirect competition and their potential for undermining a firm's strategic position.

Organizations researchers have devoted primary attention to indirect competition that is strategic, which involves firms serving the same market but in different ways (Miles and Snow 1978; Porter 1980). This perspective presumes management's interest is minimizing competitive pressures by finding services, unique product characteristics, and interorganizational linking mechanisms that define market segments for which there is little competition (Child 1972; Pfeffer and Salancik 1978; Pfeffer 1982). The result is not the elimination of competitive pressures but stable and predictable competition that can be anticipated and controlled (Thompson 1967).

Indirect competition also exists in the form of a diffuse threat that varies across industries and technologies. As commonly used, it exists in all activities conducted beyond the organizational boundary, including those of buyers, suppliers, and firms in related lines of business (Porter 1980). For instance, the introduction of desktop publishing hardware and software is a threat to traditional printers because customers can now do their own printing—that is, the customers' in-house capability is taking over the printing market (Williamson 1975). Similarly, electronic-component suppliers may expand into markets where the devices they produce are a significant part of the total product, a possibility that encourages many electronics firms to maintain economically inefficient integrated circuit manufacturing facilities (Brittain and Freeman 1980).

Interorganizational influence models that focus on a single type of competitive interaction will not perform well because "the competition" includes multiple indirect and direct exchange relationships, resource interdependencies, and dynamic interactions.[3] Because potential competition is diverse, it is best modeled as a community-level phenomenon, or *competitive structure* . This specification includes the full range of competitive, cooperative, neutral, parasitic, and predatory interactions that impact organizational actions and outcomes (Hannan and Freeman 1977; Freeman 1982) and also provides a framework for incorporating evolutionary changes associated with market and technical change (Brittain and Freeman 1980; Carroll 1985).

Competitive Structure

The dimension underlying any competitive structure, and hence industrial community, is resource interdependence. The resources that define interorganizational relationships vary across industries and economies, but the list generally includes raw materials, professional employees, technical knowledge, and market share. Even under conditions of monopolistic competition, firms typically share common suppliers, design expertise, and production knowledge. The interdependencies that result may not drive firms out of business, but they can make business more difficult and inhibit new entry by causing raw materials prices to increase, creating design talent shortages, and producing backlogs in the delivery of production equipment.

The effect of these resource interdependencies is consistent for firms with common patterns of resource utilization, while varying across other organizational populations. Although it is possible to characterize competitive structure in terms of firm-level communities, this pattern of variance coupled with the findings that firms actively avoid direct competition suggests a community specification built around organizational populations. Organizational ecology gives explicit attention to the relationship between competition and community structure (Hannan and Freeman 1977; Aldrich 1979; Carroll 1984; Wholey and Brittain 1986) and also provides a framework for characterizing the asymmetries in interorganizational networks.

Organizational ecology captures competitive structure with the Lotka-Volterra differential equation system (Hannan and Freeman 1977). The basic form of the equations is

$$\frac{dN_i}{dt} = r_iN_i \left[\frac{K_i - N_i + \sum_{j \neq i} \alpha_{ij}N_j}{K_i} \right] \qquad (11.1)$$

The variables in the equation are:

N_i = number of firms[4] in population i;
K_i = environmental carrying capacity for population i;
r_i = instantaneous growth parameter for population i;
a_{ij} = interaction coefficient, effect of population j on population i.

This equation describes the *growth rate* for an organizational population, where growth is potentially influenced by the expansion and contraction of populations of firms pursuing different business strategies.

The environmental carrying capacity is the maximum number of firms of a given type that a market can support. Where it is exceeded $(N_i > K_i)$, population size decreases until it is at or below this resource limit $(N_i \leq K_i)$. The carrying capacity is usually modeled as a function of exogenous factors affecting market size, such as human population (Carroll 1981; Carroll and Delacroix 1982), total labor force (Hannan and Freeman 1987), and industrial consumption (Brittain and Sterns 1985). By implication, this specification treats direct competition as a barrier to entry (Bain 1956), an assumption that is supported by research findings (Delacroix and Carroll 1983; Hannan and Freeman 1987) and arguments in industrial economics (Porter 1980).

The instantaneous growth parameter and interaction coefficients are the key parameters that characterize ecological competitive structures. The growth parameter is the rate of population increase occurring in the absence of competitive constraints. When this parameter is large, the population is very responsive to carrying capacity opportunities, a result that holds even in the face of competition if the competing population cannot expand rapidly to seize new resources—that is, has a lower r value. The result can be sudden growth for *first-mover* populations when the business environment is disrupted by technical innovations or dramatic market fluctuations, both of which create opportunities outside the existing competitive structure.

The interaction coefficient is a continuous measure of the impact one population has on another and may be either positive or negative. The parameters for each population in a community are unique, so the coefficients for two populations are not necessarily symmetric. We use the following designations (based on Pianka 1978) to identify the types of interactions possible between populations I and J, where the signs are for (a_{ij}, a_{ji}):

$(-, -)$ *Full competition:* Presence of I or J suppresses other's growth.
$(-, 0)$ *Partial competition:* I's growth rate is decreased, J's is unaffected.
$(+, -)$ *Predatory competition:* I expands at expense of J.
$(0, 0)$ *Neutrality:* I and J do not affect one another.
$(+, 0)$ *Commensalism:* I benefits from presence of J, but J is unaffected by I.
$(+, +)$ *Symbiosis:* Both I and J benefit from presence of other.

Each population in a community has a vector of interaction coefficients that together determine how the population is impacted by indirect competition.

The asymmetries in industrial communities reflect different levels of resource control and responsiveness to environmental change. The environment's impact on community structure depends jointly on the carrying capacity effects for individual populations and their responsiveness to opportunity, as well as the net effect of competitive constraints. Where the environment is relatively stable, the net impact of interpopulation relationships is constant and organizations can adopt strategies to minimize direct competition (Pfeffer and Salancik 1978; Perrow 1979). Competition is typically played out in successive environmental states that produce variations in population size, however, and as a result we expect competitive density and indirect competition will significantly influence community structure.

There has been relatively little research to date examining community-level competitive interactions (Carroll 1984). A number of studies have shown that populations within a community have different levels of responsiveness to environmental variations (Wholey and Brittain 1986), but none look specifically at interpopulation competitive relationships. In the section that follows, we estimate the competitive structure for the electronic components industry, showing how variations in competitive density and interpopulation asymmetries impact the strategic diversity that develops over time in the industry.

ELECTRONIC COMPONENTS

Electronic components manufacturing includes a wide array of products used in electronic instruments, computers, medical equipment, defense systems, and consumer goods. Electronic components are *active* devices that alter electrical signals to produce the operating characteristics of an electronic system. This includes receiving tubes, rectifiers, transistors, and integrated circuits, but not *passive* electrical products such as wires, resistors, indicator lights, and so forth. The receiving tube, which was discovered in 1904, was the first electronic component with commercial potential. Various technical problems and a convoluted patent situation prevented any manufacturing until the 1920s, when General Electric, AT&T, and Westinghouse transferred their patents to a newly created joint venture, RCA (MacLaurin 1949).

Until the 1950s, the industry was dominated by RCA, Sylvania, and General Electric, which together controlled 75 percent of the receiving tube market (Webbink 1977). The invention of the transistor in 1947 was the first in a series of technological breakthroughs in solid state components that would fundamentally change electronics manufacturing (Braun and MacDonald 1978) and as a result the markets for electronic components. Within twenty years of this discovery, the receiving tube was virtually obsolete, and the components industry was transformed from a stable oligopoly to a turbulent, commodities market driven by relentless pricing pressures and technical change.

The importance of technical innovation can be seen in the sales (in real dollars, 1967 = 100) of different components shown in Figure 11–1. Because the transistor was initially expensive and technically limited, receiving tubes were the largest selling component until 1959 (line T in Figure 11–1). The semiconductor developments introduced throughout the 1950s significantly lowered costs and expanded applications, and as a result solid state transistors and diodes (D for discrete in Figure 11–1) began displacing receiving tubes in the late 1950s. Discrete components dominated industry

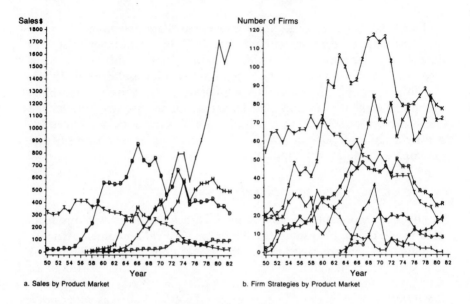

Figure 11–1.   Sales and Firm Strategies by Market.

sales until the 1970s, when they were surpassed by integrated circuits (*I* in Figure 11–1), which are now the most important class of products in the industry. Besides the devices already mentioned, major markets also exist for hybrid components, which join several devices within a single package (*H* in Figure 11–1), and optoelectronic devices, which are both light producing and photosensitive (*P* in Figure 11–1).

Total component sales went from $266 million in 1950 to $20 billion in 1984 (actual dollars). This rate of growth is even more phenomenal in light of the large learning economies that characterize the industry's production technology. These are derived from the knowledge accumulated in the course of manufacturing and as a consequence are a direct function of cumulative units produced. In semiconductors, these come from two types of learning by doing. One source is the process and machinery improvements developed as successful designs move into large-scale production. In some cases these can be incorporated into dedicated production facilities, leading to decreased machine changeover and downtime costs. The second is yield improvements associated with manufacturing experience. These are partly a function of process improvements but are also due to increased operator proficiency and decreased error rates. These can be substantial, with yields improving from 1 to 5 percent when a device first enters production to over 90 percent within two years.

These learning economies are used for strategic advantage, with device prices following production costs down the learning curve. For some devices prices have declined as much as 90 percent in the first year of production (Tilton 1971; Wilson, Ashton, and Egan 1980). For instance, the silicon transistor was introduced at a selling price of $24 but was available in 1964 for $1.50. In 1983 a similar device with enhanced performance and reliability cost $0.12. This decline includes supply and demand influences, but the overall drop in prices gives an indication of the learning economies that characterize the production process.

Although the industry as a whole has experienced a large expansion in sales, this has not come without hard times. The components business is essentially industrial commodities, and as a consequence the industry is vulnerable to business cycle fluctuations. This has been exacerbated in the past by the companies' willingness to cut prices to maintain production levels during downturns. Not surprisingly, these periods of cut-throat pricing are critical for most firms and are associated with large numbers of firm failures (Brittain and Freeman 1980).

The growth in the electronic components industry over the past thirty years has been accompanied by rapid technical change in product designs and production processes. This market's expansion has provided opportunities for firm entry, but the rate of technical change has proven to be an equally great barrier to success. The success of firms in the industry is largely dependent on their technological position but is not independent of their market position. Previous studies of firms operating in the industry (Brittain and Freeman 1980; Wilson, Ashton, and Egan 1980) have identified an array of strategies used successfully by firms to maintain a presence in the industry but have not examined the role of community structure in determining how firm participation has evolved over time and how the conditions for success are influenced by competitive structure.

Strategic Diversity

The rapid rate of technical change, drastic learning economies, and competitive pressures make participation in electronic components, and particularly semiconductor manufacturing, challenging to say the least. One solution to these problems is technical leadership, which can have tremendous payoffs as a result of the first-mover advantages associated with learning economies and the creation of design standards (Brittain and Freeman 1980). Early entrants in new product markets avoid competition by virtue of the market growth associated with the early stages of the product life cycle (Nelson and Winter 1982), while later entrants must develop operating efficiencies to compete with other firms in order to be successful. This is termed an r-strategy because it relies on quick movement to take advantage of newly available resources, which means a relatively large value of the instantaneous adjustment parameter in the Lotka-Volterra equation.

The difficulty, of course, is successfully innovating and then moving quickly down the learning curve to prevent other firms from entering the market. An alternative approach is using productive muscle to create learning economies as a rapid follower. Although this strategy may entail some losses as production moves to scale, the savings in development costs associated with new designs is considerable. This is termed a K-strategy because it attempts to derive competitive advantages under conditions of high density (Brittain and Freeman 1980).

Although the r-K dimension captures relative technological position, firms also use the market strategies of specialism and generalism to gain competitive advantage (Freeman and Hannan 1983). The market strategy of specializing in a single technology allows firms to focus their research efforts on technical avenues that are promising given the customers served and to focus competitive efforts on achieving the learning economies specific to a single production technology. The drawback of this approach is its vulnerability to major technical changes like the development of the integrated circuit, which seriously cut into the sales dominance of discrete components.

The alternative market strategy is pursuing competitive positions in all market segments—that is, to diversify (Chandler 1962). This spreads the risk of strategic change across several products and allows the firm to apply production lessons learned in one product area to other lines (Mansfield 1968). Although this has an obvious intuitive appeal, it is difficult to implement. The problem is achieving a competitive presence in several product markets, especially in an industry that trades heavily on technical sophistication. A related difficulty is the dilution of research effort involved in tracking multiple technologies. Certainly the risks of a single technical failure undermining the firm are reduced, but the possibility of multiple failures is significant. Furthermore, firms pursuing this strategy frequently encounter capital allocation difficulties when they encounter a winner and must consider the opportunity costs of utilizing financial resources on speculative ventures.

Firms have successfully used all combinations of these technological and market strategies in components manufacturing (Brittain and Freeman 1980; Wilson, Ashton and Egan 1980). The pattern of firm participation with each is shown in Figure 11–1 B. The populations included in the figure are:

T = Specialists, receiving tubes
1 = r-specialists, discrete components

2 = K-specialists, discrete components
3 = r-specialists, integrated circuits
4 = K-specialists, integrated circuits
R = r-generalists
K = K-generalists

Each population's developmental history tracks the industry's growth in a unique manner. One possible explanation for the different growth patterns is change in market size, but if this were the case, one would expect the specialists to more closely follow one another based on market participation. There is certainly some evidence of market effects in the decline of specialist firms producing receiving tubes, but even this is not a perfect correlation. We use these data—and data for hybrid and optoelectronic devices—to estimate the competitive structure for the populations producing electronic components over the years 1949 to 1981. We then use these estimates to discuss strategic diversity in the industry, the role of innovation in strategic success, and the importance of competitive asymmetries in determining the industry's overall structure.

Estimation Procedures

We use the dynamic modelling technique developed by Carroll (1981) to produce estimates of the interaction parameters for the firm populations manufacturing electronic components. This estimation method uses a vector of independent variables to characterize the carrying capacity for each population, population size of all other strategy groups to capture competitive effects, and change in population size as a dependent variable.[5] The specification of the Lotka-Volterra system used in this approach is

$$\left(\frac{1}{N_i}\right)\left(\frac{dN_i}{dt}\right) = r_i + c_iN_i + \sum_{j\neq i} a_{ij}S_j + \sum_{k\neq i} a_{ik}D_k \qquad (11.2)$$

where

N_i = number of firms in population i;
r_i = instantaneous growth parameter for population i;
c_i = suppression effect[6] from current population size, population i;
a_{im} = interaction coefficient[7] effect of population m on population i;
S_j = number of strategic competitor firms, population j;
D_k = number of diffuse competitor firms, population k.

The advantage of this form of the Lotka-Volterra system is that the model parameters can be estimated with regression methods (Pielou 1977).

The equation system we use to characterize the competitive structure in electronic components manufacturing encompasses eleven firm populations. Because market position in high technology involves both technical and market breadth dimensions, these populations were defined on two strategic dimensions: specialism/generalism (Hannan and Freeman 1977) and first-mover/late-entrant, or r/K-strategy (Brittain and Freeman 1980). Firms were classified according to their *realized* market strategy (Mintzberg 1978)—that is, what the firm has actually achieved in the marketplace.[8]

This strategic assessment was made for every firm operating in the industry for the years 1949–81 using information from the *Electronics Buyers' Guide* published by McGraw-Hill. The *Buyers' Guide* is a reference volume used by engineers, purchasing agents, and salesmen for information on device availability. Its listings are free to all electronics manufacturers and include information on every product offered by a firm. These data were checked against directories of manufacturers for the New England states, California, Arizona, and Texas, which have the largest concentrations of semiconductor producers in the United States (Webbink 1977), and were found to include approximately 97 percent of the firms in those states. This response rate is impressive relative to the standards of survey designs. The missing firms identified in this effort were added to the data base to bring the total number of firms to 1492, with a maximum of 382 firms in any given year and a mean of 243.

Information was collected on the manufacturers of eighty-seven different active electronic devices, including receiving tubes, discrete devices, integrated circuits, and optoelectronic devices. The eighty-seven products are grouped into twelve product classes that are internally homogeneous in terms of common design requirements, manufacturing methods, customer base, and a shared technical history and are consistent with general usage in the industry and in prior research (Tilton 1971; Webbink 1977; Braun and MacDonald 1978; Wilson, Ashton, and Egan 1980). The disaggregated form of the data is used to assess each firm's position relative to the technical frontier of the industry, while the product class data are used to assess the firm's breadth of participation.

The logic of the product groupings is best illustrated with an example from integrated circuit manufacturing. Integrated circuit designs are transferred to masks that are used to project the circuit image onto a silicon wafer treated with photo-sensitive chemicals. The image is developed through a series of production steps that create electrical islands on the wafer surface. This cycle is repeated several times to form individual devices and all the interconnections necessary for a complete circuit. The process and associated production equipment are identical for all integrated circuits; what differs are the masks, or product designs. Designing power transistors (another product group) requires quite different engineering skills that cannot be transferred to or from integrated circuit work, and the production of these devices involves completely separate processing machinery. Because of these capital and design differences, it is generally easier and cheaper for a firm to produce multiple types of integrated circuits (that is, to expand within a product group) than to diversify into another product group.

The r-K strategic dimension involves order of entry and is assigned with the disaggregate product information coded from the *Electronics Buyers' Guide,* supplemented by material gathered from various sources that report on industry history. The r-K operationalization captures how quickly a firm responds to new market opportunities, an issue of timing that is distinct from the specialism/generalism measure of breadth of market participation. The disaggregate product data is used to evaluate this dimension because it more accurately reflects the specific product expertise underlying the r-K distinction. First-mover options are the result of technical innovations that free customers previously tied into other technologies, creating rapid growth opportunities for firms that can move in and address market demand. It is appropriate, then, that first-mover characteristics be evaluated at the product market level. Furthermore, using this detailed information keeps the strategic dimensions operationally distinct.

An earlier study of the industry found that the dramatic price declines indicating emerging competition did not develop in any market within the first three years after the product was introduced (U.S. Department of Commerce 1979), which suggests that firms entering in the first three years achieve returns that can potentially fund other developments. Based on this finding, first-movers were defined as firms entering a product category in the three years following the initial market introduction (t to $t + 2$). This time lag exists because engineering knowledge about new devices does not instantly diffuse to customers, device adoption requires prior customer testing and performance assessments, production only gradually reaches levels sufficient to make fixed delivery commitments, and it takes time for firms pursuing similar lines of development to create compatible devices.[9]

The first-mover advantages associated with early entry diminish as a product advances through its life cycle. To account for this, the r designation for each product expires when the product's real dollar sales per firm reaches a plateau or begins to decline. Although unit volumes may continue to rise, sales per firm decline when pricing pressures develop. Maintaining a presence in such a market requires a shift to production efficiencies (Brittain and Freeman 1980), which means that the strategic problems are those of a K-strategist. The time to expiration varies across product categories, with some products reaching saturation within four years, while the apparent margins for other products continue to expand for up to ten years.

Given the multiple products a firm might manufacture, the question arises as to where the cut-off is made in assigning a summary r and K designation. One possibility is to treat "r-ness" as a continuous variable by operationalizing it as the percentage of products for which the firm is a first-mover. This is not workable substantively because sales of certain chips depend on the availability of complementary support chips in which the firm may not be a first-mover (for example, micro-processors need compatible memory devices). In other instances manufacturers offer standard commodity chips to discourage their customers from developing relationships with competing firms, but this should not dilute the strategic evaluation. The solution adopted here is to treat the r-K dimension as dichotomous, classifying a firm as a r-strategist if it is a first-mover in any product. Because the returns from a single innovative product can have an enormous impact on firm success and overwhelm the consequences of all other markets, this seems justified.

This strategic classification framework produces eleven organizational populations: K specialists[10] in receiving tubes; r and K specialists in discrete components (semiconductor diodes and transistors); r and K specialists in hybrid components (products that mix components), integrated circuits, and optoelectronics; and r and K generalists. An equation was estimated for each of these dependent variables that includes carrying capacity effects on growth, the effects of strategic competitors in the same product market, and diffuse competition from all other populations in the industry. For the market specialists, strategic interaction coefficients were estimated for generalists participating in the same market, while generalists in other markets were included as diffuse competitors.

The estimating form of equation 11.2 includes lagged size, which introduces possible autocorrelation problems, while the simultaneity of effects can result in biased OLS estimates. We deal with both of these issues by using a generalized least squares estimation procedure with a structural model (SYSREG procedure in SAS). The results are in Table 11-1, which presents all the Lotka-Volterra parameter estimates by strategy and market. The R-squares listed in the table are for the regression equations, not the Lotka-Volterra transformation. The system R-square is .99, but this reflects the inclusion of lagged values in the estimation equations, as do the R-squares for the individual equations.

Parameter Estimates

The first parameter of interest is the speed of adjustment, or instantaneous growth rate, which determines how fast the population expands in the absence of competitive and resource constraints. This is larger for the r-strategists, which indicates that our classification system is capturing basic differences in the strategic populations' responsiveness to opportunities. An additional, and unanticipated, finding is the historical progression of these values from receiving tubes to discrete components and hybrid devices, which are based in a similar technology, to integrated circuits (ICs) and optoelectronics, both of which emerged at about the same time (Braun and MacDonald 1978). This pattern is consistent for both the r-strategy (rS) and K-strategy (KS) groups, which leads us to believe it is not an analytic anomaly. Furthermore, an accumulated experience effect is evidenced in the fact that the values for the K-specialists in integrated circuits and optoelectronic circuits approach the r-strategist values in older technologies, a finding that is consistent with the industry learning effects identified in other ecological studies (Delacroix and Carroll 1983; Wholey and Brittain 1986).

The adjustment value for K-generalists is at approximately the mean value for the corresponding specialists, which is consistent with what one would expect from a group of diversified firms. The parameter value for r-generalists, on the other hand, is high relative to the r-specialist populations. This is partly because established r-specialists are both in a position to learn about emerging technologies and to become generalists by adding product lines. In addition, companies that successfully innovate and capture the monopoly profits associated with first-mover advantages have the financial resources to invest in further innovation and market expansion (Brittain and Freeman 1980). This adaptive form of population growth is the most frequent strategic change involving innovation in the period studied, accounting for 52 percent of the adaptive moves and 30 percent of all entries into the r-generalist category.

The carrying capacity equation includes variables that have a straightforward impact on the potential number of firms operating in the United States: U.S. component sales, foreign sales, and the percentage of worldwide sales by foreign competitors. The effect of each of these variables on the various population growth rates is given at the bottom of Table 11–1. It is not surprising that market size has a uniformly positive effect because sales are the primary resource for profit-based organizations. This is also true for overseas sales, while the percentage of sales by foreign competitors generally has a negative impact on U.S. firms. There are two exceptions to the foreign market size and competition generalization, K-specialists in discrete components and r-generalists. These two populations grew prior to 1965 when foreign markets were small, and so it appears were not positioned to move into foreign markets but benefitted from the effect of foreign competition on domestic competitors. Although we did not expect this result, it is consistent with our competitive structure findings.

The competition coefficients listed in Table 11–1 indicate a complicated pattern of interpopulation competition that reflects the history of technological innovation, relative economies of scale in production,

Table 11–1. Lotka-Volterra Estimates, Electronic Components Strategic Populations.

Variable	rS-Discrete	rS-Hybrid	rS-ICs	rS-Opto	r-Generalist	KS-Tubes	KS-Discrete	KS-Hybrid	KS-ICs	KS-Opto	K-Generalist
Speed of adjustment	.2788	.2336	.3143	.3868	.3328	.0288	.1387	.1310	.2194	.2179	.1773
Competition coefficients											
K-specialist-tubes	.0015[a]	.0019	.0024[a]	.0028	-.0107[a]	—	.0033[a]	-.0014[a]	-.0022[a]	.0070[a]	-.0048[a]
r-generalist-tubes						.0157[a]					
K-generalist-tubes						.0150[a]					
r-specialist-discrete	—	.0128[a]	.0008	.0097	.0059[a]	-.0020[a]	.0134[a]	.0037[a]	.0128[a]	.0157[a]	-.0195[a]
K-specialist-discrete	-.0400[a]	.0027	-.0009[a]	-.0025	.0098[a]	.0021[a]	—	-.0018[a]	-.0032[a]	.0022[a]	.0104[a]
r-generalist-discrete	.1756[a]						.0097[a]				
K-generalist-discrete	.0146[a]						-.0064[a]				
r-specialist-hybrid	.9869[a]	—	.7166[a]	.2113[a]	.6108[a]	.0598[a]	-.0185[a]	—	-.2753[a]	-.1401[a]	-.2299[a]
K-specialist-hybrid	.0289[a]	.0081[a]	-.0202[a]	-.0001	-.0194[a]	-.0045[a]	.0081[a]		-.0026[a]	.0152[a]	.0103[a]
r-generalist-hybrid		.0035						.0643[a]			
K-generalist-hybrid		-.0133[a]						.0142[a]			
r-specialist-ICs	-.2413[a]	.0271[a]	—	.0006	-.1069[a]	-.0009[a]	.0034[a]	.0377[a]	-.0791[a]	-.0099[a]	.0167[a]
K-specialist-ICs	-.0517[a]	.0036	-.0696[a]	.0045	-.0173[a]	-.0069[a]	.0106[a]	-.0413[a]	—	.0105[a]	.0199[a]
r-generalist-ICs			-.0216[a]						.0136[a]		
K-generalist-ICs			.0837[a]						.1040[a]		
r-specialist-Opto	-.4881[a]	-.0120	.0022	—	.0115	.1062[a]	-.0672[a]	.0516[a]	.1456[a]	.1017[a]	.0935[a]
K-specialist-Opto	-.0101[a]	-.0917[a]	.3664[a]	.0095	.0095[a]	-.0040[a]	-.0353[a]	-.1228[a]	-.0965[a]	—	-.0260[a]
r-generalist-Opto				.0188[a]						-.0317[a]	
K-generalist-Opto				-.0096						.0453	

Other r-generalists	-.0920[a]	-.0143[a]	.0264[a]	-.0168[a]		.0140[a]	.0177[a]	-.0031[a]	-.0073[a]	-.0172[a]
Other K-generalists	.0745[a]	-.0028	.0378[a]	.0040		.0052[a]	-.0066[a]	.0040[a]	.0059[a]	-.0154[a]
All r-generalists					—						.0157[a]
All K-generalists					.0310[a]						—
Carrying capacity[b]										
Market size	.0049	.0840	.9740	.0839	66.0819	12.1303	.2950	1.1296	1.0239	.7043	14.0720
Non-U.S. sales	.6897	.9221	.2886	1.6973	-.0829	.3625	-.1222	3.9286	3.0647	.7408	.1997
Foreign competition	-.7681	-1.7431	-.3969	-2.4171	.0328	-.3799	.1294	-5.5364	-4.1804	-1.8643	-.4382
Regression R-square	.93	.86	.99	.72	.78	.99	.98	.99	.99	.96	.92

[a]Competition coefficient times maximum population size equals at least plus or minus one unit.
[b]The variables in the carrying capacity equation are inverse values. See Carroll (1981) for details.

population densities at key points in the industry's history, and technological barriers to entry. For instance in the case of receiving tubes, there is a symbiotic relationship (+,+) with the two generalist populations that are strategic competitors and K-specialist discrete producers, but the populations that arose with new technologies show a pattern of predatory competition (+,−). In hybrid markets, on the other hand, the structure of relationships is mixed, reflecting the fact that hybrid products depend on technological developments in other component areas (hybrids are special purpose combinations of other components) but are also sensitive to displacement by new technologies. This is clear in the contrasting competitive structures for r and K-specialists. The r-specialists are embedded in mainly symbiotic (+,+) relationships—with the exception of preying on the K-specialist market and being in a position of full competition with respect to K-generalists—while the K-specialists are faced with full competition (−,−) from their indirect K-specialist competitors.

Figure 11–1a indicates that the major components markets have historically been discrete products and integrated circuits. The market for solid state devices really developed after 1954. The r-specialist population expanded along with it in the 1950s, but then faded (line 1 in Figure 11–1b). It is apparent in looking at the pattern of competitive relationships in Table 11–1 that this is the result of two sources of predatory competition. One is strategic competition from an expanding population of K-specialists, while the second is diffuse competition rooted in the development of the integrated circuit.

Although it is possible to glean a basic understanding of the effects of competitive structure from Table 11–1, the competition coefficients alone are not sufficient for understanding how the expansion of one population impacts another's growth. Figure 11–2 presents a graphic analysis of the relationship between competitive structure and population density, where C is the dampening parameter effect in equation 11.2, D is the diffuse competition effect, R and K are the strategic relationships with r and K-generalists, and S is the strategic competition attributable to the opposite specialist population in the same market. The Y-axis shows how the interacting population(s) are impacting the growth rate of the population in question, with the actual figures indicating a percentage change in size. In the case of the r-specialist population in discrete components (11–2c), it is clear that the population declined as a result of the joint negative effect of increased density for the K-specialist population and the expanding number of firms producing integrated circuits, which are included in the diffuse competition figures.

The strategic difference associated with K-specialism is clear in Figure 11–2d. The K-specialist population in discrete components is the largest in the industry (see 2 in Figure 11–1b) and is apparently only limited by the suppressing effects of its own size. It is also apparently subject to the pressures of strategic competition from K-generalists operating in the market, but this is largely counterbalanced by the parasitic predatory relationship $(+,-)$ that exists with specialists in integrated circuits. This relationship reflects the price pressures from discrete components during the early period of integrated circuit development, and the fact that the expansion of integrated circuit use from 1970 produced an ancillary demand for competitively priced discrete components, which are still necessary in most circuit designs. Although the population of firms pursuing this strategy has declined with the dollar value of discrete sales, the market is still an active one. Competition in this sector is primarily on the basis of price, which has effectively eliminated any r-specialist competition.

The r and K-specialists in integrated circuits have a contrasting interaction pattern that reflects historical differences in the industry's development, knowledge base, and competitive density. Unlike discrete components, integrated circuit production was pioneered by r-generalists who remained a significant competitive force. As a result, markets were defined that K-specialists could exploit with a predatory strategy $(+,-)$, while r-specialists were forced to go head-to-head in full competition $(-,-)$ with established innovators. The r-generalist population dominated this market early on, forcing the specialist populations into niche markets on the periphery in a fashion similar to what Carroll (1985) uncovered in newspaper publishing. The result was a competitive struggle $(-,-)$ along price-performance dimensions that prevented either population from achieving the market penetration of their counterparts in discrete components. The effect of K-generalists has been the opposite, however, since their effect on both specialist populations is symbiotic (see Figures 11–2e and 11–2f).

The generalist populations have a symbiotic relationship but differ sharply in their relationship with other populations. The r-generalist population was constrained by its carrying capacity when the industry was dominated by discrete components but has been subjected to considerable competitive pressures with the entry of specialist populations in integrated circuits. K-generalists have not been exposed to the same degree of indirect competition but have been plateaued at their apparent carrying capacity since integrated circuits became the dominant technology (see K in Figure 11–1b).

The roles the two generalist populations filled in the industry's competitive structure reversed after integrated circuits were introduced. The r-generalists had a symbiotic interaction pattern with the specialist populations that emerged in discrete components, while the K-generalists of the time, which were primarily involved with receiving tubes, were the object of predatory competition from r-specialists and in turn exploited

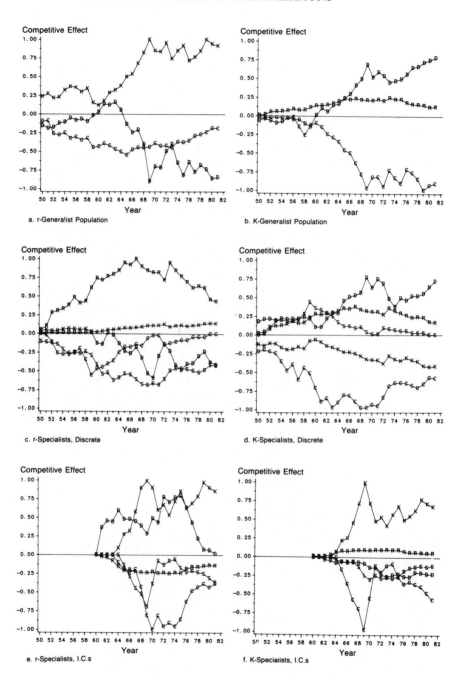

Figure 11–2.   Direct, Strategic, and Diffuse Competition.

the markets established by the K-specialists. Contrary to the situation with discrete components and receiving tubes, integrated circuits are not a technological substitute for discrete devices, and as a result the specialists in ICs have a symbiotic relationship with the K-generalist population. However, as we discussed earlier, the r-generalist's initial domination in ICs resulted in a competitive relationship with both specialist populations.

Summary

The speed of adjustment and carrying capacity results are generally consistent with prior expectations and indicate that the strategic classification framework we use captures the population growth characteristics identified by organizational ecologists. The competitive structure, however, is neither simple nor straightforward, but it is also not *ad hoc*. Although the pattern of findings does not lend itself to simple relational statements about strategic performance, it clearly indicates that strategic success is linked with the one idea that is common to all discussions of competitive strategy (Porter 1980)—that is, it depends on who the competitors are. This principle connects several themes that run throughout our discussion, including the ideas that strategic population growth is related to timing of entry, competitive density, population response to opportunity, and population resistance to diffuse competition. Translated to the firm level, this implies that strategic success depends on when a firm enters a market, who is already there, who grows fastest, and who comes along later.[11] We discuss these findings further in the next section.

COMMUNITY COMPETITIVE DYNAMICS

Our analysis of the Lotka-Volterra parameters indicates that the competitive dynamic in electronic components includes the simultaneous effects of technological change, market expansion, and changing population densities. The resulting competitive structure is an amalgam of symbiotic, predatory, and competitive relationships involving both strategic and technological competition. Although the industry would generally be considered competitive, this has not led to any dramatic population dislocations over the industry's history. Rather, the industry-level participation by firms falling into our four basic strategic categories is stable relative to the population discontinuities that are apparent in Figure 11–1b.

Similar patterns of industry-level stability in participation have been used as counter arguments to organizational ecology's selection logic by advocates of strategic choice theory (Snow and Hrebiniak 1980). As is evidenced in the analysis above, the existence of multiple strategies within a particular industry does not indicate that competitive pressures are not operating, but this does not explain the coexistence of these populations. One contributing factor is the symbiotic and commensal interactions that exist in the competitive structure, but these do not fully balance the competitive and predatory relationships that are apparent in the industry's core markets. Another possible factor might be the adaptation of firms from one market to another as technologies evolve, but other studies show that such adaptive moves account for only 11.7 percent of the firm-level events during the period 1949–81. The role of symbiotic and adaptive effects should not be ignored, but a complete explanation must also include the dynamic effects of competitive structure.

Competitive Coexistence

There are two general limitations on the growth of organizational populations. The first is density-dependent selection (K-selection), which refers to selection mechanisms that change as a function of population size. For instance, the carrying capacity and inter-population competitive effects discussed above have their greatest impact when the populations in a market are near carrying capacity levels. Under these circumstances, coexistence depends directly on the values of the competition coefficients, which will be relatively low for populations competing in peripheral markets and high where they are going head-to-head. What this means is that even under conditions of full competition ($-,-$), it is the value of the coefficient that is the measure of effect, not just its sign. The degree of effect is apparent in Figure 11–2, which also makes it clear that direct competition generally has the greatest effect in suppressing population growth.

The second general limitation on population growth is produced by exogenous factors—often of a catastrophic nature—that cause fluctuations in the environmental carrying capacity. This includes events such as major technological changes, unanticipated economic downturns, revolutions (Carroll and Delacroix 1982), labor disputes, local political battles (see Chapter 10), and other business and organizational catastrophes that undercut existing populations or strengthen a population at the expense of competing organizations. This is generally termed density-independent selection because it is not related to current population size but nevertheless impacts it (Brittain and Freeman 1980).

Density-independence is also referred to as r-selection because populations with large instantaneous growth parameters have an advantage in responding to these situations. This responsiveness usually depends on slack resources that can be redeployed to quickly take advantage of emerging opportunities (Cyert and March 1963). The slack resources commonly used by electronic components firms include state-of-the-art but technologically underutilized productive capacity, underemployed professionals, and unproductive capital allocated to research and development. These resources are expensive to maintain and as a consequence must generate the kind of returns available from first-mover advantages.

Firms that rely on r-strategies are vulnerable to the competitive pressures that develop as the total organizational population in a market nears carrying capacity levels. Populations of r-strategists exhibit high levels of volatility as a result because they respond rapidly to opportunity and suffer when competition emerges. This is the case in the components industry, as Figure 11–3 indicates. These graphs show the net competitive effect

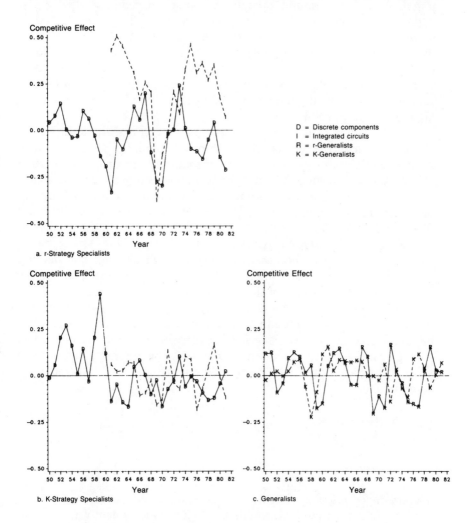

Figure 11–3. Net Competitive Effects.

(right-hand side of equation 11.2) for the specialist populations in discrete components and integrated circuits, as well as for the generalist populations. The summed time series for r-specialists in discretes has a standard deviation of .14, while it is .22 for ICs. This compares with standard deviations of .07 and .09 for the same respective K-specialists, .11 for r-generalists, and .08 for K-generalists.[12]

The volatility in the r-strategy populations is indicative of their responsiveness to technological change and market opportunities. Environmental disruptions that limit competitive densities afford opportunities for populations that respond quickly to obtain first-mover advantages. Although K-strategists also move into emerging markets, their growth is more tightly coupled with market expansion and occurs at a slower rate— that is, they are not creating sales, they are responding to demand. Coexistence is normal in such situations because environmental changes occur with sufficient regularity to maintain r-strategy populations. This is not a characteristic of all industrial communities but is common in the high-technology sectors.

Technical change not only disrupts existing competitive densities but also creates new competitive relationships as populations enter developing markets. The ecological framework introduced by Hannan and Freeman (1977) is based on environmental variation between two recurring states, which results in competitive dominance for one organizational population. When this is extended to include variation between successive states (Brittain and Freeman 1980), it becomes apparent that density-independent effects can produce a dynamic coexistence based on strategic succession. This occurs because competitive densities do not develop immediately, which creates opportunities for organizational populations to expand in the absence of density-dependent constraints.

The introduction of major design and product innovations in electronics manufacturing has resulted in a pattern of strategic succession that has maintained strategic diversity in the community, even though some strategies are replaced in individual markets. The graphs in Figure 11–4 show this process occurring in discrete components and integrated circuits, where

1 = r-specialists
2 = K-specialists
R = r-generalists
K = K-generalists

The predicted number of firms was generated with regression equations that use time, time squared, and time cubed as independent variables and was included to provide a clearer picture of the succession process (R^2

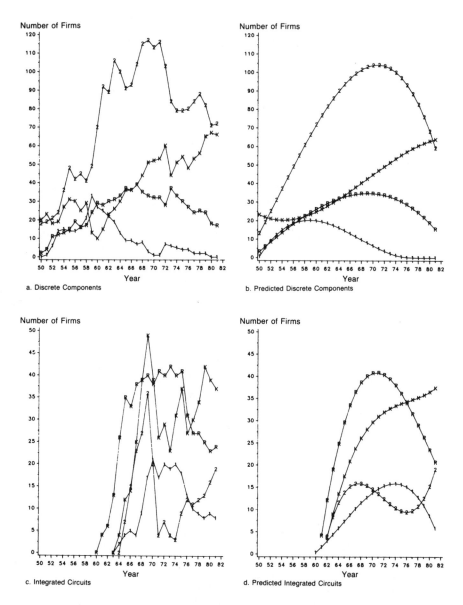

Figure 11–4. Actual and Predicted Number of Firms.

values ranged from .80 to .95, except for the K-specialist population in integrated circuits, which had a value of .47).

A population of K-strategists producing older types of discrete devices existed when semiconductor components were first introduced. Of these, it was the K-generalists, which were principally receiving tube firms, that were most directly impacted by the initial expansion of the semiconductor market (Figures 11–4a and 11–4b). The wave in the predicted curve is indicative of the predatory competitive relationship that exists between r-specialists and K-generalists in this market. The peak in the r-specialist curve is in 1959, which also coincides with a period when the K-specialist population begins to grow rapidly (Figure 11–4a). The number of r-generalists in the industry continued to expand, however, until the mid-1960s, when a growing number of r-specialists began emerging in integrated circuits and product innovation slowed in discrete components.

The competitive structure in the industry was further complicated when firms producing integrated circuits began to appear. The charge was led by r-generalists, who reaped the benefits of their quick start well into the late 1970s. The r-specialist population appeared later around innovations in large-scale ICs, which contributed to the levelling of the r-generalist population's growth. This second wave of innovation is also associated with a rapid decline in the K-specialist population, which later recovered.

The majority of ecological studies to date have emphasized density-dependent selection (Wholey and Brittain 1986). Density-dependent effects are important where resource competition is stable (Hannan and Freeman, 1987) but do not capture the complexities of ecological competition in evolving high-technology markets. Density-independent factors such as market segmentation, technical change, and applications developments play a central role in the competitive asymmetries and pattern of ecological succession that characterize the dynamics of coexistence and competition in the electronic components industry and are likely to be critical in other technology-driven markets. The strength of the competitive constraints operating at any time is a function of population density (see Chapter 2), but the structure of competitive relationships depends on the pattern of environmental change and the timing of historical events. The strength of the ecological model is that it can simultaneously capture all of these effects in a dynamic framework.

CONCLUSION

Although the competitive structure of the semiconductor industry is complex, it is also easily modeled. The complexities involve the ways in which new product designs and production technologies are used strategically by firms operating in the industry, and the ways in which new product and process opportunities effect established firms (Brittain and Freeman 1980). By modeling this structure, the complexity becomes amenable to sophisticated scenario analysis and the underlying dynamic processes of density-independent selection and strategic succession become apparent (Tuma and Hannan 1984). This process knowledge is a tool for anticipating how exogenous events will influence an industry's competitive structure and firm competitive positions, issues of great concern for managers, investors, and government planners.

Organization theory has been strangely quiet on the subject of competitive effects, which has limited its importance in the formation of social policy and its relevance to firm-level strategy formulation. The analysis presented here suggests that firm outcomes and industry structure can both be better understood if the conceptualization of competition is broadened to include the full range of direct, strategic, and diffuse competitive effects. The strategic role of management is not in question; it is the boundaries of the strategic problem that are of interest from the standpoint of ecological theory. Organization theory will be well served if organizational ecology can address this larger issue.

NOTES

1. The dynamic insight in the speeder-racer example is the result of a shift in analytic focus from the *interaction* between organizations, to the organizational *relationship to the interaction*. In other words, the issue is no longer whether a race/relationship exists, but how individual drivers/organizations are driving/ behaving relative to other drivers/organizations. From this standpoint, the relationship is not a nominal category, but a continuous measure of association.

2. The relative importance attached to competitive survival differs across theoretical approaches. Competition is a central management problem in approaches that emphasize efficiency (Williamson 1975; Ouchi 1980) and is equally important, although sometimes less explicit, in contingency theories (Thompson 1967; Hannan and Freeman 1977). The strategic choice perspective discusses the threat of competitive failure (Child 1972) but puts greater emphasis on managing interdependence (Pfeffer and Salancik 1978) and system integration (Lawrence and Lorsch 1978; Miles and Snow 1978), both of which are subject to greater direct managerial control. Regardless of emphasis, however, all these perspectives acknowledge that competition influences organizational action under some circumstances.

3. Our findings indicate firm actions are influenced by a range of interorganizational competitive and cooperative effects. When such a system is analyzed in terms of a single dyadic relationship, the potential for specification bias is large. Furthermore, dismissing direct competition without controlling for the effects of indirect interactions may understate cooperation's role as a counterbalancing influence on social structure. We avoid this misspecification by looking at the entire range of interactions influencing organizational outcomes.

4. The logistic system used in this chapter relies on comparative population size but can also be used to model comparative market share, sales, or any other measure of relative competitive strength (Brittain and Sterns 1985).

5. Estimating the model parameters involves complex functions of the coefficients taken from a regression equation, and as a result it is not possible to provide significance tests with this particular procedure (Carroll 1981).

6. This negative feedback parameter is equal to $- r_i/K_i$. The carrying capacity portion is modelled as a function of variables impacting market size.

7. The interaction coefficient in this specification is equal to $- c_i a_{ij}$.

8. This can be different from what management intends, but it is market accomplishments that determine success. In addition, the actions of the firm in the market are more readily and reliably observed than managerial aspirations.

9. Even if a competing firm has a device that is identical, it often has to be modified to achieve what is referred to as pin compatibility. This involves designing the input/output relationships so they use the same connections, or mounting pins. Firms vary in how important they regard this feature to be, since a different pin structure can lock in customers once they adopt. Late entrants do not have this option and must use a standard pin structure.

10. No r-specialists were observed in receiving tubes. Historical accounts indicate that they did exist at one time but were displaced in the period prior to our time series (MacLaurin 1949).

11. These are also suitable guidelines for evaluating whether a cocktail party is worth cultivating or fleeing, although drinking is usually substituted for growing at such events.

12. The figure for the discrete K-specialists was calculated with the data for 1960–81 because the expansion in the 1950s is in an ecological vacuum, and as a result is not representative of the population's general characteristics.

12 CRAFTING AN INSTITUTIONALLY INFORMED ECOLOGY OF ORGANIZATIONS

Charles J. Fombrun

Studies of organization from an ecological perspective have drawn heavily on Hannan and Freeman's (1977) translation of concepts from bioecology. Despite considerable success in pointing to the influence of population-level selection pressures on individual organizations, however, both empirical accounts and theoretical treatments have also been strongly chastised. Perrow (1986), for one, claimed that ecological analyses favored an uncritical acceptance of historically specific outcomes and, as such, were little more than a quantitatively disguised apology for the status quo. Betton and Dess (1985) pointed to some of the difficulties involved in articulating an ecology of organizations that relied on a competitive process to explain the differential survival of favorable variations. By emulating biological formulations, they argued, ecological models of organizations overstate the inertial characteristics of organizations and fail to specify the process by which variations propagate, thereby lacking a suitable analog to genetic inheritance in organisms. Astley and Fombrun (1983a) attended to the processes binding firms into distinct collectivities whose joint actions could significantly modify the forces of selection. Finally, Astley (1985) elaborated a community-level argument to redress population

I have greatly benefited from ongoing work with Bill Starbuck (NYU) and provocative discussions with Glenn Carroll (Berkeley) in preparing this manuscript. Many thanks. The development of this paper was supported in part by a grant from the Tenneco Fund Program at the Graduate School of Business Administration, New York University.

ecology's overemphasis on the regulatory role of selection and its neglect of variation and punctuation in the study of industrial change.

To date, ecological theorists have only partially responded to these diverse criticisms. In their strongest rebuttal to date, Hannan and Freeman (1984) strongly defended and extended their initial position on inertia as a genetic analog for organizations. They did this by introducing an institutional context that favors organizations with high degrees of repro-ducibility and accountability and therefore fosters organizational inertia. If so, it is possible to also argue that environments must vary in—and hence can be rank-ordered by—the degree to which these selection criteria ac-tually prevail. What then of the process of change in those environments that do *not* favor high reproducibility and accountability? A critical defi-ciency of their analysis is its failure to specify how these criteria themselves come to attain the status of institutionalized norms in the industrial or societal superstructure (Fombrun 1986).

Due, in part, to such lingering conceptual difficulties in the formulation of ecological theories, some have taken the opportunity to charge organiza-tional ecology with a multitude of sins, not least of which is the claim that ecologists are either evolutionists or apologists. As the chapters in this book clearly demonstrate, to do so is clearly to misrepresent current ecological research: Most empirical studies of organizational populations now systematically reject notions of either stability or evolution in favor of understanding the forces that animate change in the particular char-acteristics of firms in the population (Carroll 1984). Indeed, the chang-ing mix of characteristics in surviving organizations is increasingly regarded as a joint effect of both institutional and ecological influences.

This chapter takes as its point of departure the belief that theoretical development in organizational ecology now lags empirical research. As researchers introduce institutional content into the study of the ecologies within which organizations thrive, they stretch the limits of the prevailing theory of change by Darwinian selection. Organizational ecology therefore requires a theoretical framework that departs significantly from that of bioecology, one that not only accommodates but incorporates the institu-tional character of both organizations and environments.

In fact, the problems that organizational ecology confronts are not unrelated to those with which biologists wrestle as they too struggle to extend the neo-Darwinian framework of biotic evolution. Despite the inherently social nature of organizational phenomena, biologists' concerns prove surprisingly appropriate to students of organizations. Thus, devel-opments in bioecology and paleology suggest a view of evolution as both projective and adaptive, punctuational and gradual. This chapter proposes that similar conclusions are warranted in organizational ecology. If we follow biologists' lead in questioning the underlying neo-Darwinian framework of ecological change for organizations, then it becomes apparent that a suitable theoretical framework for organizational ecology should encompass (1) the hierarchical embeddedness of organizations in structured fields; (2) the social mechanisms through which organizations project themselves into the environment; and (3) the interactive processes through which organizations actively learn and collectively construct the environments to which they then respond.

DARWIN'S LEGACY

In 1836 Darwin deduced from his own observations of nature and from Malthus's 1798 *Essay on Population* the conclusion that "in the struggle for survival in the face of scarce resources, those best adapted to their environment will, on average, survive and breed at the expense of the less well endowed, who will tend to be eliminated" (in Dowdeswell 1984: 47). Selection is therefore a two-step process that acts, first, on the transient characteristics of organisms—phenotypes—and, second, through the differential reproductive success of these traits, on genetic characteristics of organisms—genotypes (Mayr 1982). In this neo-Darwinian formulation, "species do not evolve in an active sense; they only get evolved by an external natural selector. They do not have causal roles in their own evolution" (Campbell 1985: 133).

From a theoretical standpoint, most organizational ecologists are heavily invested in this two-step, neo-Darwinian model of adaptive evolution. In the first stage, selection sifts through organizations in the resource niche: In the struggle to acquire resources, unfit organizations are winnowed out. Key features of surviving organizations (such as their structure or form) spread through the niche over time because density-dependent selection systematically eliminates rivals without these features (Hannan and Freeman 1977; Freeman and Hannan 1983).

The second stage of selection occurs through the reproductive success of selected forms. Environments overwhelm organizations because of assumed levels of inertia that inhibit learning and voluntaristic transformation. Inertia not only induces the disbanding of unfit organizations, it also makes it possible for fit organizations to perpetuate themselves through time. Hannan and Freeman (1984) argued, for instance, that institutional pressures for accountability and reliability in organizational performance induce structural inertia, with the consequence that environments favor organizations that sustain these characteristics through time. Thus, inertia serves as an organizational analog to the genetic structures of organisms. Winter (1964, 1975) and Nelson and Winter (1982) also contend that organizations develop such a repertoire of routines (their collective memory) to transmit learning to successive generations of participants. In fact, organizations draw on a common pool of skills and competencies within a population, and this pool fulfills the retention function for populations that inertia plays for organizations (McKelvey 1982).

Not surprisingly this two-step sequence remains unconvincing to many critics. For one, it seems difficult to reconcile its caricature of organizations as isolated, inertial entities, with the visible intrusions that organizations make—either singly, collectively, or through institutional relationships with powerful actors—into the environments to which they are said to respond (Perrow 1986; Astley and Fombrun 1983a; Betton and Dess 1985). Thus, it appears to distort the complex interrelationship between the economic substructure and the societal superstructure within which organizations are embedded (Fombrun 1986).

More problematic, however, is the observation that these ecological formulations rely heavily on a concept of fitness to explain the progressive accomodation of organizations to environments. In this, they call to mind the problems that biologists confront in claiming that surviving organisms are necessarily more fit than those that failed (Campbell 1985); that economists face when they are accused of "naturalism" in their defense of the inherent efficiency of competitive markets (Robbins 1985); that social theorists brave when they defend social outcomes as "functional" (Merton 1967); and that historians tackle when they try to formulate a science of history (Gould 1986). They are charged with teleology, with constructing elaborate rationalizations for historically specific outcomes, with theorizing "as if God does the negative and positive selecting" (Perrow 1986: 213).

In response, most organizational ecologists now dispense with teleological arguments altogether. As the papers in this volume demonstrate, to conduct ecological research increasingly means to search for patterned changes in environmental and organizational characteristics that make reference neither to evolution nor to fitness in explaining these changes (Carroll 1984). Much as sociologists have challenged notions of advancement in theories of societal evolution (Granovetter 1979), so have organizational ecologists turned to contextualist theories of the middle range. Though this may appease those critics who fear evolutionism in ecological theorizing (Perrow 1986), it only reinforces the view that the neo-Darwinian framework to which organizational ecology implicitly subscribes should be carefully scrutinized if we are to maintain consistency in the development of theories that accommodate institutional processes.

CHALLENGING THE NEO-DARWINIAN SYNTHESIS

Neo-Darwinism has come under attack from both modern genetics and paleology. The conclusions of theorists and researchers, and the directions they are taking suggest some interesting parallels for students of organizational ecology. In particular, they propose that in the study of biological organisms, the Darwinian legacy must be extended in two directions: (1) to address the projective characteristics of organisms and (2) to encompass the punctuated changes that transform populations of organisms. As I will argue, similar recommendations can be made in the study of organizations.

Outrunning the Red Queen

Developments in molecular biology increasingly point to the endogenous forces unleashed by the molecular structure of organisms themselves. For modern geneticists, the hereditary material of organisms does not consist of static and particulate units of information faithfully handed down from generation to generation. Rather, genes display significant degrees of internal structure that can be and are deliberately altered by organisms. Indeed, complex genes appear to develop sensors that bring relevant information from the environment to the constituent DNA molecules within genes—thereby suggesting that genes themselves 'learn.' So, it may be that, contrary to neo-Darwinian assumptions, "genetic structures do not adapt the organism to its evironment. Instead, they have evolved to promote and direct the process of evolution. They function to enhance the capacity of the species to evolve" (Campbell 1985: 137).

But even the coding of evolutionary functions into genetic structures need not increase the competitive fitness of any individual organism. Van Valen (1973) proposed the Red Queen paradox as a way of conceptualizing the dynamic aspect adaptation. In Lewis Carroll's *Alice through the Looking Glass*, the Red Queen tells Alice that, even though they are all running at top speed, they really should not expect to get anywhere. This is because inhabitants of Looking Glass Land are obliged to run as fast as they can just to stay where they are and, to get anywhere, they would have to run ever so much faster.

Organizations face the same dilemma. The paradox of the Red Queen suggests that organizations must not only cope with current environmental conditions, they must out-evolve competing organizations over time. As Campbell (1985: 139) put it: "Ultimately, evolutionary success for each competitor comes from acquiring tricks, skills, and strategies to evolve faster and more effectively than the competition."

For organizations, this points to the importance of modeling the search processes through which managers acquire information about environments with which they then imitate competitors. As Dutton, Freedman, and Subbanarasimha (1987) report, the incidence of industrial espionage is higher in rapidly growing industries: imitation prevails. Not suprisingly, it is precisely in these environments that managers strive to institutionalize innovative behaviors by developing shared frames of reference that cultivate innovation, flexibility, and adaptability (Nelson and Winter 1982). A better understanding of imitative processes may help explain how a firm buffers itself from the action of selection by elaborating a complex internal structure that maximizes information gathering and enables it to outcompete firms with structures that would otherwise appear more efficient in the short-run. Like organisms, organizations project themselves into their environments in order to anticipate future contigencies. To recognize and encompass these anticipatory features of organizations is to extend the reach of ecological research beyond the current neo-Darwinian framework.

Hierarchical Inclusion in Nested Systems

Biologists claim that an organism is adapted to its environment when it displays characteristics that enhance its ability to outperform rivals in the quest for resources. As Brandon (1985: 81) points out, however: "to claim that something is an adaptation is . . . to make a claim about the causal history of that thing and, so to say, how its existence is to be causally explained. In a sense, adaptations are explained in terms of the good they confer on some entities." The question that begs answering is: For the good of what?

In the neo-Darwinian framework, adaptations are strictly for the good of the organisms possessing them. Biologists increasingly recognize, however, that these adaptations also occur at levels other than that of individual organisms (Arnold and Fristrup 1982; Brandon 1985). This is because living systems are highly complex, ordered systems. Hence many of their properties are emergent and cannot be deduced from their components. If the boundaries separating systems from larger systems are artificially drawn, then what unit does selection act upon?

Sociobiologists use a group-level concept of fitness to explain the emergence of altruism in hymenoptera (Wilson 1975). They suggest that selection involves "thinking of the animal as playing a 'game' against other members of its species, and asking what 'strategy' would maximize its inclusive fitness, subject to the environmental constraints facing it" (May and Seger 1986: 265). Although this argument may seem less relevant to organizational ecologists studying selection processes in Western capitalist states where individualism and self-interest are institutionalized, it may prove more germane in explaining organizational processes in less fragmented, more centralized economies where collective well-being is emphasized (Meyer and Rowan 1983). Not only are the fitness criteria likely to be different under different political regimes, selection itself may act at an interorganizational level of analysis.

Paleobiologists provide the most complete view of the embeddedness of single organisms in nested systems. Gould (1980: 121), for instance, proposed a hierarchical view of the world:

> constructed not as a smooth and seamless continuum, permitting simple extrapolation from the lowest level to the highest, but as a series of ascending levels, each bound to the one below it in some ways and independent in others. Discontinuities and seams characterize the transitions; "emergent" features not implicit in the operation of processes at lower levels, may control events at higher levels.

Indeed, the evolution of species and higher order groupings in biology (macroevolution) displays emergent properties that, Gould (1980) contends, make it an entirely autonomous field of study from microevolution, the gradual succession of organisms (Gould 1980). Discontinuities separate the development of local populations from the origination and development of whole species (Eldredge and Gould 1972), and fundamentally different explanations of historical patterns result depending on which particular level is stressed (Vrba and Eldredge 1984).

Organizations are also nested in higher-order collectivities. An ecology of organizations might therefore specify the various sorting and branching processes that interrelate organizations as they are nested in populations, species, communities, and ecosystems. In this light, most of the existing empirical research on organizations dwells on quantifying the study of sorting processes within populations. Although important, such gradualist models cannot explain the wholesale appearance and disappearance of entire sectors of activity, such as the displacement of manufacturing by information services in the United States (Piore and Sabel 1984) or more generally the process of creative destruction of industries by new technologies (Schumpeter 1958).

EXTENDING THE REACH
OF ECOLOGICAL RESEARCH

Biologists propose that mounting evidence in the organismic realm requires revision of the neo-Darwinian framework to encompass, on the one hand, the projective properties of organisms and, on the other hand, the hierarchical structure within which organisms survive. Applied to organizations, this line of thinking suggests that a revised ecological framework should encompass (1) the voluntaristic transformation of organizations through strategic change and (2) the embeddedness of organizations in higher-order collectivities. Some organizational ecologists have begun to address these points empirically: Singh, House, and Tucker (1986) assessed the relative influence of strategic change against selection pressure on survival rates, while in Chapter 11 of this volume, Brittain and Wholey tackled the nested structure of organizations and populations in the electronics manufacturing community.

Additionally, current ecological explanations of organizational change tend to disregard some important social processes: (3) They artificially separate organizations from their environments; and (4) they distort the systemic relationships between organizations and environments. As we struggle to extend the neo-Darwinian model of change, these four concerns taken jointly are likely to be central to the research program of organizational ecology for many years to come.

Formulating a Theory of Strategic Change

Current ecological theory makes three assumptions to explain how populations are transformed: (1) that particular characteristics have direct implications for organizational performance and hence the survival of organizations; (2) that external environments judiciously discriminate between high and low performers, favoring those organizations that conform to specifiable criteria of performance and systematically withdrawing support from those organizations that do not conform; and (3) that characteristics propagate across populations principally through differential rates of foundings and closures. These assumptions are problematic because they distort important features of the institutional contexts in which organizations operate and that doubtless condition their actions (Granovetter 1985).

The adoption of a particular characteristic by any single organization or set of organizations, for instance, might have little effect on a populationwide measure of organizational performance. This could occur, for instance, if a change in one characteristic is matched by a compensatory change in another characteristic. So, equifinality in social systems implies that centralization, formalized control, and low training might be interchangeable with decentralization, participation, and intensive socialization, with no net effect on either performance or survival rates. This would explain in part why many contingency theories of structure have had a difficult time demonstrating the impact of particular organizational characteristics on performance (Miller and Friesen 1984).

Organizations might also adopt particular characteristics for purely faddish reasons. Just as garment manufacturers select new designs each season to capture the interest of customer groups, so may organizations make changes to signal to external constituencies that they too are on the cutting edge, trendy, and hence legitimate (Abrahamson 1987; Meyer and Rowan 1983). Existing organizations follow suit so as not to be left behind, with no net change in either organization or population performance. Following Hannan and Freeman (1984), if we distinguish core from periphery characteristics, then perhaps peripheral characteristics are most apt to display such faddish cyclicality. Yet the characteristics that organizational ecologists sometimes monitor are not always core characteristics (cf. Carroll 1984: note 2).

Environments might also be either unable or unwilling to discriminate between high- and low-performing organizations. Even when organizations choose characteristics that do affect their performance, the existence of multiple stakeholders in their environments means that external evaluators often disagree on the merits of those characteristics. Inefficient or illegitimate organizations might therefore elicit social supports even though they adopt characteristics that do not enhance their short-run performance. Indeed, characteristics have only a probabilistic impact on any measure of performance: They develop into advantages and disadvantages to an adopting organization only in the future. Because prediction is difficult at best, both organizations and environmental stakeholders may therefore disagree about the long-run effects of particular choices, and particular changes in some of an organization's characteristics are likely to be only loosely coupled to its short-run performance and survival.

Moreover, strategic imitation may overwhelm structural inertia. Although Hannan and Freeman (1977, 1984) assert that newly formed organizations are disproportionately likely to adopt the advantageous characteristics of surviving organizations, such a theory of propagation creates a quandary: If advantageous characteristics can be imitated, then characteristics that were initially advantageous to adopting organizations cannot remain advantageous for long. Just as visitors to Looking Glass Land are obliged to run as fast as they can just to stay where they are, so are organizations compelled to adopt new characteristics just to remain competitive. If so, then the advantages that particular characteristics confer on organizations should show periodicity, decaying as imitation proceeds and rising as new characteristics are adopted that confer temporary advantages to innovating organizations. This suggests that when survival rates are plotted as a function of a particular organizational characteristic, some cyclicality should be observed.

Unfortunately, the neo-Darwinian framework resists the introduction of either strategic or faddish imitation. From this perspective, survival achieved by the voluntary change efforts of existing organizations is actually an anomaly: Only through selection do populations change (Hannan and Freeman 1984). *Prima facie,* such an extreme statement seems difficult to maintain, given the radical transformations many organizations appear to undergo, both in their core technologies and in their managerial practices. Adhering to this assumption merely reflects organizational ecology's roots in the neo-Darwinian framework. Although it may adequately describe the presence of long-lasting, genetic constraints on change for organisms, it appears less convincing in the context of a theory of organizational change (Betton and Dess 1985).

Treating change as a purely Darwinian process of selection ultimately obscures the fact that variation itself is probably more Lamarckian than Darwinian (McKelvey 1982). There are strong incentives for imitation even by large organizations, witness the explicit emphasis that firms place on industrial espionage even in concentrated industries, particularly in high-growth niches (Dutton, Freedman, and Subbanarasimha 1987). In order to accommodate the existence of strategic and faddish imitation in organizational populations, we therefore have to make important modifications to the neo-Darwinian framework imported from bioecology. Chapter 2 in this volume took a first step in this direction. By defining founding rates and disbanding rates in terms of both competition and legitimacy—each one a function of the proportion of existing organizations of a specific form—Hannan and Freeman allow for an important aspect of the institutional embeddedness of organizations. Tucker, Singh, Meinhard, and House report in Chapter 8 supportive evidence for such a nonmonotonic influence of density on founding and disbanding rates. In so doing, ecological theory is clearly extended beyond the neo-Darwinian framework because a definition of legitimacy in terms of the density of existing forms can enter the Lotka-Volterra equations not only through foundings and closings but through a process of strategic imitation.

Blurring the Boundaries of Organizations and Environments

A second problem of existing ecological models results from an understanding that organizations and environments interpenetrate through a wide range of formal and informal interlocks. People may belong to the same organization by day and to different organizations by night. Ambiguous boundaries make it unclear whether a social arrangement constitutes an organization, when an organization came into being, or whether it has in fact ceased to exist (Starbuck and Nystrom 1981). As such, to distinguish organizations from their environments is not a trivial task.

Because organizations are social constructions, their existence depends as much on collective consensus, legal definition, and the institutional environment as it does on objective properties (Zucker 1983). To infer results from historical outcomes is therefore problematic because the interpretations of what constitutes an organization and what constitutes an environment are themselves specific to time and place. To conduct an ecological analysis of organizations is therefore to raise considerations frequently addressed by historians, particularly their appreciation of the time bound meanings of events.

Finally, the characteristics of organizations themselves vary widely based on the criteria the researcher applies to them. An organization may appear centralized on some dimensions and democratic on others, highly structured on some dimensions and chaotic on others (Starbuck 1976). To isolate a correspondence between a single organizational characteristic and a particular environmental state is therefore to risk misrepresenting the multidimensionality of both organizations and environments. Viewing organizations and environments as joint configurations of characteristics (Miller and Friesen, 1984) might enhance the power of future ecological research. Students of industrial organization (Caves and Porter 1979), for instance, suggest that organizations coalesce into "strategic groups" with common configurations of characteristics. To ecologists, this clearly suggests that strategic groups describe organizational membership in distinct niches. Ecological models have the capacity to explain how an isomorphic process jointly comes to define niches and groups of similarly configured firms. This would afford a natural point of convergence for ecological theory with models of industrial organization theory and competitive strategy (Scherer 1980; Caves and Porter 1979).

Embedding Organizations in Higher-Order Collectivities

Even if we continue to forge a conceptual distinction between organization and environment, ecological models could benefit from acknowledging that cooperative relationships also bind organizations and individuals into collectivities with emergent properties. In the pursuit of profit, stability, growth, or legitimacy, organizations sign agreements, form industry associations, engage in joint ventures, exchange personnel, and sometimes collude (Scherer 1980). So seemingly competitive organizations are fused into groups, networks, and social circles, capable of counterinfluence on environments in ways that thwart the forces of selection (Astley and Fombrun 1983a).

As cooperative relationships stabilize, competition may shift from population to network: What was once competition between organizations could become competition between networks. The rivalry between the leading automobile manufacturers (General Motors, Ford, and Chrysler), for instance, actually takes place between intricate networks of loosely coordinated suppliers, dealers, parts manufacturers, assemblers, data processors, advertising agencies, designers, and labor unions. Indeed, the Japanese formally organize such networks into "groups": The Mitsubishi group, for instance, joins hundreds of nominally independent organizations into a coordinated network. Modeling the degree of competition between networks may prove useful as we turn our attention away from the study of organizational forms to the study of interorganizational structures (Fombrun 1986).

In turn, these buffered networks fuse into loosely articulated configurations that Schön (1971) labeled *business systems* and that Gerlach and Palmer (1981: 364) called Segmented Polycentric Integrated Networks (SPINs). SPINs, they claimed, create evolutionary advantages for member organizations by maximizing heterogeneity, increasing reliability, and protecting against suppression and cooptation.

Much as biologists have claimed that organisms fit into nested systems, networks are the building blocks of organizational communities; like the food webs of bioecology, they fuse populations into higher-order collectivities (Astley and Fombrun 1987). By linking organizations into such ecosystems, networks can distort the selection pressures that organizations face, making it difficult to account for changing organizational characteristics in terms of selection at the population level. So Astley and Fombrun (1983b) described how the ecology of the motion-picture industry converged into the ecologies of neighboring industries, suggesting the potential value of viewing these diverse industries as constituent members of a single telecommunications community subject to communitywide selection. Indeed, entirely different processes may operate on the ebb and flow of organizations and populations experiencing communitywide selection (Astley 1985). For instance, although Zucker's (1983) account documented the rise of the corporate form in the United States as a process of gradual change, Astley and Fombrun (1987) argued that the adoption of the corporate form actually went through a punctuated sequence in which the modal organizational form changed from the horizontal trust, to the vertically integrated functional form, to the multidivisional form. Far more research is needed to substantiate this punctuated model of community change.

Beyond its ability to address radical change, the community perspective also enables modeling the effects of cooperative action on survival rates. In Chapter 7, for instance, Aldrich and Staber demonstrated how trade associations foundings and dissolutions might be explained in terms of a niche-width model with a finite carrying capacity. A provocative extension of their analysis would overlay the rise of trade associations within particular industries against the foundings and dissolutions of *firms* within those industries. Because trade associations represent a form of collective action, this would enable discussion of the moderating effects of institutional acts on population dynamics. Other forms of community-level acts—such as contracts or joint ventures that span industry boundaries— could be modeled in this way.

Recognizing That Systemic Relationships Induce Contradictions

A final problem that future ecological models will have to grapple with is their tendency to ignore the complex interactions that characterize the social system within which organizations are embedded. Thus, the actions of organizations invariably beget reactions from competitors and other environmental actors. For instance, an organization that chooses a practice that confers it some advantage quickly elicits imitation and hence a round of intensified competition that soon eliminates the advantage. This suggests that imitation by individual organizations creates a compensatory increase in the degree of rivalry in the population as a whole: A population that succeeds in generating above-normal profits because of its managerial practices both fosters shirking behavior by existing members of the population and encourages imitation by competitors and new entrants, thereby driving down the profitability of the niche.

These systemic effects are widely acknowledged. Less obvious, however, are the fundamental contradictions between the activities organizations engage in and the outcomes of those activities for different groups of firms in a population. For instance, Brittain and Freeman (1980) pointed out how established firms sow the seeds of increased population rivalry by spawning entrepreneurs who use the training, knowledge, and information they acquired as employees to compete with their former employers. Similarly, Astley and Fombrun (1987) indicated how the attempts by firms to absorb horizontal, then vertical, and finally diagonal interdependence led not only to radical transformations of the modal organizational form from trusts, to vertically integrated functional structures, to the M-form, but to a proliferation of contracts, joint ventures, and other forms of interfirm networking. As Fombrun (1986) argued, organization-environment complexes were transformed by an emergent contradiction between the self-interested motivation of single organizations to reduce interdependence, and the resulting proliferation of interorganizational relationships that actually increased interdependence: To pursue a convergence between economic activity and social relationships is to also evoke a contradiction that undermines the convergence.

If relationships within and between organizations and environments develop both through processes of convergence and through processes of divergence, then clearly ecological models have taken a one-sided view of the processes that drive population change. By dwelling on the competitive and institutional forces that foster isomorphism and convergence, existing ecological models are silent on the dialectical processes that also elicit a realignment of administrative practices within organizations, populations, and communities (Fombrun 1986). To date, ecological models remain wedded to a view that sees only gradual change through selection as the motor for transforming populations and exogenous technological change as the driving force of community punctuations (Astley 1985). By studying processes of divergence in an ecological framework, we are presented with a potentially rich field of inquiry for addressing how *endogenous* causal forces can propel changes in organizational populations and communities.

INFERRING CAUSALITY FROM HISTORY

Ultimately, the task of organizational ecology is to infer causal processes from historically specific outcomes. In this, the field shares many basic problems and concerns with students of history: Data collected for particular human purposes may systematically distort the processes under study; important causal influences may have gone unrecorded; recording practices and human error may vary systematically; fundamental causal processes between variables of interest may themselves be time-dependent. These are familiar pitfalls of all longitudinal research that reaches backward through time to investigate causal relationships. They caution researchers to beware of seemingly objective data whose production was embedded in a sociocultural context. For organizational researchers, this means that quantitative data describing the historical record of organizational foundings and closings should increasingly be supplemented with "thick description" (Geertz 1973), both of the data collection and the societal context in which the data were produced. Indeed, most explanations of findings, whether confirmatory or anomalous, are typically explained by recourse to such unquantified descriptive information.

Consistent with these admonitions, care must be taken to ensure that the patterned changes in organizations and environments identified by *ex post facto* methods are, in fact, causally related. Theoretically informed hypotheses should not only carefully delineate the expected causal process but also strive to identify credible null models against which to test for the presence or absence of an effect. As Connor and Simberloff (1986: 161) pointed out, "if one is unwilling to make assumptions to account for structure in the data that can be attributed to causal processes not under investigation, then posing and rejecting null hypotheses will be trivially easy and uninteresting." They propose that ecological propositions should be tested against viable, credible alternatives. Many ecological models make relatively naive tests: They do not present a systematically developed alternative process that could also generate the observed pattern. Significantly, Singh, House, and Tucker (1986) took a major step forward by carefully articulating and contrasting the predictions of an adaptive model against those of a selection model. Articulating such credible null models in future ecological research seems highly desirable to ensure greater confidence in findings generated from historical data.

In some ways, organizational ecologists are tasked to develop a science of organizational history. Here too Darwin has been influential. As Gould (1986) proposed in his recent essay, Darwin's legacy consists not only of having articulated a theory of descent by natural selection but also in having formalized a science of history. In particular, Gould (1986) identified three principles for inferring causality from historical data in Darwin's writings: (1) uniformity; (2) simultaneity; and (3) anomaly. Darwin's approaches, like the theoretical framework that he bequeathed us, must also be tailored to the needs of organizational science.

Delimiting the Principle of Uniformity

Darwin's assumption of uniformity implied that all large-scale changes arise as the extrapolated result of accumulated small-scale changes. In Darwin's view, rigorous measurements of current small-scale processes could be extrapolated into historical time to test their cumulative impact.

Caution must be exercised in applying this Darwinian principle to organizational research. Uniformity suggests that careful study of the microlevel processes that produce foundings and closings—when aggregated across organizations and over time—could help apprehend the role that organizations play in producing large-scale social change. This gradualist hypothesis may still bear fruit if carefully applied over relatively short time spans or in circumscribed institutional contexts. However, if we accept the greater relative malleability of organizations, punctuational processes may better explain the metamorphic transformations that organizations also appear to undergo, whether it be the systemwide adoption and diffusion of bureaucracy (Zucker 1983; DiMaggio and Powell 1983); the shifting allegiance of business to the single function, vertically integrated, and multidivisional forms; or the wholesale disappearance of populations (Piore and Sabel 1984).

Developing Comparative Ecologies

Darwin's principle of simultaneity holds that all the stages of the historical process existed somewhere in the world at any one time. Just as astronomers could infer the course of a star's life by finding different stars in various stages of a general process, so could evolutionary processes, he reasoned, be inferred by comparing different organisms in various stages of development.

For the most part, organizational ecologists no longer adhere to developmental theories that propose a sequential ordering of either environmental states or organizations. Nonetheless, even if contexts are not thought to be progressively interrelated, much can still be inferred about organizational change from comparing the ecologies of either the same population in distinct time periods, multiple populations in similar environments, or similar populations in multiple cities, states, or countries as they contend with comparable sets of causal forces. This requires that we carefully define the relevant parameters of the local setting before we engage in quantitative comparisons of organizational processes. In Chapter 10, Carroll and Huo convincingly demonstrated how social processes leading to foundings of local assemblies of the Knights of Labor varied in different time periods. Similarly, in Chapter 5, McCarthy, Wolfson, Baker, and Mosakowski presented a well-grounded contrast between local communities in their attempt to explain the founding of social movement organizations. Finally, in Chapter 6, Miller, McPherson and Smith-Lovin indicated how country-specific data regarding economic development and class structure can shed light on the nature of competition for affiliation in the voluntary sectors of five different countries. Thus, even though we may have abandoned notions of advancement in social theory (Granovetter 1979), comparative ecologies enable us to untangle potentially important contextual effects.

Identifying Anomalies

Finally, Darwin claimed that the historical record was full of anomalies—traces of the past that linger on despite changed environmental circumstances. Like the inefficient but workable false thumb of the panda, organizations may also support antiquated appendages that are traces of previous responses to environmental constraints (Meyer and Rowan 1977). When aggregated across organizational populations, these anomalies may reveal common contingencies that organizations responded to at the same time—Stinchcombe's (1965) hypothesis that organizational properties may be imprinted at founding.

Some of these anomalies could appear as sudden bursts or blips in a time series of organizational changes. Because these jolts disrupt stability, they could prove useful to students of ecology by revealing the hidden forces that stabilize the ecologies of organizations (Meyer 1982). More careful, thick descriptions of such seemingly anomalous changes are needed if we are to understand how macrolevel influences translate into microlevel effects.

CONCLUSION

Although empirical research now largely defines *organizational ecology* as the study of patterned changes in organizational characteristics and environmental states, most theoretical treatments reflect a lingering allegiance to the conceptual baggage of the neo-Darwinian frame of reference. This chapter has argued that organizational ecology stands to benefit from explicitly addressing the deficiencies of neo-Darwinism in formulating a theory of change. In such a revised framework, selection should contend with strategic change, the hierarchical embeddedness of organizations in an institutional matrix should be recognized, and the problematic nature of causal inference based on historical data should be examined.

Various chapters in this book have pointed us in this direction. In one form or another, a modified interpretation of Darwin's historical principles have informed the research they report. As the empirical results of these and other ecological studies cumulate, perhaps in the years to come a theoretical articulation of organizational ecology can be attempted that successfully extends the neo-Darwinian framework and incorporates a stronger set of institutional assumptions about the environments in which organizations thrive.

REFERENCES

Abrahamson, Eric. 1987. "Managerial Fashion." Unpublished paper, School of Business, New York University.

Adams, L.D. 1978. *The Wines of America*. 2d ed. New York: McGraw-Hill.

Alapuro, R. 1982. "Finland: An Interface Periphery." In *The Politics of Territorial Identity: Studies in European Regionalism*, edited by Stein Rokkan and Derek W. Urwin, pp. 113–64. London: Sage.

Alchian, Armen A. 1950. "Uncertainty, Evolution and Economic Theory." *Journal of Political Economy* 58: 211–22.

Aldrich, Howard E. 1979. *Organizations and Environments*. Englewood Cliffs, N.J.: Prentice-Hall.

Aldrich, Howard, and Ellen R. Auster. 1986. "Even Dwarfs Started Small: Liabilities of Age and Size and Their Strategic Implications." In *Research in Organizational Behavior*, vol. 8, edited by Barry Staw and L.L. Cummings, pp. 165–98. Greenwich, Conn.: JAI.

Aldrich, Howard, and Udo Staber. 1983. "The Organization of Business Interest Associations." Unpublished paper, Department of Sociology, University of North Carolina, Chapel Hill.

———. 1984. "The Creation and Persistence of Business Interest Associations: An Ecological Approach." Unpublished paper, Department of Sociology, University of North Carolina, Chapel Hill.

Aldrich, Howard, and Robert Stern. 1983. "Resource Mobilization and the Creation of U.S. Producers' Cooperatives, 1835–1935." *Economic and Industrial Democracy* 4: 371–406.

Allardt, E., and P. Pesonen. 1967. "Cleavages in Finnish Politics." In *Party Systems and Voter Alignments: Cross-National Perspectives*, edited by Seymour M. Lipset and Stein Rokkan, pp. 326–66. New York: Free Press.

Almond, G.A., and S. Verba. 1963. *The Civic Culture: Political Attitudes and Democracy in Five Nations*. Princeton, N.J.: Princeton University Press.

———. 1968. *The Five Nation Study*. Ann Arbor: Interuniversity Consortium for Political Research.

Amburgey, Terry L. 1986a. "Multivariate Point Process Models in Social Research. *Social Science Research* 15: 190–207.

———. 1986b. "The Strategy of Serendipity: Tactical and Strategic Opportunism in Organizations." Unpublished paper, Northwestern University, Evanston, Illinois.

Amburgey, Terry L., and Dawn Kelly. 1985. "Transformation and Selection in Organizational Populations." Unpublished paper, Northwestern University, Evanston, Illinois.

Andrews, K.R. 1971. *The Concept of Corporate Strategy*. Homewood, Ill.: Irwin.

Ansoff, H.I., and J. Stewart. 1967. "Strategies for a Technology-Based Business." *Harvard Business Review* 45: 71–83.

Arnold, Anthony, J., and Kurt Fristrup. 1982. "The Theory of Evolution by Natural Selection: A Hierarchical Expansion." *Paleobiology* 8: 113–29.

Astley, W. Graham. 1985. "The Two Ecologies: Microevolutionary and Macroevolutionary Perspectives on Organizational Change." *Administrative Science Quarterly* 30: 224–41.

Astley, W. Graham, and Charles J. Fombrun. 1983a. "Collective Strategy: The Social Ecology of Organizational Environments." *Academy of Management Review* 8: 576–87.

———. 1983b. "Technological Innovation and Industrial Structure." In *Advances in Strategic Management*, 1, edited by Robert Lamb, pp. 205–29. Greenwich, Conn.: JAI.

———. 1987. "Organizational Communities: An Ecological Perspective." In *Research in the Sociology of Organizations*, edited by Samuel Bacharach and Nancy DiTomaso. Greenwich, Conn. JAI. Forthcoming.

Bain, Joseph S. 1956. *Barriers to New Competition* Cambridge: Harvard University Press.

Baker, David P.; Mark Wolfson; John D. McCarthy; and Elaine M. Mosakowski. 1986. "Social and Demographic Environmental Determinants of Social Movement Organization Founding: The Case of Local Citizens' Organizations Opposing Drunken Driving." Paper presented at the Annual Meetings of the American Sociological Association, New York, N.Y., August 30–September 3.

Baron, James N.; Frank R. Dobbin; and P. Devereaux Jennings. 1986. "War and Peace: The Evolution of Modern Personnel Administration in U.S. Industry." *American Journal of Sociology* 92: 350–83.

Bauer, Raymond; Ithiel de Sola Pool; and Lewis Dexter. 1963. *American Business and Public Policy*. New York: Atherton.

Beard, Mary R. 1930. "Knights of Labor." In *Encyclopaedia of the Social Sciences*, edited by Edwin R. Seligman, pp. 581–84. New York: Macmillan.

Bell, Wendel. 1954. "A Probability Model of the Measurement of Ecological Segregation." *Social Forces* 32: 357–64.

Best, Robert S. 1974. "Youth Policy." In *Issues in Canadian Public Policy*, edited by G. Bruce Doern and V. Seymour Wilson, pp. 137–65. Toronto: Macmillan.

Betton, John, and Gregory G. Dess. 1984. "The Application of Population Ecology Models to the Study of Organizations." *Academy of Management Review* 10: 750–57.

Beyme, Klaus von. 1983. "Neo-Corporatism: A New Nut in an Old Shell?" *International Political Science Review* 4: 173–96.

Bidwell, Charles E., and John D. Kasarda. 1985. *The Organization and Its Ecosystem.* Greenwich, Conn.: JAI.

Birdsall, William C. 1953. "The Problem of Structure in the Knights of Labor." *Industrial and Labor Relations Review* 6: 532–46.

Blau, Peter M., and W. Richard Scott. 1961. *Formal Organizations.* San Francisco: Chandler.

Bleyer, W.G. 1927. *Main Currents in the History of Journalism.* Cambridge, Mass.: Riverside Press.

Bollen, Kenneth R. 1979. "Political Democracy and the Timing of Development." *American Sociological Review* 44: 572–87.

———. 1980. "Comparative Measurement of Political Democracy." *American Sociological Review* 45: 370–90.

———. 1983. "World System Position, Dependency, and Democracy." *American Sociological Review* 48: 468–79.

Borg, O. 1966. "Basic Dimensions of Finnish Party Ideologies: A Factor Analytic Study." *Scandinavian Political Studies* 1: 94–120.

Borrus, Michael; James Millstein; and John Zysman. 1982. *International Competition in Advanced Industrial Sectors: Trade and Development in the Semiconductor Industry.* Berkeley: Institute of International Studies.

Boswell, C. 1973. *The Rise and Fall of Small Firms.* London: Allen and Unwin.

Brandon, Robert N. 1985. "Adaptation Explanations: Are Adaptations for the Good of Replicators or Interactors?" In *Evolution at a Crossroads: The New Biology and the New Philosophy of Science*, edited by David J. Depew and Bruce H. Weber, pp. 81–96. Cambridge, Mass.: MIT Press.

Braun, Ernest, and Stuart MacDonald. 1978. *Revolution in Miniature.* Cambridge, England: Cambridge University Press.

Brittain, Jack W., and John Freeman. 1980. "Organizational Proliferation and Density Dependent Selection." In *The Organizational Life Cycle*, edited by John Kimberly and Robert H. Miles, pp. 291–338. San Francisco: Jossey-Bass.

Brittain, Jack W., and Timothy W. Stearns. 1985. "Competitive Dynamics and Organizational Diversity: Strategic Interactions in Semiconductor Components." In *Proceedings of the Southwest Division of the Academy of Management*, pp. 186–90. New Orleans, La.: Southwest Division, Academy of Management.

Brown, John L., and Rodney Schneck. 1979. "A Structuralist Comparison between Canadian and American Industrial Organizations." *Administrative Science Quarterly* 24:24–47.

Bucklin, R.; R. Caves; and A. Lo. 1985. "Games of Survival in the Newspaper Industry." Unpublished paper.

Buhle, Paul. 1978. "The Knights of Labor in Rhode Island." *Radical History Review* 5: 39–73.

Bureau of the Census. 1984a. *County Statistics File 1* (CO-STAT 1) (Machine-readable data file). Washington, D.C.: Bureau of the Census (producer and distributor).

———. 1984b. *County Statistics File I* (CO-STAT 1), Technical Documentation. Washington, D.C.: Bureau of the Census (producer and distributor).

Burt, Ronald 1982. "A Note on Cooptation and Definitions of Constraint." In *Social Structure and Network Analysis*, edited by Peter V. Marsden and Nan Lin, pp. 219–34. Beverly Hills: Sage.

Campbell, John H. 1985. "An Organizational Interpretation of Evolution.." In *Evolution and a Crossroads: The New Biology and the New Philosophy of Science*, edited by David J. Depew and Bruce H. Weber, pp. 133–68. Cambridge, Mass.: MIT Press.

Carroll, Glenn R. 1981. "Dynamics of Organizational Expansion in National Systems of Education." *American Sociological Review* 46: 585–99.

———. 1983. "A Stochastic Model of Organizational Mortality: Review and Reanalysis." *Social Science Research* 12: 303–29.

———. 1984. "Organizational Ecology." *Annual Review of Sociology* 10: 71–93.

———. 1985. "Concentration and Specialization: Dynamics of Niche Width in Populations of Organizations." *American Journal of Sociology* 90: 1262–83.

———. 1987. *Publish and Perish: The Organizational Ecology of Newspaper Industries*. Greenwich, Conn.: JAI.

Carroll, Glenn R., and Jacques Delacroix. 1982. "Organizational Mortality in the Newspaper Industries of Argentina and Ireland: An Ecological Approach." *Administrative Science Quarterly* 27: 169–98.

Carroll, Glenn R.; Jacques Delacroix; and Jerry Goodstein. 1988. "The Political Environments of Organizations: An Ecological View." *Research in Organizational Behavior* 10, edited by Barry Staw and Larry Cummings. Greenwich, Conn.: JAI.

Carroll, Glenn R., and Yangchung Paul Huo. 1985. "Losing by Winning: The Paradox of Electoral Success by Organized Labor Parties in the Knights of Labor Era." Technical Report No., OBIR-6. Center for Research in Management, University of California, Berkeley.

———. 1986. "Organizational Task and Institutional Environments in Ecological Perspective: Findings from the Local Newspaper Industry." *American Journal of Sociology* 91: 838–73.

Cassity, Michael J. 1979. "Modernization and Social Crisis: The Knights of Labor and a Midwest Community, 1885–1886." *Journal of American History* 66: 41–61.

Castaldi, M.A., and P.J. Folwell. 1986. "Washington Winery Investments." *Wines and Vines* (November): 56–57.

Caves, Richard E., and Michael E. Porter. 1979. "From Entry Barriers to Mobility Barriers." *Quarterly Journal of Economics* 91: 421–34.

Chandler, Alfred D. 1962. *Strategy and Structure*. Cambridge, Mass.: MIT Press.

———. 1977. *The Visible Hand: The Managerial Revolution in American Business*. Cambridge, Mass.: Harvard University Press.

Child, John. 1972. "Organizational Structure, Environment and Performance: The Role of Strategic Choice." *Sociology* 6: 1–22.

Choldin, M.T. 1985. *Fence around the Empire: Russian Censorship of Western Ideas under the Tsars*. Durham: Duke University Press.

Clark, B.R. 1972. "The Organizational Saga in Higher Education." *Administrative Science Quarterly* 17: 178–84.

Clark, G.K. 1967. *The Critical Historian*. London: Heinemann Educational Books.

Clemments, F.E. 1936. "Nature and Structure of the Climax." *Journal of Ecology* 24, no. 2: 252–84.

Colgate, Craig, Jr. 1966 to 1984. *Directory of National and Professional Associations in the U.S.* Washington, D.C.: Columbia.

Collins, O.F., and D.G. Moore. 1970. *The Organization Makers.* New York: Meredith.

Committee on Youth. 1971. *A Report to the Secretary of State. It's Your Turn.* Ottawa: Information Canada.

Conell, Carol, and C. Kim Voss. 1982. "Craft Organization and Class Formation: The Impact of Craft Locals on Working Class Organization in the Knights of Labor." Unpublished manuscript, Stanford University.

Connor, Edward F., and Daniel Simberloff. 1986. "Competition, Scientific Method, and Null Models in Ecology." *American Scientist* 74: 155–62.

Cooper, A.C. 1971. "Spin-offs and Technical Entrepreneurship." *IEEE Transactions on Engineering Management* 18.

Cornfield, Daniel. 1984. "Organizational Aging in a Population of Local Labor Unions." Paper presented at the American Sociological Association meetings, August San Antonio, Texas.

Cox, D.R. 1972. "Regression Models and Life Tables." *Journal of the Royal Statistical Society* B34: 187–220.

———. 1975. "Partial Likelihood." *Biometrika* 62: 269–76.

Curran, J. 1978. "The Press as an Agency of Social Control: An Historical Perspective." In *Newspaper History: From the 17th Century to the Present Day*, edited by George Boyce, James Curran and Pauline Wingate, pp. 51–75. Beverly Hills: Sage.

Cyert, Richard M., and James G. March. 1963. *A Behavioral Theory of the Firm.* Englewood Cliffs, N.J.: Prentice-Hall.

Daft, Richard L. 1983. *Organizational Theory and Design.* St. Paul: West.

Dataquest. 1984. "Semiconductor Startups since 1977." *Internal Company Memo.*

Delacroix, Jacques. 1984. "Export Strategies for Small American Firms." *California Management Review* 3: 138–53.

Delacroix, Jacques, and Glenn R. Carroll. 1983. "Organizational Foundings: An Ecological Study of the Newspaper Industries of Argentina and Ireland." *Administrative Science Quarterly* 28: 274–91.

Department of Commerce. 1939. *Survey of Current Business*: 17–18.

———. 1961. *Survey of Current Business Supplement: Business Statistics*: 130–31.

———. 1984. *Survey of Current Business: Business Statistics*: 94–95.

DiMaggio, Paul J., and Walter W. Powell. 1983. "The Iron Cage Revisited: Institutional Isomorphism and Collective Rationality in Organizational Fields." *American Sociological Review* 48: 147–60.

Dowdeswell, W.H. 1984. *Evolution: A Modern Synthesis.* London: Heinemann.

Duncan, Robert B. 1972. "Characteristics of Organizational Environments and Perceived Environmental Uncertainty." *Administrative Science Quarterly* 17: 313–27.

Dunham, A.C. 1886. "The Knights of Labor." *New England and Yale Review* 195: 490–97.

Dutton, John M.; Richard D. Freedman, and P.N. Subbanarasimha. 1987. "Why Spy? Industrial Espionage and Firms' Strategies." Unpublished paper, School of Business, New York University.

Economic Council of Canada. 1976. *People and Jobs: A Study of the Canadian Labour Market*. Ottawa: Information Canada.

———. 1977. *Into the 80s*. Ottawa: Information Canada.

Edelman, Murray. 1967. *The Symbolic Uses of Politics*. Chicago: University of Illinois Press.

Efron, Bradley. 1977. "The Efficiency of Cox's Likelihood Function for Censored Data." *Journal of the American Statistical Association* 72, no. 359: 557–65.

Eldredge, N., and Stephen J. Gould. 1972. "Punctuated Equilibria: An Alternative to Phyletic Gradualism." In *Models of Paleobiology*, edited by T.J.M. Schoff, pp. 82–115. San Francisco: W.H. Freeman.

Elton, Charles. 1927. *Animal Ecology*. London: Sidgwick and Jackson.

Encyclopedia of Associations. 1955–85. Detroit: Gale.

Fell, James C. 1983. "Alcohol Involvement in United States Traffic Accidents: Where It Is Changing." Washington, D.C.: U.S. Department of Transportation, National Highway Traffic Safety Administration.

Fierman, J. 1986. "How Gallo Crushes the Competition." *Fortune* (September): 24–31.

Fink, Leon. 1983. *Workingmen's Democracy: The Knights of Labor and American Politics*. Urbana: University of Illinois Press.

Fombrun, Charles J. 1986. "Structural Dynamics Within and Between Organizations." *Administrative Science Quarterly* 31: 403–21.

Foner, Philip S. 1947. *The History of the Labor Movement of the United States*, Volume 1. New York: International.

———. 1955. *The History of the Labor Movement of the United States*, Volume 2. New York: International.

Freeman, John. 1978. "The Unit of Analysis in Organizational Research." In *Environments and Organizations*, edited by M. Meyer and Associates, pp. 335–51. San Francisco: Jossey-Bass.

———. 1979. "Going to the Well: School District Administrative Intensity and Environmental Constraint." *Administrative Science Quarterly* 24: 119–33.

———. 1982. "Organizational Life Cycles and Natural Selection Processes." In *Research in Organizational Behavior*, vol. 4, edited by Barry M. Staw and Larry L. Cummings, pp. 1–32. Greenwich, Conn.: JAI.

———. 1984. *Entrepreneurs as Organizational Products*. Paper presented at the 1984 Business/Academic Dialogue, Karl Eller Center, University of Arizona, November 1984.

Freeman, John, and Jack W. Brittain. 1977. "Union Merger Process and Industrial Environment." *Industrial Relations* 16: 173–85.

Freeman, John; Glenn R. Carroll; and Michael T. Hannan. 1983. "The Liability of Newness: Age Dependence in Organizational Death Rates." *American Sociological Review* 48: 692–710.

Freeman, John, and Michael T. Hannan. 1983. "Niche Width and the Dynamics of Organizations Populations." *American Journal of Sociology* 88: 1116–45.

Gais, Thomas L.; Mark A. Peterson; and Jack L. Walker. 1983. "Interest Groups, Iron Triangles and Representative Institutions in American National Government." *British Journal of Political Science* 4: 161–85.

Gamson, William. 1975. *The Strategy of Social Protest*. Homewood, Ill.: Dorsey.

Garlock, Jonathan. 1973. *User's Guide to the Knights of Labor Data Bank*. Ann Arbor: InterUniversity Consortium for Political and Social Research.

──────. 1974. *A Structural Analysis of the Knights of Labor: A Prolegomenon to the History of the Producing Classes*. Ph.D. dissertation, University of Rochester.

Gartner, W.B. 1985. "A Conceptual Framework for Describing the Phenomenon of New Venture Creation." *Academy of Management Review* 10: 696–706.

Gause, G.F. 1934. *The Struggle for Existence*. Baltimore: Williams and Wilkens.

Geertz, Clifford. 1973. *The Interpretation of Cultures*. New York: Basic Books.

Gerlach, Luther P., and Gary B. Palmer. 1981. "Adaptation through Evolving Interdependence." In *Handbook of Organization Design*, vol. 1, edited by Paul C. Nystrom and William H. Starbuck, pp. 323–81. New York: Oxford.

Gould, Stephen J. 1980. "Is a New General Theory of Evolution Emerging?" *Paleobiology* 6: 119–30.

──────. 1986. "Evolution and the Triumph of Homology, or Why History Matters." *American Scientist* 74: 60–69.

Granovetter, Mark. 1978. "Threshold Models of Collective Behavior." *American Journal of Sociology* 83, no. 6: 1420–43.

──────. 1979. "The Idea of 'Advancement' in Theories of Social Evolution and Development." *American Journal of Sociology* 85: 489–515.

──────. 1985. "Economic Action and Social Structure: The Problem of Embeddedness." *American Journal of Sociology* 91: 481–510.

Grant, Verne. 1985. *The Evolutionary Process*. New York: Columbia University Press.

Greiner, L.E. 1972. "Evolution and Revolution as Organizations Grow." *Harvard Business Review* 50: 37–46.

Grob, Gerald N. 1958. "The Knights of Labor and the Trade Unions, 1878–1886." *Journal of Economic History* 18: 176–92.

──────. 1961. *Workers and Utopia*. Evanston: Northwestern University Press.

Gusfield, Joseph. 1975. "Categories of Ownership and Responsibility in Social Issues: Alcohol Abuse and Automobile Use." *Journal of Drug Issues* 5: 285–303.

──────. 1981. *The Culture of Public Problems*. Chicago: University of Chicago Press.

Guth, W.D., and R. Taguri. 1965. "Personal Values and Corporate Strategy." *Harvard Business Review* 43: 123–32.

Gywn, Sandra. 1972. "The Great Ottawa Grant Boom (and How It Grew)." *Saturday Night* 87, no. 10: 7–20.

Hamblin, R.; R.B. Jacobsen; and J.L.L. Miller. 1973. *A Mathematical Theory of Social Change*. New York: Wiley.

Hambrick, D.C. 1980. "Operationalizing the Concept of Business-Level Strategy in Research." *Academy of Management Review* 5: 567–75.

──────. 1981. "Environment, Strategy and Power within Top Management Teams." *Administrative Science Quarterly* 26: 253–76.

Hannan, Michael T. 1986. "Uncertainty, Diversity and Organizational Change." In *Behavioral and Social Science: Fifty Years of Discovery*, edited by Neil Smelser and Dean Gerstein, pp. 73–94. Washington: National Academy Press.

──────. In press. "A Model of Competitive and Institutional Processes in Organizational Ecology." In *Sociological Theories in Progress*, vol. 3, edited by Joseph Berger and Morris Zelditch. Pittsburgh: University of Pittsburgh Press.

Hannan, Michael T., and John Freeman. 1974. "Environment and the Structure of Organizations." Paper presented at the Annual Meetings of the American Sociological Association, August, Montreal, Quebec.

Hannan, Michael T., and John Freeman. 1977. "The Population Ecology of Organizations." *American Journal of Sociology* 82: 929–64.

———. 1984. "Structural Inertia and Organizational Change." *American Sociological Review* 49: 149–64.

———. 1986. "Where Do Organizational Forms Come From?" *Sociological Forum* 1: 50–72.

———. 1987. "The Ecology of Organizational Founding: American Labor Unions, 1836–1985." *American Journal of Sociology* 92: 910–43.

———. In press. "The Ecology of Organizational Mortality: American Labor Unions, 1836–1985." *American Journal of Sociology*.

Hanson, Dirk. 1982. *The New Alchemists.* Boston: Little, Brown.

Hanushek, E.A., and J.E. Jackson. 1977. *Statistical Methods for Social Scientists.* New York: Academic Press.

Harvey, A.C. 1981. *The Econometric Analysis of Time Series.* New York: Wiley.

Hawley, Amos H. 1950. *Human Ecology: A Theory of Community Structure.* New York: Ronald Press.

———. 1968a. "Human Ecology." *International Encyclopedia of the Social Sciences*, Vol. 4, edited by David Sills, pp. 328–37. New York: Free Press.

———. 1986b. *Human Ecology: A Theoretical Synthesis.* Chicago: University of Chicago Press.

Hayes, Michael T. 1981. *Lobbyists and Legislators: A Theory of Political Markets.* New Bruswick: Rutgers University Press.

Hay, George, and Daniel Kelley. 1974. "An Empirical Survey of Price Fixing Conspiracies." *Journal of Law and Economics* 17: 13–38.

Hervouet, V., and D. Blandford. 1986. "Determinants of the Volume and Structure of U.S. Still Wine Imports from France." Unpublished paper, Department of Agricultural Economics, Cornell University.

Himmelberg, Robert. 1976. *The Origin of the National Recovery Administration.* New York: Fordham University Press.

Hofstadter, Richard. 1955. *The Age of Reform.* New York: Vintage.

Houston, Lorne F. 1972. "The Flowers of Power: A Critique of OFY and LIP Programmes." *Our Generation* 7: 52–61.

Høyer, S. 1975. "Temporal Patterns and Political Factors in the Diffusion of Newspaper Publishing: The Case of Norway." *Scandinavian Political Studies* 10: 157–71.

Høyer, S.; S. Hadenius; and L. Weibull. 1975. *The Politics and Economics of the Press: A Developmental Perspective.* London: Sage.

Hutchinson, G. Evelyn. 1957. "Concluding Remarks." *Cold Spring Harbor Symposium on Quantitative Biology* 22: 415–27.

Jacek, Henry J. 1983. "The Organization and Activities of Business Interest Associations in North America: A Comparative Study of Their Relations with the State and Organized Labor." Paper presented at the Annual Meeting of the American Political Science Association, September 1–4, Chicago, Illinois.

Johnston, John. 1972. *Econometric Methods.* 2d ed. New York: McGraw-Hill.

Judkins, C.J. 1942. *Trade and Professional Associations of the U.S.* U.S. Department of Commerce, USGPO.

———. 1949. *Trade and Professional Associations of the U.S.* U.S. Department of Commerce, USGPO.

Kaarna, V., and K. Winter. 1965. *Bibliography of the Finnish Newspapers 1771–1963*. Helsinki: Tampereem Kaupunginkirjaste.

Kastari, P. 1969. "The Position of the President in the Finnish Political System." *Scandinavian Political Studies* 4: 151–59.

Kaufman, Herbert. 1985. *Time, Chance, and Organization*. Chatham, N.J.: Chatham House.

Kemmerer, Donald C., and Edward D. Wickersham. 1950. "The Reasons for the Growth of the Knights of Labor in 1885–1886." *Industrial and Labor Relations Review* 3: 213–20.

Kent, C.A.; D.L. Sexton; and K.H. Vesper. 1982. *The Encyclopedia of Entrepreneurship*. Englewood Cliffs, N.J.: Prentice Hall.

Kesselman, Mark. 1982. "The Conflictual Evolution of American Political Science: From Apologetic Pluralism to Trilaterialism and Marxism." In *Public Values and Private Power in American Politics*, edited by J. David Greenstone, pp. 34–67. Chicago: University of Chicago Press.

Kim, K. 1978. "Multivariate Analysis of Ordinal Variables Revisited." *American Journal of Sociology* 81: 261–98.

Kimberly, John. 1975. "Environmental Constraints and Organizational Structure: A Comparative Analysis of Rehabilitation Organizations." *Administrative Science Quarterly* 20: 1–9.

———. 1979. "Issues in the Creation of Organizations: Initiation, Innovation and Institutionalization." *Academy of Management Journal* 22: 437–57.

Kline, Morris. 1985. *Mathematics and the Search for Knowledge*. New York: Oxford.

Kramer, Ralph M. 1981. *Voluntary Agencies in the Welfare State*. Berkeley: University of California Press.

Krebs, Charles J. 1978. *Ecology: The Experimental Analysis of Distribution and Abundance*. 2d ed. New York: Harper & Row.

Krueger, Anne O., and B. Tuncer. 1982. "An Empirical Test of the Infant Industry Argument." *American Economic Review* 72: 1143–52.

Kurian, G.T. 1982. "Finland." In *World Press Encyclopedia*, edited by George T. Kurian, pp. 331–39. London: Mansell.

Labovitz, S. 1970. "The Assignment of Numbers to Rank Order Categories." *American Sociological Review* 35: 515–24.

Langton, John. 1984. "The Ecological Theory of Bureaucracy: The Case of Josiah Wedgewood and the British Pottery Industry." *Administrative Science Quarterly* 29: 330–54.

Langton, Nancy. 1982. "Selection and Adaptation in Service Sector Labor Unions." Unpublished paper, Department of Sociology, University of Oklahoma.

Lawrence, Paul R., and Jay W. Lorsch. 1967. *Organization and Environment*. Cambridge, Mass.: Harvard University Press.

Lester, M. 1980. "Generating Newsworthiness." *American Sociological Review* 45: 984–94.

Levin, Simon. 1970. "Community Equilibria and Stability, and an Extension of the Competitive Exclusion Principle." *American Naturalist* 104: 413–23.

Lindblom, Charles. 1977. *Politics and Markets: The World's Political-Economic Systems*. New York: Basic Books.

Lincoln, James R. 1977. "The Urban Distribution of Voluntary Organizations." *Social Science Quarterly* 58, no. 3: 472–80.

Litvak, Isaiah. 1982. "National Trade Associations: Business-Government Intermediaries." *Business Quarterly* (Autumn): 34–42.

Loney, Martin. 1977. "The Political Economy of Citizen Participation." In *The Canadian State: Political Economy and Political Power*, edited by Leo Panitch, pp. 346–72. Toronto: University of Toronto Press.

Lotka, Alfred. 1925. *Elements of Mathematical Biology*. New York: Dover.

Lowi, Theodore J. 1964. "American Business, Public Policy, Case Studies, and Political Theory." *World Politics* 17: 675–715.

———. 1970. "Decision Making vs. Policy Making: Toward an Antidote for Technocracy." *Public Administration Review* 30: 298–310.

———. 1972. "Four Systems of Policy, Politics, and Choice." *Public Administration Review* 32: 314–25.

MacArthur, Robert H. 1968. "The Theory of the Niche." In *Population Biology and Evolution*, edited by R.C. Leowontin, pp. 159–76. Syracuse: Syracuse University Press.

———. 1970. "Species Packing and Competitive Equilibrium for Many Species." *Theoretical Population Biology* 1: 1–11.

MacArthur, Robert H., and Edward O. Wilson. 1967. *The Theory of Island Biogeography*. Princeton: Princeton University Press.

MacAvoy, Paul. 1965. *The Economic Effects of Regulation*. Cambridge, Mass.: MIT Press.

MacLaurin, W. Rupert. 1949. *Invention and Innovation in the Radio Industry*. New York: Macmillan.

Maidique, M., and P. Patch. "Corporate Strategy and Technological Policy." In *Readings in the Management of Innovation*, edited by M. Tushman and W. Moore, pp. 273–85. Marshfield, Mass.: Pitman, 1982.

Mansfield, Edwin. 1968. *The Economics of Technological Change*. New York: Norton.

Marrett, Cora B. 1980. "Influences on the Rise of New Organizations: The Formation of Women's Medical Societies." *Administrative Science Quarterly* 25: 185–99.

May, Robert M., and Jon Seger. 1986. "Ideas in Ecology." *American Scientist* 74: 256–67.

Mayr, Ernst. 1982. *The Growth of Biological Thought*. Cambridge, Mass.: Harvard University.

McCarthy, John D., and Mayer N. Zald. 1977. "Resource Mobilization and Social Movements: A Partial Theory." *American Journal of Sociology* 82, no. 6: 1212–41.

McConnell, Grant. 1966. *Private Power and American Democracy*. New York: Vintage.

McKelvey, Bill. 1982. *Organizational Systematics*. Berkeley: University of California Press.

McKelvey, Bill, and Howard Aldrich. 1983. "Populations, Natural Selection, and Applied Organizational Science." *Administrative Science Quarterly* 28: 101–28.

McKeough, W.D. 1975. *Ontario Budget 1975*. Toronto: Ministry of Treasury: Economics and Intergovernmental Affairs.

———. 1976. *Ontario Budget 1976*. Toronto: Ministry of Treasury, Economics and Intergovernmental Affairs.

McPherson, J. Miller. 1981. "A Dynamic Model of Voluntary Affiliation." *Social Forces* 59, no. 3: 705–28.

———. 1982. "Hypernetwork Sampling: Duality and Differentiation among Voluntary Organizations." *Social Networks* 3, no. 4: 225–50.

———. 1983. "An Ecology of Affiliation." *American Sociological Review* 48, no. 4: 519–32.

McPherson, J. Miller, and Lynn Smith-Lovin. 1982. "Women and Weak Ties: Differences by Sex in the Size of Voluntary Associations." *American Journal of Sociology* 87, no. 4: 883–904.

———. 1986. "Sex Segregation in Voluntary Associations."- *American Sociological Review* 51, no. 1: 61–79.

Merton, Robert. 1967. *On Theoretical Sociology*. New York: Free Press.

Meyer, Alan D. 1982. "Responding to Environmental Jolts." *Administrative Science Quarterly* 27: 515–37.

Meyer, John W., and Brian Rowan. 1977. "Institutionalized Organizations: Formal Structures as Myth and Reality." *American Journal of Sociology* 83: 340–63.

Meyer, John W., and W. Richard Scott, eds. 1983. *Organizational Environments: Ritual and Rationality*. Beverly Hills: Sage.

Meyers, Frederic. 1940. "The Knights of Labor in the South." *Southern Economic Journal* 6: 479–87.

Miles, Raymond E., and Charles C. Snow. 1978. *Organizational Strategy, Structure, and Process*. New York: McGraw-Hill.

Miles, R.H., and W.A. Randolph. 1980. "Influence of Organizational Learning Styles on Early Development." In *The Organizational Life Cycle*, edited by J. Kimberly and R. Miles, pp. 44–82. San Francisco: Jossey-Bass.

Miller, Danny, and Peter Friesen. 1984. *Organizations: A Quantum View*. Englewood Cliffs, N.J.: Prentice-Hall.

Miller, Frank S. 1980. *Ontario Budget 1980*. Toronto: Ministry of Treasury and Economics.

Mintzberg, Henry. 1978. "Patterns in Strategy Formation." *Management Science* 24: 934–48.

Moe, Terry. 1980. *The Organization of Interests*. Chicago: University of Chicago Press.

Morse, D.H. 1980. *Behavioral Mechanisms in Ecology*. Cambridge: Harvard University Press.

Naroll, R. 1962. *Data Quality Control*. Glencoe, Ill.: Free Press.

National Association of Beverage Importers. *Quarterly Bulletin*. Washington, D.C.: National Association of Beverage Importers. Various issues.

Nelson, Richard R., and Sidney G. Winter. 1982. *An Evolutionary Theory of Economic Change*. Cambridge, Mass.: Harvard University Press.

Nie, N.H.; G.B. Powell; and K. Prewitt. 1969a. "Social Structure and Political Participation: Developmental Relationships I." *American Political Science Review* 63: 361–78.

Nie, N.H.; G.B. Powell; and K. Prewitt, 1969b. "Social Structure and Political Participation: Developmental Relationships II." *American Political Science Review* 63: 808–33.

Nielsen, François, and Michael T. Hannan. 1977. "The Expansion of National Educational Systems: Tests of a Population Ecology Model." *American Sociological Review* 42: 479–90.

Oberschall, Anthony. 1973. *Social Conflict and Social Change*. Englewood Cliffs, N.J.: Prentice-Hall.

Offe, Claus. 1985. *Disorganized Capitalism?* Cambridge, Mass.: Polity Press.

Offe, Claus, and Helmut Wiesenthal. 1979. "Two Logics of Collective Action." *Political Power and Social Theory* 1 67–115.

Olson, Mancur. 1965. *The Logic of Collective Action*. Cambridge, Mass.: Harvard University Press.

Olson, Mancur. 1982. *The Rise and Decline of Nations*. New Haven, Conn.: Yale University Press.

Olzak, Susan. 1986. "Causes of Ethnic Collective Action in Urban America, 1877–1914." Technical Report 86–14, Department of Sociology, Cornell University, Ithaca, New York.

Oster, S. 1982. "Intraindustry Structure and the Ease of Strategic Change." *Review of Economics and Statistics* 64: 376–84.

Ouchi, William G. 1980. "Markets, Bureaucracies and Clans." *Administrative Science Quarterly* 25: 129–41.

Palmer, M. 1978. "The British Press and International News, 1851–99: Of Agencies and Newspapers." In *Newspaper History: From the 17th Century to the Present Day*, edited by George Boyce, James Curran, and Pauline Wingate, pp. 205–19. London: Sage.

Paris, Edna. 1972. "Are There Really Any Opportunities for Youth?" *MacLean's* (September): 34.

Park, Robert E. 1922.. *The Immigrant Press and Its Control*. New York: Harper.

Peet, R.K., and O.L. Loucks. 1977. "A Gradient Analysis of Southern Wisconsin Forests." *Ecology* 58, no. 3: 485–99.

Pennings, Johannes M. 1980. "Environmental Influences on the Creation Process." In *The Organizational Life Cycle*, edited by J. Kimberly and R. Miles, pp. 134–63. San Francisco: Jossey-Bass.

———. 1982. "Organizational Birth Frequencies: An Empirical Investigation." *Administrative Science Quarterly* 27, no. 1: 120–44.

Perlman, Selig. 1918. "Upheaval and Reorganization." In *History of Labor in the United States*, vol. 2, edited by John R. Commons and Associates, pp. 195–587. New York: Macmillan.

Perrow, Charles. 1979. *Complex Organizations, A Critical Essay*. 2d ed. Palo Alto: Scott, Foresman.

———. 1985. "Comments on Langton's Ecological Theory of Bureaucracy." *Administrative Science Quarterly* 30: 278–83.

———. 1986. *Complex Organizations: A Critical Essay*. 3d ed. New York: Random House.

Pettigrew, A.M. 1979. "On Studying Organizational Cultures." *Administrative Science Quarterly* 24: 570–81.

Pfeffer, Jeffrey. 1972. "Merger as a Response to Organizational Interdependence." *Administrative Science Quarterly* 17: 382–94.

———. 1981. *Power in Organizations*. Marshfield, Mass.: Pitman.

———. 1982. *Organizations and Organization Theory*. Marshfield, Mass.: Pitman.

Pfeffer, Jeffrey, and Gerald R. Salancik. 1978. *The External Control of Organizations*. San Francisco: Harper & Row.

Phillips, Almarin. 1960. "A Theory of Interfirm Organization." *Quarterly Journal of Economics* 74: 602–13.

Pianka, Eric R. 1976. "Competition and Niche Theory." In *Theoretical Ecology*, edited by Robert M. May, pp. 167–96. Oxford: Blackwell.

———. 1978. *Evolutionary Ecology*. 2d ed. New York: Harper & Row.

Pielou, E.C. 1977. *Mathematical Ecology*. New York: Wiley.

Piore, Michael J., and Charles F. Sabel. 1984. *The Second Industrial Divide: Possibilities for Prosperity*. New York: Basic Books.

Piven, Frances Fox, and Richard A. Cloward. 1977. *Poor People's Movements*. New York: Pantheon Books.

Porter, Michael E. 1980. *Competitive Strategy*. New York: Free Press.

Posner, Richard. 1974. *Antitrust: Cases, Economic Notes, and Other Materials*. St. Paul: West.

Potorski, J. 1985. "The Impact of Foreign Competition on the American Wine Industry." In *The Impact of Foreign Competition on Selected American Industries*, edited by Matthew C. Sonfield, pp. 450–84. New York: Hofstra University, Yearbook of Business.

Powers, Charles H. 1987. *Vilfredo Pareto*. Thousand Oaks, Calif.: Sage.

Puckett, Tom, and David J. Tucker. 1976. "Hard Times for Ontario's Social Services." *Canadian Welfare* 52: 8–11.

Rantala, O. 1969. "Finland." In *International Guide to Electoral Statistics*, edited by Stein Rokkan and Jean Meyriat, pp. 79–101. The Hague: Mouton.

Reinarman, Craig. 1985. "Social Movements and Social Problems: 'Mothers Against Drunk Driving,' Restrictive Alcohol Laws and Social Control in the 1980s." Paper presented at the Society for the Study of Social Problems Annual Meeting, Washington, D.C., August 23–26.

Ricklefs, R.E. 1979. *Ecology*. New York: Chiron Press.

Robins, James A. 1985. "Organizations and Economics." *Proceedings of the Forty-fifth Academy of Management Meetings*. Wichita, Kans.: Academy of Management, pp. 181–185.

Rogers, J. 1919. *Building Newspaper Advertising*. New York: Harper.

Rokkan, Stein. 1970. "The Growth and Structuring of Mass Politics in Western Europe: Reflections of Possible Models of Explanation." *Scandinavian Political Studies* 5: 65–83.

———. 1975. "Dimensions of State Formation and Nation-Building: A Possible Paradigm for Research on Variations within Europe." In *The Formation of National States in Western Europe*, edited by Charles Tilly, pp. 562–600. Princeton: Princeton University Press.

Rokkan, Stein, and D.W. Urwin. 1983. *Economy, Territory, Identity: Politics of West European Peripheries*. London: Sage.

Rosse, James R.; B.M. Owen; and J.R. Dertouzos. 1978. "Trends in the Daily Newspaper Industry, 1923–1973." Technical Report, *Studies in Industry Economics*. Stanford: Stanford University.

Rothenberg, T. 1946. *The Newspaper: A Study in the Workings of the Daily Press and Its Laws*. New York: Staples Press.

Roughgarden, Jonathan. 1979. *Theory of Population Genetics and Evolutionary Ecology*. New York: Macmillan.

Rowan, Brian. 1982. "Organizational Structure and the Institutional Environment: The Case of Public Schools." *Administrative Science Quarterly* 27: 259–79.

Roy, William. 1981. "The Process of Bureaucratization in the U.S. State Department and the Vesting of Economic Interests, 1886–1905." *Administrative Science Quarterly* 26: 419–33.

Sabatier, Paul. 1975. "Social Movements and Regulatory Agencies; Toward a More Adequate—and Less Pessimistic—Theory of 'Clientele Capture.' " *Policy Sciences* 6: 301–42.

Salisbury, Robert H. 1984. "Interest Representation: The Dominance of Institutions." *American Political Science Review* 78: 64–76.

Salisbury, Robert H., and John Heinz. 1970. "A Theory of Policy Analysis and Some Preliminary Applications." In *Policy Analysis in Political Science*, edited by Ira Sharkansky, pp. 39–60. Chicago: Markham.

Salisbury, Robert H.; John P. Heinz; Edward O. Laumann; and Robert L. Nelson. 1984. "Soaking and Poking among the Movers and Shakers: Quantitative Ethnography Along the K Street Corridor." Paper presented at the annual meeting of the American Political Science Association, Washington, D.C.

Salmelin, P. 1968. "The Transition of the Finnish Workers Papers to the Social Democratic Press." *Scandinavian Political Studies* 3: 70–84.

Samuelson, Paul A. 1980. *Economics*. 11th ed. New York: McGraw-Hill.

Sankiaho, R. 1970. "Voting Strength in the Finnish Parliament 1951–1966." *Scandinavian Political Studies* 5: 119–28.

Sarason, S.B. 1972. *The Creation of Settings and the Future Societies*. San Francisco: Jossey-Bass.

Schein, E. 1983. "The Role of the Founder in Creating Organizational Culture." *Organizational Dynamics* (Summer): 13–28.

———. 1985. *Organizational Culture and Leadership*. San Francisco: Jossey-Bass.

Scherer, F.M. 1980. *Industrial Market Structure and Economic Performance*. Chicago: Rand-McNally.

Schlozman, Kay Lehman. 1984. "What Accent the Heavenly Chorus? Political Equality and the American Pressure System." Department of Political Science, Boston College. Unpublished manuscript.

Schlozman, Kay Lehman, and John T. Tierney. 1983. "More of the Same: Washington Pressure Group Activity in a Decade of Change." *Journal of Politics* 45: 351–77.

———. 1986. *Organized Interests and American Democracy*. New York: Harper & Row.

Schmitter, Phillippe C., and Donald Brand. 1979. "Organizing Capitalists in the United States: The Advantages and Disadvantages of Exceptionalism." Paper presented at the American Political Science Association meetings, August 17–21.

Schmitter, Phillippe, and Wolfgang Streeck. 1981. "The Organization of Business Interests." Unpublished paper, International Institute of Management, West Berlin.

Schneider, B. 1985. "The People Make the Place." Paper presented at the Annual Convention of the Society for Industrial and Organizational Psychology, American Psychological Association, Los Angeles, California.

Schön, Donald. 1971. *Beyond the Stable State*. New York: Norton.

Schumpeter, Joseph 1934. *The Theory of Economic Development*. Cambridge, Mass.: Harvard University Press.

——. 1958. *Capitalism, Socialism and Democracy*. New York: Simon and Schuster.

Scott, W. Richard. 1981. *Organizations: Rational, Natural, and Open Systems*. Englewood Cliffs, N.J.: Prentice-Hall.

——. 1983. "The Organization of Environments: Network, Cultural, and Historical Elements." In *Organizational Environments: Ritual and Rationality*, edited by John W. Meyer and W. Richard Scott, pp. 155–75. Beverly Hills: Sage.

Scott, W. Richard, and John W. Meyer. 1983. "The Organization of Societal Sectors." In *Organizational Environments: Ritual and Rationality*, edited by John W. Meyer and W. Richard Scott, pp. 129–54. Beverly Hills: Sage.

Secretary of State. 1971. *Evaluation of the Opportunities for Youth Program, 1971*. Ottawa: Secretary of State.

Selznick, Philip. 1949. *TVA and the Grass Roots*. Berkeley: University of California Press.

Shimwell, D.W. 1971. *Description and Classification of Vegetation*. Seattle: University of Washington Press.

Silk, Leonard, and David Vogel. 1976. *Ethics and Profits: The Crisis of Confidence in American Business*. New York: Simon and Schuster.

Singh, Jitendra; David J. Tucker; and Robert J. House. 1986. "Organizational Legitimacy and the Liability of Newness." *Administrative Science Quarterly* 31: 171–93.

Singh, Jitendra; Robert J. House; and David J. Tucker. 1986. "Organizational Change and Organizational Mortality." *Administrative Science Quarterly* 31: 587–611.

Smith, A. 1978. "The Long Road to Objectivity and Back Again: The Kinds of Truth We Get in Journalism." In *Newspaper History: From the 17th Century to the Present Day*, edited by George Boyce, James Curran, and Pauline Wingate, pp. 153–71. Beverly Hills: Sage.

Smith, C., and A. Freedman. 1972. *Voluntary Associations: Perspectives on the Literature*. Cambridge, Mass.: Harvard University Press.

Smith, D.H., ed. 1973. *Voluntary Action Research 1973*. Lexington, Mass.: Heath.

Snow, Charles C., and Lawrence G. Hrebiniak. 1980. "Strategy, Distinctive Competence, and Organizational Performance." *Administrative Science Quarterly* 25: 317–36.

Social Planning Council of Metropolitan Toronto. 1976. *In Search of a Framework*. Toronto: Social Planning Council of Metropolitan Toronto.

——. 1984. *Caring for Profit: The Commercialization of Human Services in Ontario*. Toronto: Social Planning Council of Metropolitan Toronto.

Sonfield, M.C. 1985. *The Impact of Foreign Competition on Selected American Industries*. Hempstead, N.Y.: Hofstra University, Yearbook of Business.

Splane, Richard. 1965. *Social Welfare in Ontario, 1791–1893*. Toronto: University of Toronto Press.

Staber, Udo. 1982. *The Organizational Properties of Trade Associations*. Ph.D. dissertation, Cornell University.

Staber, Udo, and Howard Aldrich. 1983. "Trade Association Stability and Public Policy." In *Organizational Theory and Public Policy*, edited by Richard Hall and Robert Quinn, pp. 163–78. Beverly Hills: Sage.

Starbuck, William H. 1976. "Organizations and Their Environments." In *Handbook of Industrial and Organizational Psychology* edited by Marvin D. Dunnette, pp. 1069–1123. Chicago: Rand-McNally.

Starbuck, William H., and Paul C. Nystrom. 1981. "Designing and Understanding Organizations." In *Handbook of Organizational Design*, vol. 1, edited by Paul C. Nystrom and William H. Starbuck, pp. ix–xxii. New York: Oxford.

Stinchcombe, Arthur L. 1965. "Organizations and Social Structure." In *Handbook of Organizations*, edited by James G. March, pp. 153–93. Chicago: Rand-McNally.

———. 1968. *Constructing Social Theories*. New York: Harcourt, Brace, Jovanovitch.

Teiser, R., and C. Harrown. 1981. *Wine Making in California*. New York: McGraw-Hill.

Temporary National Economic Committee. 1941. *Investigation of Concentration of Economic Power*. Washington, D.C.: Department of Commerce.

Thompson, James D. 1967. *Organizations in Action*. New York: McGraw-Hill.

Tilly, Charles. 1978. *From Mobilization to Revolution*. Reading, Mass.: Addison-Wesley.

Tilton, John E. 1971. *International Diffusion of Technology: The Case of Semiconductors*. Washington, D.C.: Brookings Institution.

Timberlake, M., and K.R. Williams. 1984. "Dependence, Political Exclusion, and Government Repression." *American Sociological Review* 49: 141–46.

Tolbert, Pamela, and Lynne G. Zucker. 1983. "Institutional Sources of Change in the Formal Structures of Organizations: The Diffusion of Civil Service Reform." *Administrative Science Quarterly* 28: 22–39.

Tornudd, K. 1969. "Composition of Cabinets in Finland 1917–1968." *Scandinavian Political Studies* 4: 58–70.

Tucker, David J. 1981. "Voluntary Auspices and the Behavior of Social Service Organizations." *Social Service Review* 55: 603–27.

Tucker, David; Jitendra Singh; and Robert House. 1984. "The Liability of Newness in Voluntary Social Service Organizations." Paper presented at the American Sociological Association meetings, August, San Antonio, Texas.

Tuma, Nancy Brandon. 1980. *Invoking Rate*. Menlo Park, Calif.: SRI.

Tuma, Nancy Brandon, and Michael T. Hannan. 1984. *Social Dynamics: Models and Methods*. Orlando: Academic Press.

Tuma, Nancy B.; Michael T. Hannan; and Lyle P. Groeneveld. 1979. "Dynamic Analysis of Event Histories." *American Journal of Sociology* 84: 820–54.

Ulman, Lloyd. 1961. "The Development of Trades and Labor Unions." In *American Economic History*, edited by Seymour E. Harris, pp. 366–419. New York: McGraw-Hill.

Ungerleider, Steven; Steven A. Bloch; and Ross F. Conner. 1986. "Report from the Drunk Driving Prevention Project." Eugene, Ore.: Integrated Research Services.

U.S. Department of Commerce. 1979. *Report on the U.S. Semiconductor Industry*. Washington, D.C.: U.S. Government Printing Office.

U.S. Department of Transportation. 1980. *Fatal Accident Reporting System* (Machine-readable data file). Washington, D.C.: National Highway Traffic Safety Administration.

Van Valen, L.M. 1973. "A New Evolutionary Law." *Evolutionary Theory* 1: 1–30.

Vogel, David. 1978. "Why Businessmen Distrust Their State; The Political Consciousness of American Corporate Executives." *British Journal of Political Science* 8: 45–78.

————. 1980–81. "The Public-Interest Movement and the American Reform Tradition." *Political Science Quarterly* 95: 607–27.

Volterra, Vito. 1927/1978. "Variations and Fluctuations in the Number of Coexisting Species." In *The Golden Age of Theoretical Ecology: 1923–1940*, edited by F.M. Scudo and J.R. Ziegler, pp. 65–236. New York: Springer-Verlag.

Vrba, Elisabeth S., and Niles Eldredge. 1984. "Individuals, Hierarchies and Processes: Towards a More Complete Evolutionary Theory." *Paleobiology* 10: 146–71.

Walker, Jack L. 1983. "The Origins and Maintenance of Interest Groups in America." *American Political Science Review* 77: 390–406.

Ware, Norman J. 1929. *The Labor Movement in the United States 1860–1895: A Study in Democracy*. New York: Appleton.

Webb, Sidney, and Beatrice Webb. 1912. *The Prevention of Destitution*. London: Longsman, Green.

Webbink, D.W. 1977. *The Semiconductor Industry*. Washington, D.C.: Federal Trade Commission.

Weber, Max. 1947. *The Theory of Social and Economic Organization*. Trans. A.M. Henderson and T. Parsons. New York: Oxford University Press.

Weed, Frank J. 1985. "Grass-Roots Activism and the Drunk Driving Issue: A Survey of MADD Chapters." Paper presented at the 80th annual meeting of the American Sociological Association, Washington, D.C., August 26–30.

Weidenbaum, Murray. 1981. *Business, Government, and the Public*. 2d ed. Englewood Cliffs, N.J.: Prentice-Hall.

Weston, J.F., and T.E.. Copeland. 1986. *Managerial Finance*. 8th ed. Chicago: CBS.

Wharf, Brian, and Novia Carter. 1972. *Planning for Social Services: Canadian Experiences*. Ottawa: Canadian Council on Social Development.

Wholey, Douglas R., and Jack W. Brittain. 1986. "Organizational Ecology: Findings and Implications." *Academy of Management Review* 11: 513–33.

Wilensky, Harold, and Charles Lebeaux. 1957. *Industrial Society and Social Welfare*. New York: Free Press.

Williams R. 1978. "The Press and Popular Culture: An Historical Perspective." In *Newspaper History: From the 17th Century to the Present Day*, edited by George Boyce, James Curran, and Pauline Wingate, pp. 41–50. Beverly Hills: Sage.

Williamson, Oliver E. 1975. *Markets and Hierarchies: Analysis and Anti-trust Implications*. New York: Free Press.

Wilson, Edward O. 1975. *Sociobiology*. Cambridge, Mass.: Harvard University Press.

Wilson, Edward O., and William H. Bossert. 1971. *A Primer of Population Biology*. Stamford, Conn.: Sinauer Associates.

Wilson, Graham. 1981. *Interest Groups in the United States*. Oxford: Clarendon Press.

Wilson, Robert W.; Peter K. Ashton; and Thomas P. Egan. 1980. *Innovation, Competition, and Government Policy in the Semiconductor Industry*. Lexington, Mass.: Heath.

Wines and Vines. Various issues. *Annual Directory* and *Wineries and Vineyard Industry Suppliers of North America*. San Rafael: Hiaring.

Winter, Sidney G. 1964. "Economic 'Natural Selection' and the Theory of the Firm." *Yale Economic Essays* 4: 225–72.

————. 1975. "Optimization and Evolution in the Theory of the Firm." In *Adaptive Economic Models*, edited by R.H. Day and T. Groves, pp. 73–118. New York: Academic Press.

Wohlgenant, M.K. 1985. "An Econometric Model of the U.S. Wine Industry." *Bulletin B1507.* College Station: Texas Agricultural Experiment Station (September).

Wohlgenant, M.K., and R.D. Knutson. 1985. "Impact of Wine Imports on the U.S. Wine Industry." *Report to the American Grapegrowers Alliance* (September). Fresno, Calif.

Wright, Carroll D. 1887. "An Historical Sketch of the Knights of Labor." *Quarterly Journal of Economics* 1: 137–68.

Zald, Mayer, N., and John D. McCarthy. 1980. "Social Movement Industries: Competition and Cooperation among Movement Organizations." *Social Movements, Conflicts and Change* 3: 1–20.

Zucker, Lynne G. 1983. "Organizations as Institutions." *Research in the Sociology of Organizations* 2: 1–47.

———. 1986. "Production of Trust: Institutional Sources of Economic Structure." *Research in Organizational Behavior* 8: 53–111.

NAME INDEX

SUBJECT INDEX

ABOUT THE EDITOR

Glenn R. Carroll is an associate professor in the School of Business Administration at the University of California, Berkeley. He is also an affiliated faculty member with the University's Department of Sociology and a research associate at the Institute for Industrial Relations. His *Publish and Perish* summarizes research that he and his colleagues have conducted on the organizational ecology of newspaper industries. Editorial work on *Ecological Models of Organizations* was completed while Carroll was a Fellow at the Center for Advanced Study in the Behavioral Sciences in Palo Alto. During that period, financial support was provided by National Science Foundation grant #BNS-8700864.

ABOUT THE CONTRIBUTORS

Howard Aldrich is a professor of sociology at the University of North Carolina, Chapel Hill. His *Organizations and Environments* was one of the first major statements of organizational ecology. His other work has been published widely, including in such journals as *Administrative Science Quarterly, American Sociological Review,* and *American Journal of Sociology.* With Udo Staber, he is continuing his research on business associations.

Terry Amburgey received his Ph.D. in sociology from Stanford University. He is currently an assistant professor of business policy and strategy at the University of Texas at Dallas. In 1988 he will become an assistant professor at the University of Wisconsin, Madison.

David P. Baker is an assistant professor at the Catholic University of America, where he holds joint appointments in the Department of Sociology and the Center for the Study of Youth Development. His research interests include education and the comparative study of immigration and human development. He is currently engaged in a historical analysis of organization building by immigrants to the United States from 1870 to 1930.

Warren P. Boeker is an assistant professor at the Graduate School of Business, Columbia University. His teaching and research interests include strategic management and business policy, organization theory, entrepreneurship, innovation, and dynamic models of organizational strategy. He was previously employed as a strategic planner for Texas Instruments and received his Ph.D. from the University of California, Berkeley.

Jack W. Brittain is a visiting assistant professor in the Department of Management and Policy at the University of Arizona. His primary research interest is in the implications of rapid environmental change for organizational design. He is currently completing a number of studies on the historical development of the semiconductor industry, including research on entrepreneurial spinoffs, the development of strategic diversity in the industry, and the implications of firm innovation for subsequent firm success. He is also involved in other joint projects with Doug Wholey, including a study of the relationship between environmental dynamics and firm structure that examines staffing adjustments over time.

Jacques Delacroix received his Ph.D. in sociology from Stanford University in 1974. His early research focused on the sociology of economic development and was published in such journals as *American Sociological Review* and *American Journal of Sociology*. For six years he operated a private practice specializing in international trade. Currently, he is an associate professor in the Leavey School of Business Administration at Santa Clara University, where he teaches international management.

Charles J. Fombrun is an associate professor of Management and Organizational Behavior at New York University's Graduate School of Business Administration. A graduate of Columbia University, where he obtained his Ph.D. in 1980, he is active in research on organizational evolution, environmental construction, and strategy-making. He is the author of articles that have appeared in *Administrative Science Quarterly, Academy of Management Journal, Academy of Management Review,* and the *American Journal of Sociology*. Dr. Fombrun also serves on the editorial boards of *Human Resource Planning, Human Resource Management,* and *Academy of Management Journal*.

John Freeman is a professor at Cornell University, where he is in the Johnson Graduate School of Management and the Department of Sociology. Currently, he serves as the editor of *Administrative Science Quarterly*. Professor Freeman has published widely on the topic of organizational ecology, and his article with Michael T. Hannan, "The Population Ecology of Organizations," *American Journal of Sociology* (1977), is commonly credited with reviving interest in ecological theory. He and Professor Hannan have also written a forthcoming book on organizational ecology.

Michael T. Hannan is the Henry Scarborough Professor of Social Sciences at Cornell University. His books include *Aggregation and Disaggregation in Sociology, National Development and the World System* (coedited with John Meyer), and *Social Dynamics: Models and Methods* (with Nancy Brandon Tuma). With John Freeman, his *Organizational Ecology* is forthcoming.

Amos H. Hawley is the Kenan Professor Emeritus of Sociology at the University of North Carolina, Chapel Hill. Among his many scholarly and professional achievements, Professor Hawley has served as the president of the American Sociology Association. His *Human Ecology* is considered the classic statement of ecological theory in sociology. More recently, his *Human Ecology: A Theoretical Synthesis* addressed newer questions of interest to ecological theorists.

Robert J. House is a professor in the Faculty of Management at the University of Toronto. His research interests include leadership, executive succession, and power in complex organizations, as well as ecological processes relevant to organizational founding, adaptation and mortality. He is a fellow of the Academy of Management and the American Psychological Association and a past member of the editorial review boards of *Administrative Science Quarterly, Academy of Management Journal,* and *Academy of Management Review.* He is the author of a number of articles in learned organizational journals, including a forthcoming chapter in *The Annual Review of Psychology.* He received his M.B.A. from the University of Detroit and his Ph.D. from the Ohio State University.

Yangchung Paul Huo is an assistant professor of business administration at California State University, Chico. He received his Ph.D. in organizational behavior from the University of California, Berkeley. His thesis examined the diffusion of innovations in microprocessors among personal computer manufacturers.

Dawn Kelly is an assistant professor of organization and strategic management at the University of Wisconsin-Milwaukee. She received her Ph.D. from Northwestern University's Kellogg Graduate School of Management. Her areas of interest include the ecology, evolution, and regulation of organizations.

Marjo-Ritta Lehtisalo received her Ph.D. in marketing from Northwestern University in 1986. She is currently a visiting professor of marketing at the Norwegian School of Economics and Business Administration.

John D. McCarthy is an associate professor, the chair of the Department of Sociology, and a member of the Center for the Study of Youth Development at the Catholic University of America. His recent research has included longitudinal analyses of adolescent self-evaluation processes, investigation of the varying levels of social and political organization of professional occupational groups, and the project on the Citizens' Movement Against Drunken Driving, of which he is director. His writing on resource mobilization understandings of social movements with Mayer N. Zald are collected with some new essays in the recently published *Social Movements in an Organizational Society.*

J. Miller McPherson is a visiting professor in the Department of Sociology at Cornell University. He is analyzing data generated from a representative sample of organizations in ten communities and examining ideas about the population ecology of associations, social networks generated by these groups, determinants of the groups' composition, and how best to measure organizational characteristics.

Agnes G. Meinhard is an assistant professor in the Department of Sociology, Brock University, Ontario. Her research interests include organizational ecology, women in organizations, group processes and intergroup relations, and the use of advanced multivariate statistical procedures in the analysis of longitudinal social data. Her publications have appeared in *International Journal of Communication Research, Social Review,* and *Journal of Welfare and Social Security Studies.* She received her M.A. from Carleton University, Ottawa, Canada, and her Ph.D. in social psychology from the University of Tel Aviv.

Elaine Mosakowski is completing a Ph.D. in business administration at the University of California, Berkeley. Her research interests include entrepreneurship, innovation, and business strategy. In 1988 she will become an assistant professor at the University of Minnesota.

Jitendra V. Singh is an associate professor in the Department of Management at The Wharton School, University of Pennsylvania. His research interests center around models of organizational adaptation and ecological processes in organizational populations, and organizational slack. His articles have appeared in *Administrative Science Quarterly, Academy of Management Journal, Annual Review of Psychology, American Sociological Review,* and *Journal of Occupational Behavior.* He received his M.B.A. from the Indian Institute of Management, Adhmedabad, India, and his Ph.D. in organization theory and behavior from the Graduate School of Business, Stanford University.

Lynn Smith-Lovin is a visiting associate professor in the Department of Sociology at Cornell University. She continues research into the relationship of affective meaning to the production of social action. Recent work was included in a special issue of the *Journal of Mathematical Sociology* describing the theoretical model and a study of impression formation and behavior expectations among adolescents in Northern Ireland. She is also doing work on gender differences in networks, organizational behavior, and small group interaction.

Michael E. Solt is an assistant professor of business and administration at Santa Clara University. He received a D.B.A. in 1978 from Indiana University. His research has examined the impact of inflation on financial market rates of return and the determination of components of equity market returns. His articles have appeared in such journals as the *Journal of Business, Journal of Portfolio Management, Journal of Financial Research, Journal of Business Research, American Real Estate and Urban Economics Journal,* and *American Business Law Journal.*

Udo Staber received his M.A. in industrial relations from Rutgers University and his Ph.D. in organizational theory from the New York State School of Industrial and Labor Relations at Cornell University. He previously taught at Cornell University and the Pennsylvania State University and is currently an assistant professor in the Faculty of Administration at the University of New Brunswick. His forthcoming publications include "A Population Ecology Perspective on Underemployment in Alternative Organizations," *International Journal of Sociology and Social Policy,* with Howard Aldrich, and "Corporatism and the Governance Structure of American Trade Associations," *Political Studies.*

David J. Tucker is an associate professor in the School of Social Work at McMaster University, Hamilton, Ontario. His research interests include the structural analysis of interorganizational service delivery systems, the ecology of human service organizations, the application of longitudinal data analysis procedures to selected social problems, and the critical analysis of selected public policy issues. His publications have appeared in *Administrative Science Quarterly, Social Service Review, Administrative in Social Work, Social Work Research and Abstracts, Canada Public Policy,* and *Canadian Social Work Review.* He received his M.S.W. from McGill University, Montreal, and his Ph.D. in social work from the University of Toronto.

Douglas R. Wholey is an assistant professor in the Management and Policy Department at the University of Arizona. He is currently studying organizational ecology and is particularly interested in the relationship between organizational ecology and organizational labor markets. He received his Ph.D. in organizational behavior and industrial relations from the Graduate School of Business Administration at the University of California, Berkeley.

Mark Wolfson is a Ph.D. candidate in sociology at the Catholic University of America. His interests include social control of nonprofit organizations and community influences on the birth and growth of social movement organizations.